The Difference Is Spreading

Fifty Contemporary Poets

on Fifty Poems

The Difference Is Spreading

EDITED BY

Al Filreis and Anna Strong Safford

PENN

University of Pennsylvania Press

Philadelphia

Published by
University of Pennsylvania Press
Philadelphia, Pennsylvania 19104-4112
www.upenn.edu/pennpress

Printed in the United States of America on acid-free paper
10 9 8 7 6 5 4 3 2 1

Hardcover ISBN: 978-0-8122-5396-2
Paperback ISBN: 978-0-8122-5323-8
eBook ISBN: 978-0-8122-9971-7

Library of Congress Cataloging-in-Publication Data
    Names: Filreis, Alan, editor. | Safford, Anna Strong, editor.
Title: The difference is spreading : fifty contemporary poets on fifty poems /
    edited by Al Filreis and Anna Strong Safford.
Description: 1st edition. | Philadelphia : University of Pennsylvania Press, [2022] |
    Includes bibliographical references and index.
Identifiers: LCCN 2021033976 | ISBN 978-0-8122-5323-8 (paperback)
Subjects: LCSH: American poetry. | American poetry–History and criticism. |
    American poetry–Appreciation.
Classification: LCC PS305 .D44 2022 | DDC 811.009–dc23
LC record available at https://lccn.loc.gov/2021033976

Contents

Introduction

Al Filreis and Anna Safford

This project has its beginnings in the syllabus of our massive open
online course called ModPo (modpo.org), hosted by the Kelly Writers
House at the University of Pennsylvania in Philadelphia. Since we
began offering this free, noncredit class in the fall of 2012, some
415,000 participants from 179 countries worldwide have enrolled in
order to gain access to a survey of innovative poetry in the United
States, starting with two proto-modernists, Emily Dickinson and Walt
Whitman, and moving through to the twenty-first-century poetic
practices of Caroline Bergvall, Tracie Morris, Jena Osman, Christian
Bök, Erica Baum, Nasser Hussein, and others. All fifty poets written
about in this edition are part of the ModPo syllabus, as are many of
the fifty contemporary poets who comment upon them here; and
many of these have also been filmed in conversation with us as we
have undertaken unrehearsed collaborative close readings captured
in the videos that accompany the poems in the course. Thus one of
the two main reasons for making this book: to bring together in one
volume materials that will make for a written supplement—a companion of familiars—to the online ModPo experience.

Yet this book is not a ModPo textbook or primer. Rather—and this
point brings us to our second raison d'être—our book stands as an
effort to enact across pages something of what has made ModPo the
dynamic experiment in collaborative learning that it is: the community of learners that has formed around a shared affection for reading
and writing and incessantly talking about poems. This book is about,
but also *affirms* (and is conceptually *like*) the way those communities
commune: unexpected gatherings of poets, of readers, of learners—
of any person who has ever said to another, "let's talk about this
poem"—and in doing so have formed pairings and groupings of the
sort that are producing new readings for this volume.

The two of us join others in believing that the poems most challenging and most dynamic are the poems that are open—writings, that is to say, that ask the reader to participate in making the meaning they mean. There's a pedagogy as well as a disposition toward criticism in this. We never want to presume to offer a single reading of a poem nor to suggest that one exists. If that is what we had sought, we wouldn't offer ModPo online to everyone anywhere, nor would we put at the center of the site expansively open and ongoing discussion forums. Poetry happens when a reader and a poet come in contact with one another, when the reader is invited to do interpretive work— realizing that the poem is inert without that metapoetic convergence. When Cid Corman's speaker in his poem "It isnt for want" asks to "detain" the reader inside the poem itself, it is to invite a whole association of the two. Corman is not interested in conveying content in the conventional sense ("it isnt for want of *something to say*"); rather, the poem enacts the process of forging a relationship, an exchange, the very beginnings of something that might survive, through shared understanding of what words mean when arranged just so.

Our hope is that this book will function as an instance not only of what Corman wants and does but of what an interpretive community wants and does in response to the challenge posed by the power—supportive and risky at once—of being detained by art in such a way. Each of the fifty poems represented here is one of those open, resistant-to-a-single-reading texts, and the poets who have engaged with them represent one possible approach to the poem among many. We trust that in engaging with these essays, our readers will feel emboldened and inspired to try their own hand at close reading—will talk back, will engage, will feel something of the sheer precipitousness Lyn Hejinian and Imaad Majeed felt as they embarked on the commission to reckon, respectively, with Lydia Davis on the mown American lawn and Charles Bernstein on Manhattan as a pathless broken rock. Together the poet, the poem, and the reader who reads of the encounter of the two explore alternative paths through the underlying (il)logic of modern poetic (i.e., nonrealist and typically nonnarrative) language. Then comes the realization that this is not an end point but a necessary early step in the process of bringing collaborative intelligence to bear on the task of a collective understanding. The poems are always ultimately, in short, about the necessity of investigating such alternatives.

The spirit of that realization—that, with such mass collaboration inevitably to follow it, interpretation stands as never more than an opening—is written into each of these essays. What's more, they do not really inaugurate so much as encourage existing readings of the poems. As Wai Chee Dimock put it in an October 2017 essay in *PMLA* about ModPo, PennSound, and the Kelly Writers House as experiments in "education populism," the interpretations of experts no longer aspire to mastery but rather they "get in on the act." Thus critical reading by poets—many, as noted, themselves in the syllabus—creates "a living sequel" to "an outpouring of words ongoing and multitudinous" offered by thousands of people who already care every bit as much about what poems ask of us. "If writing is a universal entitlement," Dimock continues, "poetry is what feeds it, amplifies it, and makes it perennial. Only on this basis can this seemingly rarefied body of writing make sense in [a] radically egalitarian world." The hermeneutic, pedagogical, and democratic roles of the poets, heretofore so easily kept separate, almost entirely converge. In these essays we can all take pleasure in discerning how much each of the poets had wanted it to be that way in the first place.

We cannot help but note the additional great pleasure we as editors derived as we invited these fifty writers (forty-eight poets and two critics) each to work with us on a thousand-word essay about a single poem written by another poet. What sheer fun to curate the pairings! Our delight only increased as the pieces came in. Taken all together, these essays form a helpful overview, notwithstanding both the specificity and range inherent in the one-poet-on-one-poem model. The stances and approaches are various; and, once again, there are as many ways to read a poet writing about another's poem as there are poet-poem matches in this edition. Yet a straight-through reading of these pages will indicate emphatically the general importance in poetry of community, socio-aesthetic networks and lines of connection, and genuine expressions of affection and honor due innovative colleagues and predecessors.

Some pairings came to us from our understanding of direct influence, affinity, and literary history: for instance, Rae Armantrout on Emily Dickinson; Fred Wah on Robert Creeley; Laynie Browne on Bernadette Mayer. (These sorts of pieces, we hope, will guide readers of this book to and through a number of important poetic relationships.) Several conjunctions were in fact productively disjunctive—resistant, skeptical, or oppositional: Bob Perelman on Robert Frost; Divya Victor on Walt Whitman. Several poet-poet convergences turned out to explore the outlines and edges of poetic movements or modes: Eileen Myles on James Schuyler (New York School); Danny Snelson on Jackson Mac Low (Fluxus-style chance and constraint); Sharon Mesmer on Michael Magee (Flarf); Christian Bök on Marcel Duchamp and Baroness Elsa von Freytag-Loringhoven (Dada unoriginality); erica kaufman on Joan Retallack (Cagean poethics); Edwin Torres on Anne Waldman and Tracie Morris on Jayne Cortez (radical performance); Mark Nowak on Ruth Lechlitner (proletarian formalism).

A few couplings gave us very special pleasure precisely because they seem eccentric or counterintuitive, perhaps even surprising, speculative, or imaginative as pairings in themselves—and produce, we think, truly new critical approaches. Here we conceived our editorial work as creative. We asked Lyn Hejinian to write about a microfiction by Lydia Davis, and the effect is intensely Language-y; we doubt Davis has been written about in such a way. Lytle Shaw hears in his contemporary ear the aural rhetoric of modernist Wallace Stevens, such that you won't read "The Snow Man" the same way again after experiencing Lytle's take (and his own poem-response) here. The Sri Lankan poet Imaad Majeed approaches one of Charles Bernstein's poems about 9/11 and conveys cross-cultural ideas about the upsetting total indivisibility with which that aimless sonnet ends. When Mónica de la Torre describes her encounter with Erica Baum's photograph-poems depicting library card catalogues, we can learn how fundamentally *visual* is the approach to language of many of today's poets, and how fundamentally *ambient*—already available in the environment—are the images making their way into the experimental writing we read now.

We wish to acknowledge the generosity and wisdom of our editor at the University of Pennsylvania Press, Jerry Singerman; our colleagues at the Kelly Writers House, especially Andrew Beal, Zach Carduner, Lily Applebaum, and Chris Martin; the late and much-missed Paul K. Kelly, whose support of the Kelly Writers House and Kelly Family Professorship enabled us to provide honoraria to our essayists; and Gary and Nina Wexler, Rodger and Hillary Krouse, and Nathan and Elizabeth Leight, whose support of the Wexler Studio and online poetry projects have made possible the conversations that form the basis of this project. We are especially grateful to ModPo teaching assistants and co-teachers who have contributed essays to this book, for their deep understanding of the values of collaborative, democratic pedagogy: erica kaufman, Davy Knittle, Jake Marmer, Gabriel Ojeda-Sagué, Julia Bloch, and Amber Rose Johnson. We are indebted to the poets and their families, heirs, and executors who have given us permission to use their poems. Many of them have told us they are delighted that these poems will inspire yet further conversation.

Divya Victor

on **Walt Whitman, Canto 11 from "Song of Myself"**
(1855)

Twenty-eight young men bathe by the shore,
Twenty-eight young men, and all so friendly,
Twenty-eight years of womanly life, and all so lonesome.

She owns the fine house by the rise of the bank,
She hides handsome and richly drest aft the blinds of the
    window.

Which of the young men does she like the best?
Ah the homeliest of them is beautiful to her.

Where are you off to, lady? for I see you,
You splash in the water there, yet stay stock still in your room.

Dancing and laughing along the beach came the twenty-ninth
    bather,
The rest did not see her, but she saw them and loved them.

The beards of the young men glisten'd with wet, it ran from their
    long hair,
Little streams pass'd all over their bodies.

An unseen hand also pass'd over their bodies,
It descended tremblingly from their temples and ribs.

The young men float on their backs, their white bellies swell to
    the sun, they do not ask who seizes fast to them,
They do not know who puffs and declines with pendant and
    bending arch,
They do not think whom they souse with spray.

"Song of Myself" is a coyly corseted title for the billowing expanse of themes encompassed in the poem's 52 cantos. Neither are the cantos strictly "songs" or merely mellifluous signification set to rhythmic music, nor are these cantos merely expressions of an individual. To "sing" one's self as a "separate person" is to also "utter the word Democratic, the word En-Masse."[1] The individual is a crowd; she contains "multitudes."[2] The cantos ask us to imagine a broad stave of possibilities for what a "song" might include: the speaking voice; the brook-like rush of a giggle; the voice clasped in the throat of a voyeur; the marching anthems of war; the percussive strikes of oratory; the keeling wail; the sharp gasps of orgasm.

The eleventh canto of the long poem's fifty-two parts (which seem to count the number of weeks in any year) is especially interested in the silences and sounds of pleasure in a quotidian context. It sings itself through plain and affable speech, descriptive diction, and a full arc of action—from exposition to denouement—in eight symmetrical strophes that describe a woman watching a group of men bathing in a river, in a reversal of a more traditional structure of the dyadic gaze.

The first and last strophes are three lines each and hug six unrhymed couplets, which carry the narrative action. The opening strophe offers us exposition, describing a scene of "twenty-eight young men" frolicking in a river, watched by a twenty-eight-year-old woman, standing "lonesome." Each anaphoristic line of this strophe repeats "Twenty-eight" as a significant number, alluding to the menstrual cycle, the lunar cycle, or the Egyptian goddess Isis's embrace of her lover Osiris's twenty-eight dismembered parts, linking pleasure to the restoration of life to the body. This number also documents how desire has pervaded this woman's *entire* life—"Twenty-eight years of womanly life, and *all* so lonesome." Whitman's suggestion here decouples pleasure from sexuality and reproduction, and conjugates it with ontology.

The last line of the first strophe is almost twice as long as the first, and the speaker's attention flirts with a portrait of the woman, outlining her first only by superficial markers of class, and then slowly teases out her interiority. The second strophe develops exposition further with a couplet describing the voyeur: she is rich ("owns the fine house"); she stands apart ("by the rise of the bank"); she is well dressed; she is hidden ("aft the blinds"). She can see while remaining unseen, and she deliberates "Which of the young men does she like the best?" Her invisibility allows for discernment, thought. Whitman's speaker draws out her internal dialogue, allowing the reader to espy its contents in this private moment.

Like the second strophe, the third opens with a rhetorical question: "Where are you off to, lady? for I see you." Both the line break and the autonomously answered questions allow the reader and the speaker to gaze upon the woman as she gazes upon the bathers. We are no longer merely observing a dyad: we are participating in a triangle of relations. We are watching her watch them—are we jealous? Glad? Turned on?

When the poem gathers us to itself, the fourth strophe escalates action. The woman "splash[es] in the water" with the bathers even though she "stay[s] stock still in [her] room." In the sibilant exuberance of this strophe, the woman has slipped out and slid into a different scene, becoming a participant-voyeur—someone who can "stay stock still" in one space and also participate, through acts of fantasy, in another.

The fifth strophe complicates the action: "Dancing and laughing along the beach came the twenty-ninth bather." The strophe affixes the reader's position to the woman's previous location—in her room—even as her eyes rove. She is transformed by her desire, splits herself in two, projects herself to be with bathers. Her desire makes her ebullient; she multiplies herself. She is "dancing and laughing" rather than hidden, clothed, and "stock still." Her desire makes her visible to herself and exposes her to us. She is, however, invisible to the bathers, "but she saw them and loved them." Like the speaker in Canto 13 ("I behold the picturesque giant and love him") and in Canto 15

("I love him, though I do not know him;"), Whitman's voyeurs can love (and appropriate) by looking while remaining invisible. Yet, Canto 11 offers a female embodiment for the voyeurism that is at the heart of human transactions in "Song of Myself." There is a proliferation here—twenty-eight bathers and a twenty-ninth and a reader and a speaker. A crowd is gathering around the wet, warm, and shimmering scene. It is an erotic community building around homosocial conviviality, a splash into the selfsame, an othering frisson in an element as primordial as life itself.

Through the voyeur ventriloquized by the speaker, the reader watches on, rapt: "The beards of the young men glisten'd with wet, it ran from their long hair, / Little streams pass'd all over their bodies." The rivulets are causeways, transporting a shared gaze, from top to toe. Touch and sight are paired like "unseen hand[s]" that "pass'd all over their bodies" moving "tremblingly" downward. By the time the hands and the reader reach downward to the final strophe, the action is excited, escalating a climax of someone the men cannot see or know, someone who "puffs and declines with pendant and bending arch." Without their own knowledge they "souse with spray" the dipping and arched body, the undulation and ecstasy of the twenty-ninth bather, who is *both* among them and "soused," drenched, wet in her own room. The "puff and decline" of her body, in orgasm, is a song in the chorus of "myself"—a democracy of pleasure between self and self. Perhaps she contains *multiples* rather than multitudes. We see her and know her like this. The poem's denouement, its uncurling, depends on the young men's ignorance of this fact. They are oblivious, pregnant and floating, their "white bellies" confronting the sun with the gravid androgyny of bodies, in their own corral, private and bulging in the open. The woman, once "so lonesome," finds a kind of community in mutual privacies; we leave them to it.

NOTES

1 Walt Whitman, "One's Self I Sing," in *Leaves of Grass* (Philadelphia: David McKay Publishers, 1894), 9.

2 Canto 51, "Song of Myself," in *Leaves of Grass*.

Rae Armantrout

on **Emily Dickinson, "The Brain—is Wider than the Sky"**
(c. 1862)

The Brain—is wider than the Sky—
For—put them side by side—
The one the other will contain
With ease—and You—beside—

The Brain is deeper than the sea—
For—hold them—Blue to Blue—
The one the other will absorb—
As Sponges—Buckets—do—

The Brain is just the weight of God—
For—Heft them—Pound for Pound—
And they will differ—if they do—
As Syllable from Sound—

This is a wonderfully tricky poem. It consists of three assertions. The first is completely unproblematic, at least for people living within the Enlightenment, humanist tradition. In an almost childlike way, it asks us to imagine that something physically impossible (placing the brain alongside the sky) will be easy and that two things of very different natures can be readily compared. The common phrase "side by side" appears to normalize this process. Making such a comparison would, in fact, show off the powers of the brain. It's worth noting that she chooses to say "brain" where most writers would have said "mind." This is a mark of her greatness. And it leads us into increasingly uncharted waters.

What the second stanza says is similar to the statement made by the first. The brain is greater than the sea (this begins to sound like a mathematical formula) because the brain can "absorb" (i.e., perceive and remember) images such as that of the ocean. The poem holds them "blue to blue" (a more vivid phrase, odder than "side by side"). Consciousness, we generally imagine, is just this ability to hold a mental image of something in mind and compare it to the original. (The original will, of course, be an earlier mental image.) As the stanza continues, Dickinson gets surprisingly literal, physical, even grungy. The brain is mopping up the sea the way a housewife mops a floor. Stop a moment and picture that. What shocks it would have sent through its first readers. The presumed loftiness, perhaps spirituality, a reader might have attributed to consciousness is brusquely taken down a peg. We are leaving convention and sentiment far behind.

The third stanza is truly wild. In its first line we are casually told that God has weight, mass. That he too is physical and that his (or its) weight is oddly equivalent—pound for pound—to that of the human brain. In order to make this comparison, we must wrench both brain and God from their normal contexts or abodes. She suggests we put them on a balance scale (such as we'd find in some mercantile estab-lishment) to take their measure. This involves the mind seeing the brain as if from the outside. Long before the birth of cognitive science, Dickinson has created a grotesque and hyperreal image of what's entailed in self-consciousness. What is it, after all, but the ability to see ourselves as if from the outside. This graphic pound-for-pound measurement of the brain by the brain goes past as pertly as the ano-dyne "side by side" and the slightly odd "blue to blue." In the first two measurements, the brain came out on top. It was wider and deeper. The third stanza throws that superiority open to paradox and doubt. Difference vies with equivalence. "They will differ—*if* they do—[italics mine] / As Syllable from Sound."

Let's look at the ways similarity and difference work in the sonic structure of this poem. With her pairs of like-sounding words, Dickin-son leads us through an exploration of equality and inequality. At first, it's a question of adding same to same: "side by side," "Blue to Blue," and "Pound for Pound." This leads us unsuspecting to the final two lines, where we get the paired alliterations of "differ" and "do" and "syllable" and "Sound." It's in this last stanza, where sameness is asserted ("The Brain is just the weight of God"), that the paired words begin to differ, that is, "differ and do" and "Syllable and Sound" are clearly pairs, but they are not twins. The difference is spreading. Most of the words in this emphatic and assertive poem are just one syllable. A few are two. The only three-syllable word in the poem is, perhaps tellingly, Syllable itself—a word that represents the smallest meaningful sound.

This poem is a pointed example of a kind of spatial anxiety/obsession that permeates Dickinson's work. The small is in conversation with the enormous. Sometimes the tiny captures or undermines the great. At other times, it's obliterated. Dickinson's eyes are always fixed on Circumference (what we might now, less interestingly, call space) and its ever expanding and contracting boundary ("and I alone— / A Speck upon a Ball— / Went out upon Circumference— / Beyond the Dip of Bell—"). She is always dealing with incongruities of scale and with a desire to connect things that she sees as incommensurate. This makes her work tragicomic. In this poem "Syllable" is the (seemingly) tiny, finite thing vying with "Sound," which seems potentially infinite. She experiments with creating (forcing) an equality, one that is ultimately unstable.

So how does a syllable differ from a sound? Let me count the ways. The two here said to be equally weighty are entangled but are not identical. All syllables are (potentially) sounds, but most sounds are not syllables. Sound is a more capacious category than syllable. A sound is the raw material from which a syllable is formed. Syllables are necessarily discrete and separate while a sound can be continuous. If a believer thinks of God as infinite, then is God closer to sound in this statement? On the other hand, it is syllables that are associated with meaning. If God is on the side of the syllable in this quasi-equation, then he/she/it is small and separate. Another option remains. Perhaps the two do not differ after all. (That was left open.) Could she be saying that God is all in our heads or that each brain is a little piece of God? These two turn into One; this One turns into two. Her meaning oscillates between (im)possibilities like a radio frequency. In her completely unpretentious way she brings us, by way of measurement, to the unfathomable.

3

Ron Silliman

on **Gertrude Stein, "A Carafe, that is a Blind Glass"**
(1914)

A kind in glass and a cousin, a spectacle and nothing strange
a single hurt color and an arrangement in a system to pointing.
All this and not ordinary, not unordered in not resembling.
The difference is spreading.

Gertrude Stein was the first modernist to focus on language in the
way that readers and/or listeners actually experience the serial creation of meaning. Where Joyce's *Finnegans Wake*, for example, relied
on the nineteenth-century notion of language as philology, and
Pound's sense of disjunct juxtaposition was appropriated from the
arts of film and collage, Stein recognized that the reader (listener)
hones in on the word in front of them with a minimum of attention to
the peripheral vision of syntax. Grammar serves to connect elements
but seldom does so in practice with the magisterial articulation of
well-parsed arguments that were the ideals of the Victorian novel
or essay. Today this seems apparent, particularly in the textual representation of speech, but for a century now academics have built
careers on the demonstration in one major author after another that
we seldom mean what we say, and that ambiguity can be categorized,
diagrammed, and deconstructed. Stein, who was rarely taken seriously during her lifetime because she was a woman, a lesbian, and
a Jew, got there first and with insights so bold that she can still seem
breathtakingly opaque.

Stein was in her mid- to late thirties when she wrote *Tender Buttons*,
the same age as the famously "late-blooming" William Carlos Williams when he composed *Spring and All*, a book that owes a signifi-

cant debt to her work. Stein had by then published one book, *Three Lives*, while devoting over a decade to other projects, few of which had seen print. In this sense *Tender Buttons* is a brave and confident project, unlike anything that had appeared before in English and by an author who had to put most of her work into a drawer.

Tender Buttons is often characterized as a kind of verbal Cubism, but what it shares with this visual analog is a commitment to reveal more than what is apparent in a naïve imagist landscape. The opening phrase presents a pairing of two dissimilar phenomena, the first of which offers itself as an undecidable: do we read this as "a kind" rendered in glass or contained in glass? The traditional carafe after all is a container made of glass, simpler than a decanter, transparent unlike most vases. The noun here is not *glass* but *kind*. Its initial *k* is indeed related as a sound to the hard *c* of *cousin*. So what is transparent here: the object depicted or the capacity of a general categorical term—*kind*—to invoke the physical realm? A carafe of milk is not one of wine.

The second phrase offers a parallel conjunction with yet another undecidable: spectacles may represent a show, even a circus, but there is also the ordinary object composed of glass. Nothing strange about that.

What is strange is the absent punctuation that then "joins" these opening words to the remainder of the sentence. Again we are offered a pair of items around the fulcrum of a conjunction, in this case somewhat more complicated phrases. One of the most interesting and urgent questions of this text occurs at this point: does the reader (*should the reader*) take the "single hurt color" to refer outside itself back to the "kind in glass" of the initial phrase (maybe it is a carafe of red wine). Reference, after all, *is* "an arrangement in a system to pointing." The second sentence seems to underscore this duality, discussing the physical world as well as the language employed to discuss it. Thus something that was "nothing strange" at one level (the physical) can prove "not ordinary" at the other, precisely because our language *is* quite ordered, even when the reality it depicts has spilled. The gap between word and object is indeed spreading.

This work and the other short pieces that make up *Tender Buttons* anticipate a mode of reading inaugurated by William Empson at the start of the 1930s and soon codified as close reading by the so-called New Critics. Far more than the compulsive footnoting that the likes of Joyce, Pound, and Eliot gave rise to in their scholars, or the deeply conservative aesthetic attachments of the more conventional New Critics, Stein here demands a reader who is fully present to the language itself, each word connected to the one before and the one after, without having to reach even halfway across this short paragraph. In this way she anticipates much of the poetry of the last half of the twentieth century and the opening decades of the twenty-first. The difference, having spread, offers a firm foundation.

4

Bob Perelman

on **Robert Frost, "Mending Wall"**
(1914)

Something there is that doesn't love a wall,
That sends the frozen-ground-swell under it,
And spills the upper boulders in the sun;
And makes gaps even two can pass abreast.
The work of hunters is another thing:
I have come after them and made repair
Where they have left not one stone on a stone,
But they would have the rabbit out of hiding,
To please the yelping dogs. The gaps I mean,
No one has seen them made or heard them made,
But at spring mending-time we find them there.
I let my neighbor know beyond the hill;
And on a day we meet to walk the line
And set the wall between us once again.
We keep the wall between us as we go.
To each the boulders that have fallen to each.
And some are loaves and some so nearly balls
We have to use a spell to make them balance:
"Stay where you are until our backs are turned!"
We wear our fingers rough with handling them.
Oh, just another kind of out-door game,
One on a side. It comes to little more:
There where it is we do not need the wall:
He is all pine and I am apple orchard.
My apple trees will never get across
And eat the cones under his pines, I tell him.
He only says, "Good fences make good neighbors."
Spring is the mischief in me, and I wonder

If I could put a notion in his head:
"*Why* do they make good neighbors? Isn't it
Where there are cows? But here there are no cows.
Before I built a wall I'd ask to know
What I was walling in or walling out,
And to whom I was like to give offense.
Something there is that doesn't love a wall,
That wants it down." I could say "Elves" to him,
But it's not elves exactly, and I'd rather
He said it for himself. I see him there
Bringing a stone grasped firmly by the top
In each hand, like an old-stone savage armed.
He moves in darkness as it seems to me,
Not of woods only and the shade of trees.
He will not go behind his father's saying,
And he likes having thought of it so well
He says again, "Good fences make good neighbors."

I was introduced to "Mending Wall" in high school in the early 1960s. For a teenager from Ohio, New England stone walls were as exotic as the sheep in Wordsworth's Lake District, but Frost's opening lines were quick in explaining what was unfamiliar.

> Something there is that doesn't love a wall,
> That sends the frozen-ground-swell under it,
> And spills the upper boulders in the sun;

"Something there is" was an odd beginning, and the second half, "that doesn't love a wall," nearly as odd—who *loves* a wall? But the following lines provided an instant introduction to stone walls. In winter the ground freezes, the ice expands, the ground pushes up and jostles the upper stones, spilling them onto the ground. By this point, I was oriented to the poem.

The poem I read in the 1960s was timeless, not subject to the vicissitudes of history. For decades Robert Frost had been central to U.S. poetry and "Mending Wall" was one of his signature pieces. Like generations of students before me, I would find that the regional was universal. The poem was a vignette from rural New England in the early twentieth century, but at the same time it presented the recurring human contest between flexibility and conservatism.

We're meant to decide in favor of flexibility: it's hard to be on the side of the "old-stone savage" neighbor as opposed the imaginative speaker. But flexibility doesn't imply change. There are the moments of disruption in the poem—the ground swell, the hunters and their dogs, the mischief of spring—but they are contained by the overall cyclical repetition described in the poem (and enacted by the poem, which closes on a repeated line). The wall gets rebuilt every year: in winter it breaks; in spring it's fixed. The rural setting itself is permanent. In the poem's jokiest lines, we get a quick description:

> There where it is we do not need the wall:
> He is all pine and I am apple orchard.
> My apple trees will never get across
> And eat the cones under his pines, . . .

Pine there, apple here: to even suggest movement is absurd, like apple trees ambling over to munch on pinecones.

While nothing was going to change in "Mending Wall"—no history, no politics—I remember being taught to look for verbal change of aspect, what must have been an introduction to close reading. For all its aw-shucks tone ("Oh, just another kind of out-door game"), it's a didactic poem. Near the end, the speaker almost offers the neighbor a lesson about poetry:

> I could say "Elves" to him,
> But it's not elves exactly, and I'd rather
> He said it for himself.

The speaker doesn't actually offer this lesson and, anyway, the neighbor would flunk (he can't think for himself, he can only repeat his father's phrases). But as a young reader, I found the poem's lessons very learnable. I was told about iambic pentameter—how most lines are purely iambic ("and SPILLS / the UP / per BOUL / ders IN / the SUN), while the places where the iambic pulse is disturbed represent disturbances in the wall ("SOME-thing / there IS /"; "and MAKES / GAPS e / ven TWO"). Beyond this, I was shown how the figurative kept peeping out from the literal. The rough stones are suddenly "loaves" or "balls." Hints of magic keep recurring: the mysterious gaps no one has seen or heard made; the spell needed to balance some stones; the not-exactly Elves. On the larger horizon of suggestion, the poem balances its meaning as carefully as the loaf-stones. Is wall-mending just an outdoor game or, as the lines about the "old-stone savage" with a rock in either hand suggest, is it something like war?

While I was learning such lessons in the early 1960s, quite a different use was being made of Frost and "Mending Wall" in the wider world. By this point Robert Frost was a potent symbol of the United States. The laconic individualist in rural New England who was also a famous poet made a perfect representative of Jeffersonian agrarian democracy, American exceptionalism and universality, suitable for domestic use and for export. Frost recited "The Gift Outright" at Kennedy's inauguration in 1961 and the next year was dispatched by Kennedy to converse with Nikita Khrushchev in Moscow. Frost may have written "Mending Wall" in 1914 without thinking about history or politics, but when the Berlin Wall was built in 1961, the poem became an ideal cultural weapon in the Cold War, standing for freedom and self-reliance as over against Communist regimentation.

As I write this in the shadow of Trump's Wall and his concocted National Emergency, the poem is again being yanked into relevance. But now it's a more conflicted relevance. Perhaps "Mending Wall" could be pressed into service to provide an applause-line for a left-wing Democratic rally: "As that iconic American poet, Robert Frost, wrote, 'Something there is that doesn't love a wall!'" But the setting and implied population of the poem seem more fertile territory for Trump supporters today: "Here's an old-time America without immigration where people build stone walls and respect property."

But to pose such alternate possibilities is to read the poem anachronistically. "Mending Wall" doesn't show any of the economic, migratory, or media-amped pressures that produced Trumpism. (The burst of paranoia on the speaker's part near the end of the poem—where the neighbor is a savage moving in darkness—feels more contemporary.)

Perhaps the most anachronistic aspect of the poem itself is what first seems more natural: the cyclical climate and the unchanging landscape. With its setting of nice cold winters and unmoving stands of pine and apple, "Mending Wall" is a poem from the pre-Anthropocene: no floods, desertification, invasive species, or die-offs. But add another hundred years of global warming and the basic premise of the poem will be quaint indeed to the students of 2114.

5

Rachel Blau DuPlessis

on **H.D., "Sea Rose"**
(1916)

Rose, harsh rose,
marred and with stint of petals,
meagre flower, thin,
sparse of leaf,

more precious
than a wet rose
single on a stem—
you are caught in the drift.

Stunted, with small leaf,
you are flung on the sand,
you are lifted
in the crisp sand
that drives in the wind.

Can the spice-rose
drip such acrid fragrance
hardened in a leaf?

Reading poems is a clustered experience—you are taking in a lot of focused stimuli, sound, meaning, pictures, word choices, rhythms, and a question of how (and why) to separate all these stimuli. "Analyzing" poems is a term some readers hate, as if it spoils something. How the poem makes you feel what you are feeling, and see both through its own focus and in your focus—analytic/emotional description is my way of beginning. Analytic/emotional description doesn't concentrate only on what the poem means (that will anyway be a cluster or a range of thoughts); it's interested in how the poem does (or makes) something in words for a complex effect.

"Sea Rose" by H.D. is a short poem with short lines, minimalist work. It is first describing a rose from the outside, and the description is not very flattering (word choices—"meagre," "sparse," "marred"). However, by the time you get to the eighth line, the imagined speaker suddenly addresses the rose itself ("you")—and this is strange because you don't expect the exterior thing to be intimately addressed. In the third stanza "you" occurs twice more, really insistent. Then in the last stanza, there's a question (a rhetorical question?) as if to another person or to the speaker, as if proving something.

The poem looks like it's in quatrains but then in the two last stanzas, there is slight irregularity—a five-line stanza and a three-line stanza. In this small way the poem is illustrating the irregularity and difference of the sea rose. This kind of finding (form "imitates" content) has to be treated cautiously, because it also looks a little corny or pat.

So the poem contrasts two roses. You can make a list of words that start to prove this, and if you do, you'll find that the sea rose is given negative or suspect connotations and that many of them "rhyme" or have similar sound qualities (harsh, marred, sparse, hardened; stint, thin; stunted, flung; caught). Most of the sounds in these words are short, tight. The nicer, prettier "spice-rose" has in its name open long vowels. The other adjectives ("precious," "wet," "single") for the nice rose also use short, tight vowels, but the content relaxes with the presentation of its expected, conventional beauty. There's no intrinsic reason in the sounds themselves that this occurs; the effect is created in the context of resemblances and contrasts that H.D. has made.

With some poets (H.D. is one) you can circle vowel and consonant sounds, breaking up the words to phonemic components (if you don't think that is smashing the poem to bits) and discover a net or mesh of related and contrastive tones and sounds taking shape over the poem. This is one way of holding a poem together when it doesn't have fixed meter or regular rhyme—features that can be an expectation for poems and present another idea about holding words together.

About the line: here, you can loosely count lines of between 2 and 3 beats (short, concentrated), and the lines with 3 beats appear in no predictable pattern. This is free verse, but like much free verse poetry, it shows traces of meter. No writing or speaking occurs without expressive emphasis implied. Both meter and its traces deploy semantic emphasis within the text of poetry. Line breaks will shape the poem if you don't have rhyme or fixed meter defining the line ends and are thus vital to modern and contemporary poetry. This H.D. poem breaks the bits of the sentences into what sound like the "natural" phrases of spoken English. This is one kind of free verse; another kind makes almost every line end-stopped (with terminal punctuation); a third kind of free verse breaks the line in ways that challenge both of those modes, creating a jagged syntactic hovering among lines.

What is this contrast of two roses proving or assuming? This is where you might re-notice the arc of the argument. The sea rose is a non-conforming rose—it is near the ocean and gets blown and damaged; it's raised up by the wind and driven down by it, sometimes battered by sand. As in nature, difficult conditions make the rose resistant and tough. These observations (using paraphrase as a technique of reading) come through the realm of imagery loosely construed; in fact, H.D. is not using decorative imagery but observable occurrences. This kind of realistic imagery links to certain plainspoken modes in poetics—involving the poet's methods, choices, and poetic traditions. Even when a poet begins a poem, her page is never totally blank but houses ghosts of what poetry is, has been, and could be.

H.D. is articulating value judgments inside sound and diction (choosing specific words like "marred" rather than a possible [unused] alternative, "spoiled"). An explicit confrontation occurs between a highly valued rose (spice-rose, wet [not desiccated], and single—isolated, out of context of other forces), that is, a garden or even hothouse flower, and a survivor rose in a harsh environment. The final stanza seals the contrast with a riddle: can the "spice-rose" smell as fascinating as the sea rose with its "acrid fragrance," an essence distilled by forces of nature? The poet has set the poem up as a challenge, which ends by valuing this bitter little battered rose for being undomesticated, not conventionally beautiful, with a rarer perfume.

Writing about roses-as-beauty and imagery involving women with roses saturate poetic tradition. Roses, women—there are endless poems on this comparison, often adding love or seduction in the carpe diem motif. This poem is written by a female poet who is hardly ignorant of these materials or of the associations among beauty, womanhood, and poetry, and the effect on herself of being the cultural object of such comparisons. She uses this poem to express her subject-claiming attitude to these materials. The fact that she placed this poem first in her first book, *Sea Garden* (1916), might give a clue as to H.D.'s own debates and conclusions.

6

Yosuke Tanaka

on **Ezra Pound, "The Encounter"**
(1916)

All the while they were talking the new morality
Her eyes explored me.
And when I rose to go
Her fingers were like the tissue
Of a Japanese paper napkin.

In Ezra Pound's "The Encounter" (from the collection *Personae*,
1926), the title represents multiple aspects of "encounter," such as
those between the speaker and the woman, the East and the West,
soul and body, or metaphysics and physics. My reading favors the
last pairing, but any one of these is tenable—and they are, of course,
related. Before furthering its exploration of such binaries, let me
offer a "close reading" of this five-line poem.

The poem begins, "All the while they were talking the new morality /
Her eyes explored me." "The new morality" in the 1910s was a trendy
intellectual and social movement. It entailed overt "new" forms of
expression of sexual desire, especially by women, as Peiss and colleagues explain: "By proclaiming the existence and legitimacy of
female sexual desire, the new morality undermined the Victorian
sexual code and encouraged some women's sexual assertiveness."[1]
In the poem, the woman's exploration of the speaker, a sexual counter-
gaze, was an actual practice of liberation.

With this erotic connotation, we cannot help reading the following
lines as an escalation of the initial arrangement: "And when I rose
to go / Her fingers were like the tissue / Of a Japanese paper napkin."
The speaker stood up, felt the texture of the woman's fingers, and

likened the feeling to a paper napkin. This simile perhaps does not work in the usual way, however, since readers of the poem might be unsure of the look of such a *Japanese* napkin in particular; its certain texture is only assumed or implied, as is the relevance of its physical sense to the story told in the poem.

So what is the meaning hidden in these lines? One possibility is the poet's desire to cause the reader to sense the charged eroticism of this encounter. The erotic reading is supported by the early critical publication *A Guide to Ezra Pound's Personae* (1926, by K. K. Ruthvan), in which the author suggested that "new morality" in this poem coincided with then-new English translations of Sigmund Freud's *Three Contributions to a Theory of Sex* (1910) and *Interpretation of Dreams* (1913). But Ruthvan also wrote that "Pound, however, had never taken a creative interest in Freudian theories," so we must explore beyond this particular hidden eroticism.

"When I rose to go" is a pastiche of the famous refrain "I will arise and go now" in William Butler Yeats's poem "The Lake Isle of Innisfree" (*Rose*, 1892). Pound and Yeats studied Noh plays together at the Stone Cottage in Sussex, from 1913 to 1916. Pound introduces sexual wordplay here to Yeats's verb "arise," rendered as a past tense of "rise," simultaneously incorporating the original title *Rose* of Yeats's book and adding a double entendre on the slang "to erect."

> *I will arise and go now,* for always night and day
> I hear lake water *lapping* with low sounds by the shore;
> While I stand on the roadway, or on the pavements grey,
> I hear it in the *deep heart's core.*

In this poem the words I have italicized, among others, have no sexual implication. Yet Yeats urgently expresses a longing for the spiritual nature of the island on Ireland's Lough Gill, despite the speaker's displacement from the place, situated just then "on the pavements grey." I was first inspired by this poem when introduced to it in poetic essays of the 1980s and 1990s written by Gozo Yoshimasu, a prominent contemporary Japanese figure. My own urgent response was to "arise and go" mountain trekking in the outskirts of Tokyo and to realize, via Yeats's rather than Pound's sense of rising, displaced to the Japanese scene, that an actual translocation into the natural can awaken one's spirit.

My collaborator Andrew Houwen in Tokyo has recently studied Pound's deep immersion in traditional Japanese culture. Pound noted that *The Cantos* were inspired in part by Japanese Noh plays, which Pound had translated and published. I will mostly reserve judgment as to whether imagists' inspiration from Noh constituted a damaging cultural appropriation, but I do appreciate their insight that Eastern cultures discern multiple, complex ways of approaching the physical wilderness beyond simple eroticism.

Traditional Japanese paper napkins are called "kaishi," literally *paper in the bosom*. They can be found today only in special situations, such as in tea ceremonies. According to one napkin supply company, the napkins once carried by every Japanese person served multiple purposes, for instance, wrapping up sweets or writing a letter. The napkin of the poem works as a metaphor for the encounter between physical and metaphysical elements of life. Intellectually it wraps up simple eroticism, and discloses the vulnerability of its desired object under the guise of the modern dispensation of the supposedly new "new morality," and abets the inner strategy of the poem. If today such fragile tradition-summoning napkins emerge only rarely and specially, it's clear that Pound meant to introduce a social ordinariness, a new and yet romantically familiar convention, to such delicacy. Pound once defined an "Image" as "that which presents an intellectual and emotional complex in an instant of time."[2] The poem presents such a modern "instant" that is at once very new and very old.

NOTES

1 Kathy Lee Peiss, Christina Simmons, and Robert A. Padgug, eds., *Passion and Power: Sexuality in History* (Philadelphia: Temple University Press, 1989), 157.

2 Ezra Pound, "A Few Don'ts by an Imagiste," *Poetry* 1 (1913): 200–206.

7

Christian Bök

on **Marcel Duchamp and Elsa von Freytag-Loringhoven,
"Fountain"**
(1917)

Fountain. Philadelphia Museum of Art: 125th Anniversary Acquisition. Gift (by exchange) of Mrs. Herbert Cameron Morris, 1998, 1998-74-1 © Artists Rights Society (ARS), New York / ADAGP, Paris / Succession Marcel Duchamp.

Marcel Duchamp (according to legend) sauntered into the showroom of the J. L. Mott Iron Works in New York, where he procured a pissoir on a whim in early April 1917.[1] Duchamp then painted the signature "R. Mutt, 1917" on the urinal so as to submit the object, under the title *Fountain*, to the Society of Independent Artists—a committee that was curating the largest exhibit of artwork in the history of America, promising to accept, unjuried, any artwork by any artisan for a fee of $6.00 USD. Duchamp resigned in protest from his membership in the society when the committee refused to include *Fountain* in the salon on the grounds that the urinal did not qualify as art. An anonymous editorial published in *The Blind Man* refuted this arbitrary rejection of *Fountain*, arguing that whether or not R. Mutt sculpted the object himself did not in fact matter: "He CHOSE it"—and by doing so, he had displaced it from its mundane context, appreciating it for its artful, rather than its useful, qualities.[2] An argument of this sort thus gave any critic permission to judge artists not for the merits of their skill but for the merits of their taste.

Fountain constituted the most eminent example of a novel class of artworks invented by Marcel Duchamp, who called them "ready-mades"[3]—each one a quotidian commodity, selected from his daily life, then reframed as an artsy item, via some negligible adjustment. Alfred Stieglitz photographed *Fountain* after the scandal, but the object then went missing, requiring Duchamp to make replicas of the original in order to satisfy demand from collectors during the final years of his career. Duchamp took credit, late in his life, for the work of R. Mutt, but in 1917, he wrote to his sister, disclaiming his authorship, professing that he had submitted the urinal on behalf of a "female friend"[4] (thought now to be Elsa von Freytag-Loringhoven, who had already created a readymade titled *God*, which consisted of a plumbing trap mounted on a miter box). Glyn Thompson eventually determined that J. L. Mott neither made nor sold the urinal photographed by Alfred Stieglitz;[5] instead, the Trenton Potteries Company made the item, lending credence to the idea that Marcel Duchamp lied about his original purchase.

Elsa von Freytag-Loringhoven (an émigré from Germany) may have submitted *Fountain* as an act of protest against the declaration of war upon Germany by Woodrow Wilson in April 1917, leading her to express her fury at the Society of Independent Artists by signing the work with a pun on the German lexeme *Armut* (meaning "poverty"). Marcel Duchamp, however, professes to have signed the work with a signature that alludes to both Mott (the industrial plumber) and Mutt (the cartoonish gambler), with the "R" standing for "Richard" (meaning "moneybags" in French).[6] *Fountain* has thus become the site for a struggle of retroactive attribution (given that the life of the lady prankster ends in poverty in 1927, whereas the life of the male pretender ends in acclaim in 1968). Sotheby's has sold replicas of *Fountain* for as much as $1,762,500,[7] and artists as diverse as Brian Eno, Pierre Pinoncelli, and Kendell Geers (among others) have attempted to influence the value of the urinal by returning the readymade to its intended function, desecrating the artwork by pissing into it during its exhibition.[8]

Fountain has inspired many thinkers in the history of Art (all of them fascinated by the concept that Art must breed ideas rather than reify craft); moreover, a poll of 500 artists, dealers, and critics in 2004 concluded that this object had become the most influential of all artworks in the modern milieu.[9] Artists as diverse as Andy Warhol, Jeff Koons, Richard Prince, and Damien Hirst have all found permission for their own practice in such a readymade, appropriating artifacts from popular culture to enhance their own repertoire of aesthetic materials. Sherrie Levine, for example, has produced a replica of the readymade, doing so by recasting the urinal in bronze, then polishing the material to a sheen of gilded chrome. Scott Naismith has, likewise, produced a replica of the readymade, doing so by selecting a helmet from a storm trooper in the movie *Star Wars*, then signing the surface of the white armor with the painted moniker "R. Mutt, 1917." Even a poet like Kenneth Goldsmith has noted the importance of *Fountain* in his style of plagiarism, celebrated by writers in the literary movement called Conceptualism.[10]

Fountain discomforts philistines, who believe that no pisspot can ever qualify as a sublime artwork, but I might refute such naysayers via two fantastic scenarios. Let us teleport such a pissoir backward in time (say 5,000 years): surely, the mystery of its manufacture might induce such wonderment in a primordial civilization that the hierophants there must, perforce, enshrine this basin in a sacred space, such as a temple. Now let us teleport such a pissoir forward in time (say 5,000 years): surely, the history of its significance might induce such wonderment in a superhuman civilization that the scientists there must, perforce, enshrine this basin in a sacred space, such as a museum. In both cases, the patina of deep time can turn such a humble vessel into a valued trophy. A curator in the present, setting the urinal on a plinth, is asking us to wonder: *If this thing exists as a work of Art before its time in the distant past, and if this thing also exists as a work of Art ahead of its time in the pending ages, why not simply call this thing a work of Art right now?* (thereby relieving ourselves, so to speak, from any pissiness about it).

NOTES

1 Arturo Schwarz, *The Complete Works of Marcel Duchamp* (New York: Harry N. Abrams, 1979), 466.

2 "The Richard Mutt Case," *Blind Man* 2 (May 1917).

3 Marcel Duchamp, "Apropos of Readymades," *Art and Artists* (July 1966): 47.

4 Marcel Duchamp to Suzanne Duchamp, April 11, 1917, quoted in William A. Camfield, "Marcel Duchamp's *Fountain*: Its History and Aesthetics in the Context of 1917," *Dada/Surrealism* 16 (1987): 90.

5 Glyn Thompson, "Not Mott, Not Mutt, and Not Marcel," *Jackdaw* 125 (January/February 2016): 8–13.

6 Otto Hahn, "Passport No. G255300," *Art and Artists* (July 1966): 10.

7 Carter B. Horsley, "Contemporary Art and 14 Duchamp Readymades," https://www.thecityreview.com/s02pco1.html.

8 Paul Ingram, "Pissing in Duchamp's *Fountain*," *3:AM Magazine* (June 23, 2014), https://www.3ammagazine.com/3am/pissing-in-duchamps-fountain/.

9 Louise Jury, "*Fountain* Most Influential Piece of Modern Art," *Independent* (December 2, 2004), https://www.independent.co.uk/news/uk/this-britain/fountain-most-influential-piece-of-modern-art-673625.html.

10 Kenneth Goldsmith, "Why Appropriation?" in *Uncreative Writing* (New York: Columbia University Press, 2011), 111.

8

Tonya Foster

on Claude McKay, "If We Must Die"
(1919)

If we must die, let it not be like hogs
Hunted and penned in an inglorious spot,
While round us bark the mad and hungry dogs,
Making their mock at our accursèd lot.
If we must die, O let us nobly die,
So that our precious blood may not be shed
In vain; then even the monsters we defy
Shall be constrained to honor us though dead!
O kinsmen! we must meet the common foe!
Though far outnumbered let us show us brave,
And for their thousand blows deal one death-blow!
What though before us lies the open grave?
Like men we'll face the murderous, cowardly pack,
Pressed to the wall, dying, but fighting back!

In this remarkable Shakespearean sonnet, written in the red summer of 1919, just after the end of World War I and in the middle of an influenza pandemic that took more than 100,000,000 lives, Claude McKay draws on language and codes of honor first learned from his Jamaican father's insistence on dignity and respect in all of his dealings. His father led a collective action campaign against a duplicitous white missionary pastor. After years, despite uncertain odds, the campaign led to the pastor's withdrawal from the parish. In "If We Must Die," there is an insistence on this kind of unrelenting dignity. There is, in the poem, a clarion call for the noble death that arises from insisting on dignity despite ignoble circumstance.

In his preface to one of his first books, *Constab Ballads* (1912), McKay "confesses" that he is "so constituted that imagination outruns discretion, and it is [his] misfortune to have a most improper sympathy with wrong-doers" (7). Here, McKay recognizes and rejects conventional etiquettes. It is not incidental that many of the "wrong-doers" he would have encountered as a Kingston constable were black. McKay goes on to say that he is "by temperament, unadaptive; by which I mean that it is not in me to conform cheerfully to congenial usages. We blacks are all somewhat impatient of discipline" (7). His poetry and prose, which he presents as mechanisms to "relieve [his] feelings," interrogate how those he identifies as "wrong-doers" and who are "impatient of discipline" may present aesthetic-ethical modes of being.

What are the codes of honor that the "wrong-doers" adhere to? "If we *must* die" is the repeated conditional statement that animates the poem's dynamic psychosocial consciousness. Composed of three quatrains with an ababcdcdefef rhyme scheme and a concluding perfectly rhymed (gg) couplet, the poem's first eight lines are structured as two conditional if/then statements that center the inevitable death of the poem's expansive "we," which may be understood as both the speaker and the listener broadly addressed.

If McKay's work is to be read on a continuum, the *we* in this poem may well be comprised of wrong-doers according to social codes that mark some as always improper.

> If we must die, let it not be like hogs
> Hunted and penned in an inglorious spot,
> While round us bark the mad and hungry dogs,
> Making their mock at our accursèd lot.

In this first if/then statement, McKay draws our attention to negation— if x, then *not* y. "Then," though absent, is implicit and insistent. If the necessity of death is true, then there is a rejection of terms that dehumanize, that render one more animal than human. The *we* are hunted and penned, mocked and accursèd.

> If we must die, O let us nobly die,
> So that our precious blood may not be shed
> In vain; then even the monsters we defy
> Shall be constrained to honor us though dead!

This second if/then statement has a dramatic poetic apostrophe that addresses an idealized *we*. O! There is an exclamatory plea—if x, then O y! This is a plea that *our* (again the *we*) death not be in vain. Death without purpose is ignoble. Nobility constrains even the "monsters" from denying *us* honor because our overarching nobility remains even in the face of death. This nobility, in fact, reveals *them* who attack as monsters to be defied. When we discuss honor, which denial matters most?

The next four lines of the poem level a dramatic call to unity and for action among kinsmen.

> O kinsmen! we must meet the common foe!
> Though far outnumbered let us show us brave,
> And for their thousand blows deal one death-blow!
> What though before us lies the open grave?

What else is there to do in the face of such an inhuman assault? What dies here? What is the nature of the death? The concluding couplet turns to answering that question:

> Like men we'll face the murderous, cowardly pack,
> Pressed to the wall, dying, but fighting back!

There is a definition of manhood as collective resistance emboldened by rhythmic, iambic marching. The murderous attackers are revealed to be both monsters and an animalistic "pack" that has dehumanized itself. The poem ends, not in death or dying but in the fighting back that is imagined as evidence of the manly and the human in McKay's undisciplining configurations. It's this "fighting back" by the wrong-doers that survives the grave and lays claim to heroic dignity.

Grappling with death and white supremacist assaults on Black life and on Black peoples' autonomies, McKay's "If We Must Die" is an appeal to protest and unity. He insists that *if* we *must die*, then *we* will establish the terms of *our* deaths. The *we* of McKay's poem is at once both speaker and listener who, while recognizing that he (and the central figures are all male) may not counter the inevitability of death (*must* is an imperative that points to the nature of this situation), will/can assert and claim dignity and integrity against dehumanizing efforts. The poem's *we* is expansive enough that though it points to the particular situation of Black peoples in the United States and celebrates notions of bravery and bravado that are characteristic of the ideal soldier, the *we* also points to any group of *we*—joined under the sign of broadly determined kinship, who is potentially hunted and penned. It is a *we* that might be slaughtered (and dehumanized) as hogs by "monsters we defy."

Interestingly, the poem makes no obvious racial claims, in that it leaves the violence and the resistance to the violence racially unmarked, though the "bark of mad and hungry dogs" was a regular feature of anti-Black violence. The unmarked or unremarked in American poetry has, in the past, been largely understood as a signifier of whiteness, of the whiteness of the speaker, of the whiteness of the universal human figure and condition. In this poem, McKay situates Black resistance and protest at the center of a racially unmarked call to unity and human dignity. As it was, so it is.

9

Lytle Shaw

on **Wallace Stevens, "The Snow Man"**
(1921)

One must have a mind of winter
To regard the frost and the boughs
Of the pine-trees crusted with snow;

And have been cold a long time
To behold the junipers shagged with ice,
The spruces rough in the distant glitter

Of the January sun; and not to think
Of any misery in the sound of the wind,
In the sound of a few leaves,

Which is the sound of the land
Full of the same wind
That is blowing in the same bare place

For the listener, who listens in the snow,
And, nothing himself, beholds
Nothing that is not there and the nothing that is.

But can you not hear the dreadful screaming
all around that people usually call silence?

—Georg Büchner, *Lenz*

Forgoing carrot noses and corncob pipes, Wallace Stevens packed his "Snow Man" with prerequisites for the viewing of a winter scene that cannot be reconciled with one another.[1] To restrain oneself from projecting human emotions onto the bleak landscape (to avoid associating winter with death or the sound of the wind with misery) would be to demonstrate a "mind of winter." This mistake of humanizing the non-human world, if it is a mistake, was first given a name by John Ruskin, who termed it the pathetic fallacy. In one sense Stevens takes Ruskin a step farther, suggesting that the viewer who seems to succeed at resisting the pathetic fallacy merely awaits the charge of inhuman coldness from those who understand his refusal to humanize the landscape as a failure to be fully human. Worse, these latter viewers aren't wrong. Indeed, "one *would* have to have a mind of winter," the poem tells us. Though there's more to be said about the poem's closing barrage of nothingness, my interest in this particular snow man has taken off from this first problem Stevens sets up: what we need to learn, or unlearn, in order to see accurately, and whether we can do that.

The recursive nature of the poem's thinking on this topic might cause a humane reader to shiver: there appears to be no outside—or rather, only outside. If we could locate the poem's beholding listener a bit more specifically, perhaps we could offer blankets, a shed, some medication. But the poem gives us no real geographic coordinates: we are somewhere that has winters. We see pines, junipers, spruces. There is some distant glitter. Despite the poet's (cold?) refusal to specify the scene of this attempt to understand winter, search parties interested in Stevens have historically set off from a surprisingly concrete location: the front yard of a largish white clapboard house six down from the north end of Westerly Terrace in West Hartford, Connecticut, where the poet resided. While I want to resist this temptation to insist that knowledge about property ownership can simply cut through philosophical abstraction and bring us down to the social reality of poetry—let us name this the proprietary fallacy—still one must acknowledge that Stevens did have a singular relationship to property: he spent his life, and became relatively wealthy, insuring it, which is to say that he needed his clients to feel both connected to the ice-shagged junipers in their front yards and aware (even worried) that these property owners would be in far worse misery if the not so distant glitter they beheld was that of flames engulfing their split-level suburban homesteads. Indeed, such a scenario needed to be a real possibility that required action and investment. It couldn't be waved aside by appealing to the homeowner as a "nothing himself."

But framing things this way makes it seem like my poem "The Confessions 2" can, by attempting to ground and contextualize, give us the truth that Stevens willfully obfuscates through his orientation toward abstraction.

> One would have to have a mine of copper, and have been cold to the union's safety and wage pleas for a long while, and perhaps have amassed a cabinet of classical artifacts in a sound proof basement displayed on custom aluminum mesh grids, or have run for several city offices on a xenophobic, police-might, no more open container ticket, to hear the clean Rhone water rushing below and not to think of the literature of the sanatorium, or restorative strolls along the lake past diplomatic estates, of the institution of the nanny, of the institution of the affair, of French dressing coming without asking for it and of the smell of hay on trains. From the observation rail they look down toward my seat. "Did you say something?" "Nothing, no it's fine."[2]

In fact, I'm playing with the corrective as much as with the problem. The scene is shifted from Connecticut to French-speaking Switzerland, where I was visiting at the time I wrote the poem (on a postcard, to a friend in San Francisco). What are the preconditions necessary for seeing not a season but rather a foreign country, accurately? Jumping off from the impossible and abstract ones Stevens proposes, I give us very possible and concrete ones. Instead of a generalized mind of winter, we get a very particular cold-weather mental geography: a figure who owns and operates a toxic and dangerous resource extraction enterprise, most likely in a country where workers are even less protected than in the United States; he ignores the reasonable demands made by these workers and pours his surplus capital into overdetailed and precious display systems in his private art museums, over which he no doubt tyrannically presides. You know the type. He digs cops, hates foreigners, and wants to criminalize large subsections of public behavior. In other words, rather than say something broadly political and vaguely plausible like, this is a person who wants to maintain the status quo because he benefits from it, the poem insists far further on exactly who this figure might be—*overidentifying* with the process of grounding Stevens's abstractions, contextualizing his placelessness. Historicism and heckling rub shoulders. The supposedly virtuous scholarly activity of specifying and concretizing becomes also a matter of insinuating, projecting wildly, smearing without compunction. From the nothing surrounding Stevens's iced-over juniper bushes, his clapboard house, and his job in the insurance industry, my poem builds a kind of composite historical android whose values and activities seem to fill in the representational gaps upon which Stevens insists.

This is the kind of figure (tyrant, boss, connoisseur) who would not notice the important things to notice about Geneva (which actually turn out to be rather obscure and contingent). More sinisterly, this is a figure that somehow (we never quite find out how) maintains some key subterranean connection to Stevens (client? hero? doppelganger?). So while "The Snow Man" says that viewing will always involve projections onto the natural world and other people, and that this is finally a philosophical question, independent of time, place, and the social world, "The Confessions II" projects onto Stevens, mistranslating his poem by "updating" its 1920s philosophical orientation with a 1990s historicist would-be corrective in such a way that a startlingly concrete (and of course damning) social world emerges from within his syntax and vocabulary. Do I imagine the latter world as the final truth of the matter? Absolutely not. My interest is far more in putting these two worlds into contact, thinking their relationship.

NOTES

1 This essay itself is a repacking; I published an earlier version, "My Stevens: Impossible Preconditions for Viewing," *Wallace Stevens Journal* 35:1 (2011): 129–32.

2 Lytle Shaw, "The Confessions 2," in *The Lobe* (New York: Roof Books, 2002). Reprinted with permission of the author.

10

Julia Bloch

on **William Carlos Williams, "The rose is obsolete"**
(1923)

The rose is obsolete
but each petal ends in
an edge, the double facet
cementing the grooved
columns of air—The edge
cuts without cutting
meets—nothing—renews
itself in metal or porcelain—

whither? It ends—

But if it ends
the start is begun
so that to engage roses
becomes a geometry—

Sharper, neater, more cutting
figured in majolica—
the broken plate
glazed with a rose

Somewhere the sense
makes copper roses
steel roses—

The rose carried weight of love
but love is at an end—of roses

It is at the edge of the
petal that love waits

Crisp, worked to defeat
laboredness—fragile
plucked, moist, half-raised
cold, precise, touching

What

The place between the petal's
edge and the

From the petal's edge a line starts
that being of steel
infinitely fine, infinitely
rigid penetrates
the Milky Way
without contact—lifting
from it—neither hanging
nor pushing—

The fragility of the flower
unbruised
penetrates space

———

"The rose is obsolete"—a poem whose title derives from its opening lines—begins by jettisoning what might be the most well-worn instance of poetic representation in Western poetry. No more roses, William Carlos Williams declares: no more roses dragging their yawningly predictable baggage into our art (scattered among that baggage: female beauty, sexual availability, passionate affection). The first line simultaneously prescribes and describes; it makes a case for what ought to be but also what is already the Modernist case against received images. No more roses; only the new.[1]

But the rose reappears immediately, and *how* it reappears, through-out a series of chiseled short declaratives, manifests the most crucial aspect of Williams's poem. Here is the rose, anatomized in this very poem that obviated it. The rose is obsolete, but here are its petals (edges), stems (columns), more petals and maybe also leaves (double facet), and sliced ends hanging free in a hand, or a vase, or open air (edges that cut without cutting). The edges meet nothing; they seem to have no substance. Williams's characteristically jarring line breaks make the words jostle and scrape against each other—against each other's edges—and hang free as the poem erases the rose into "nothing." Williams's poem converts its polemic against rose into a polemic against representation itself.

The next one-line stanza, "whither? It ends—," leans off a cliff. The stanzas that follow inaugurate a new syntactical unit (note the capitalized "But"), more pottery reproducing the rose. The poem both does and does not answer the question it poses: whither? The poem answers by asking: what happens if we consider *this* rose forged in metal, or *this* rose glazed in porcelain, or *this* rose forged in copper or steel? The poem reengages the image by way of geometry: a field devoted to the study of points, lines, surfaces, and, yes, edges. What was first question and answer and question again has become an experiment in knowledge. The sensible mind can perform the alchemical or industrial operation of turning copper roses into steel ones (or, if "into" is only implied, manifesting them from nothing). Meanwhile, the rose breaks: its representation in a majolica plate, yes, but even as its symbolic weight is yanked back into the poem ("weight of love"), the object, not its mere representation, once more comes to "an end"—recalling the edges (ends) of the rose that cut nothing.

This is not to say that Williams has given up on love. Love "waits" on the end of a broken stanza. The poem returns to lovely edges, from which "The fragility of the flower / unbruised / penetrates space" (108, 109). Notice how line breaks forestall rhetorical closure. Notice only the geometry, the points and lines, the poem seems to say. Consider the startling couplet "The place between the petal's / edge and the." A gap yawns between "the" and "From," the gap itself perhaps that "place" modified by the article.[2] After that gap, the rose must be "infinitely / rigid," both fine and infinite enough to penetrate "the Milky Way / without contact" and ending, finally, "unbruised" by all this torquing, a flower that "penetrates space." Or perhaps it is the fragility that penetrates across these line breaks. The geometrical replaces the discursive: in cuts and clippings that some critics have called cubist for the way they reject traditional forms of perspective, Williams's poem describes and then enacts the sliced image.

"Crude symbolism," Williams declares elsewhere rather more didactically, "is to associate emotions with natural phenomena such as anger with lightning, flowers with love" (100). Williams sought not better symbolism but poetry that had no need for it at all: "to replace not the forms but the reality of experience with its own—" as he puts it yet elsewhere. Where is this elsewhere? Williams's dash in the preceding quote ought to be a clue. "The rose is obsolete" arrives nearly twenty pages into Williams's restlessly hybridic work *Spring and All*, which contains Williams's most famous (originally untitled) antirepresentational poem: "so much depends / upon // a red wheel / barrow" (138). First published in 1923 in France, *Spring and All* fell into obscurity until its rerelease by New Directions Books nearly ten years after Williams's death, at which point it offered a form of poetic attention that captivated poets writing in the 1970s and beyond.[3] "The rose is obsolete" takes on one of the most intractable symbols in poetry. And yet it belongs to a work that can't avoid racial and sexual botanical baggage: the very last poem in *Spring and All*, "Black eyed susan" (anthologized elsewhere as "The Wildflower"), contrasts the "white daisy" with its "dark woman" floral cousin (151). Williams's thinking reiterates culturally encoded histories of the flower even as it tries to make a case for a fragile "new" image.

"It is necessary to dwell in the imagination," Williams writes in *Spring and All*, "if the truth is to be numbered" (112). To be numbered means to be counted, recognized, or valued; it also means to be put into poetry (Pope: "I lisped in numbers, for the numbers came"). To keep that poetry resolutely skeptical in its postures toward perspective and representation demanded, for Williams, a poem on the edge— as well as, or especially, our reading of it.

NOTES

1 William Carlos Williams, *Imaginations*, ed. Webster Schott (New York: New Directions, 1971), 107. At least two crucial Modernist efforts to evacuate the rose of its literary-cultural baggage precede Williams's: H.D.'s "Sea Rose" in 1916 and Gertrude Stein's *Geography and Plays* in 1922, a collection that includes the poem "Sacred Emily" and its unforgettable line "Rose is a rose is a rose is a rose."

2 I wish to thank Amber Rose Johnson for this observation.

3 Ron Silliman: "Like [Gertrude Stein's] *Tender Buttons*, the volume that is just possibly its closest kin, *Spring and All* is a work that every young poet should be carrying around in their back pocket until it dissolves. And then they should get a new copy." *Silliman's Blog*, March 20, 2010, https://ronsilliman.blogspot.com/2010/03/its-not-here-yet-for-this-first-day-of.html. Bernadette Mayer in a letter to Alice Notley on Williams's influence on her antilyricism: "So that it always seemed to me from Williams I could deduct that the wonderful capacity for the world to exist without an I was good for me." Quoted in Alice Notley, "Doctor Williams' Heiresses" (San Francisco: Tuumba, 1980), n.p.

11

Jennifer Scappettone

on Elsa von Freytag-Loringhoven, "XRAY"
(1924)

NATURE CAUSES BRASS TO OXIDIZE
POEPLE TO CONGEST
BY DULL RADIOPENETRATED SOIL
LUXURY ORNAMENT
~~FORCES~~
DESTINNED
POLISH COSMIC HANDS ~~CROWDED~~ DYNAMIC TO
GANG
~~TO~~ POLISH   KILL
FOR FASTIDIOUS
CONTRA NATURE BRILLIANT BOSS' ᴵᴰᴱᴱ ᶠᴵˣ SUM
TOTAL
RADIANCE
~~DIVINE IDÉE FIX~~

"X RAY" is reprinted by permission of the editors and publisher of *Body Sweats: The Uncensored Writings of Elsa von Freytag-Loringhoven*, edited by Irene Gammel and Suzanne Zelazo (Cambridge, MA: MIT Press, 2011).

"NATURE CAUSES BRASS TO OXIDIZE": this deceptively baffling poem by the "mother of Dada" and "future Futurist" the "Baroness" Elsa von Freytag-Loringhoven begins with a perfectly legible state-ment, delivered in the authoritative rhythm of iambic pentameter, about the patina that develops when copper and its alloys make con-tact with oxygen in the air.[1] Nature is its protagonist; what another version of the poem calls nature's "FINISHING PROCESS" develops a coating upon the metal that—contrary to received ideas about corrosion—protects it. Nature also causes people to amass, and even to congest, as the poem's revision has it—either through the primal instincts driving sex and reproduction or through death: a congestion not only of cities but of soil such as that of the unprecedented mass graves yielded by the recent catastrophic Great War.

Despite the unwobbling start, it turns out to be taxing to evolve an idée fixe about this short poem, which exists in nine versions housed in archives at the University of Maryland and in its published form, from the October 1927 issue of Eugene and Maria Jolas's pathbreaking little magazine *transition* (with several inexplicable editorial deletions and additions); the only thing that remains the same is its opening statement, with a few minor variants. Had Elsa von Freytag-Loringhoven and her agent, literary executor, friend, and lover Djuna Barnes succeeded in pulling together a collection of her poetry before her untimely death at age fifty-three in 1927, we might have some definitive idea of the Baroness's ultimate intention for what would appear fixed on the page. Regardless, her life's work in restless, revisionary manuscript, readymades, ephemeral assemblages, and shock-costumed spontaneities at every imaginable locus—from the offices of the *Little Review* to Broadway subway stations and the French Consulate in Berlin—suggests that fixing was contrary to her nature. So does the poem itself. "BRILLIANT BOSS' IDÉE FIX"—note the lack of the final e, which renders this a translingual phrase—is closer to the slang fix of the addict than the obsession elegantly cast in perfect French. We can assume that a poet as subversive as the Baroness (a "mother" antipatriarchal and hardly maternal) would distance herself from this brilliant and, in some versions, "fastidious" boss's monomaniacal polish.[2]

Can we nevertheless conjecture as to what this short lyric, written between 1923 and its 1927 publication, is "about"? Its title provides a clue: "X RAY," or in one instance, "RADIO." X-rays had galvanized pivotal bouts of aesthetic experiment now classified as high modernism, from Futurist kineticism to Cubist transperspectivalism. "Who can still believe in the opacity of bodies, since our sharpened and multiplied sensibilities have already grasped the obscure manifestations of mediums?" asked the Futurist painters' Technical Manifesto issued in 1911. "Why should we continue to create works that don't take into account our growing visual powers which can yield results analogous to those of X rays?"[3] The year this poem was published, Arthur Holly Compton won the Nobel Prize for his discovery of the change in X-rays' wavelength when they collide with electrons in metals. Imaging experiments such as the photograms or "rayographs" made by the Baroness's contemporary and collaborator Man Ray in the 1920s would have extended the aesthetic lure of these scientific advances.

But the Baroness doesn't assume a heady Futurist reverie in the face of these advances; instead, the artist known for dressing herself in garbage grounds a seemingly ethereal medium in earth and the body. In one version, a cluster of compound riffs suggests a marriage of sun and soil through electromagnetic radiation, which is in turn wedded to radio: "SUNS RADIOINFUSED / RADIO'S SOIL / SOILSECRET SUN-MESSAGE SUNIMPREGNATED / DORMANT WITHIN SOIL FOR PROG-RESS' / DUMB [BUMB?] RADIOPENETRATED SOIL." The poet, doubt-less inspired by the advent of voice broadcasting and the rise of the commercial radio "craze" in the 1920s, conceptually extends the aural rather than visual implications of these scientific discoveries, imagin-ing the sun's electromagnetic radiation penetrating the seemingly silent, secret earth as radio "sunmessage."

Though parataxis (the stacking up of images without pinning down their relations) makes it difficult to determine exactly how the next line of manuscript, "LUXURY ORNAMENT," fits—the line was in fact deleted (by editors?) in the published poem—it compels us to re-member the Baroness's first *objet trouvé* or found object, *Enduring Ornament* (1913): a rusted iron ring that she found on the street en route to marry Baron Leo von Freytag-Loringhoven at New York's City Hall, and which she claimed as a symbol of Venus.[4] Despite or because of its rust—another process of oxidation—the Baroness's readymade nuptial ornament is "enduring," treasured in duration, a part of nature. As the makeshift crystal radios of the 1920s and World

War II demonstrate, the oxide coatings of many metal surfaces (rusty nails, corroded pennies, and other discarded objects) can act as semiconductors capable of detecting (and rectifying) radio waves. The compulsion to "POLISH" in the service of creating a "LUXURY ORNAMENT" deprives metal not only of its place in nature but of its conductive properties.

In the compressed yet audacious space of this poem, polishing metal is rendered equivalent to killing off an amassment of people—both aspects of the boss's idea-fixes that are "CONTRA NATURE" and associated in five versions of the text with "PROGRESS." Given what was about to happen in Europe, the United States, and the Pacific theater of war, this seemingly facile analogy makes a reader shudder—and wonder about the contents of the radio's "sunmessage." Compton was instrumental in initiating the Manhattan Project, which generated the first atomic bomb. And radio itself was deployed initially in the service of killing, not communicating: "Radio ... was born into a world of jittery jingoism and started life as a weapon in the commercial and military rivalries of the great powers," writes historian Daniel Headrick. "Thus do humans unfairly project their own virtues and vices upon the machines they create."[5]

In *transition*'s June 1929 issue, Eugène Jolas, renowned advocate of transcultural work such as *Finnegans Wake*, would propose that the only rejoinder to contemporary despair would be the poet's "producing adequately and violently a chemistry in words." As lyric preface he chose the verse of the late Baroness.[6]

> "Say it with— — —
> Bolts!
> Oh thunder!
> Serpentine aircurrents— — —
> Hhhhhphsssssssss! The very word penetrates![7]

These words from a poetic commentary on radio and sex subversive enough that it wasn't published until 1983 come down to us in vengefully penetrating lines. They transmute radio into what endures and exceeds any aesthetically or ideologically constrictive message: "RADIANCE."

NOTES

1 In the 1918 poem "Love—Chemical Relationship," the Baroness cast the two "characters," the young Marcel Duchamp as "A Futurist" and herself as "A Future Futurist." See Elsa von Freytag-Loringhoven, *Body Sweats: The Uncensored Writings of Elsa von Freytag-Loringhoven*, ed. Irene Gammel and Suzanne Zelazo (Cambridge, MA: MIT Press, 2011), 253. Kenneth Rexroth remembered asking Duchamp whether he considered the Baroness a Futurist or a Dadaist and the response, "She is not a Futurist. She is the future." See Kenneth Rexroth, *American Poetry in the Twentieth Century* (New York: Herder & Herder, 1971), 77.

2 See Robert Reiss, "'My Baroness': Elsa von Freytag-Loringhoven," in Rudolf E. Kuenzli, *New York Dada* (New York: Willis Locker & Owens, 1986), 81.

3 "Futurist Painting: Technical Manifesto," signed by Umberto Boccioni, Carlo Carrà, Luigi Russolo, Giacomo Balla, and Gino Severini and dated April 11, 1910. Translated in Lawrence Rainey, Christine Poggi, and Laura Wittman, eds., *Futurism: An Anthology* (New Haven, CT: Yale University Press, 2009), 65. See also Linda D. Henderson, "Modernism and Science," in *Modernism*, ed. Astradur Eysteinsson and Liska Vivian (Amsterdam: John Benjamins, 2007), 383–404. "An invisible world beyond human perception was no longer a matter of mystical or philosophical speculation, but was now established empirically by science" (385). See also Sara Danius, *The Senses of Modernism: Technology, Perception, and Aesthetics* (Ithaca, NY: Cornell University Press, 2019), 55–90.

4 Irene Gammel, *Baroness Elsa: Gender, Dada, and Everyday Modernity: A Cultural Biography* (Cambridge, MA: MIT Press, 2003), 161. She gave the work to her friends the Chicagoan pianist Allen Tanner and Russian painter Pavel Tchelitchew while living in Berlin in 1923, in gratitude for their financial support (see p. 323).

5 Daniel Headrick, *The Invisible Weapon: Telecommunications and International Politics, 1851–1945* (New York: Oxford University Press, 1991), 116.

6 "Logos," *transition* 16–17 (June 1929): 25–27. Reprinted in Eugène Jolas, *Eugene Jolas: Critical Writings, 1924–1951*, ed. Klaus H. Kiefer and Rainer Rumold, *Avant-Garde and Modernism Collection* (Evanston, IL: Northwestern University Press, 2009). See also Gammel, *Baroness Elsa*, 388.

7 From "A Dozen Cocktails—Please," in Freytag-Loringhoven, *Body Sweats*, 50.

12

Craig Dworkin

on **Bob Brown, from *GEMS***
(1931)

Come live with me, and be my ■■■,
And we will all the pleasures prove
That ■■ and ■■■, ■■■ and ■■,
And all the craggy ■■■ yields.

There will we sit upon the rocks,
And see the shepherds ■■■ their flocks

The title of Bob Brown's 1931 collection *GEMS: A Censored Anthology* alludes to the various illustrated anthologies that had been published as epitomes of wholesome literature at the height of Victorian prudery and propriety. Brown's book set out to skewer the U.S. government's censorship of Modernist literature (the notorious obscenity ruling against James Joyce's *Ulysses*, for just one indication, would stand until 1933).[1] By canceling certain words of canonical verse with a blunt black box, Brown leveraged a fallacious logical reversal: if obscene words are targeted for erasure, then redaction will suggest something obscene; "the black blot of the censor," as Brown realized, "makes anything innocent seem most reprehensible."[2] Turning the tools of the expurgator back against puritanism, Brown gleefully generated indecency through censorship.

In its unabashedly puerile spirit, *GEMS* takes part in the classic avant-garde attempt to *épater le bourgeois*, from the barely disguised "merdre [shitt]" that opens Alfred Jarry's *Ubu Roi* to the Dadaist exploits of provocateurs like Brown's friend Arthur Cravan. Visually, Brown's typography recalls the cryptic dashes of Mina Loy's 1917 "Songs to Johannes" ("as censorship becomes more common," Brown predicts, "the dash will come more and more into its own, poets themselves will make effective use of it"), but their poetics also points to a more specific tradition.[3] By working exclusively with found texts, the gems—like poetic versions of Marcel Duchamp's assisted readymades—look forward to the appropriation strategies of Conceptual Writing and the erasure poetry that thrived in the first years of the twenty-first century.[4] Brown makes his general point by so readily adducing examples; the anthology adds up to more than the sum of its parts as it speaks to the cultural logic of censorship. But specific instances generate their own local resonances.

One of Brown's "Gems" transforms the first six lines of Christopher Marlowe's late sixteenth-century lyric "The Passionate Shepherd to His Love," which opens:

> Come live with me, and be my love,
> And we will all the pleasures prove
> That hills and valleys, dale and field,
> And all the craggy mountains yields.
>
> There will we sit upon the rocks,
> And see the shepherds feed their flocks.[5]

Brown's version takes its place in a long tradition. Almost immediately, with Walter Raleigh's "Nymph's Reply," Marlowe's poem was "endlessly imitated, parodied, and answered, well into the seventeenth century." Indeed, satirical versions continued into Brown's moment, contrasting antiquated pastoralism with contemporary urban life in poems like "The Modern Lover to His Lass" (1921) and "If Marlowe Had Tried to Write It in the Office Yesterday" (1924).[6] Like these other imitators, Brown would have expected his educated, literary audience to know the Marlowe poem, perhaps by heart, and so he stages the opportunity for a kind of doubled readerly imagination: holding the memory of the original in mind while entertaining its more prurient possibilities (of the available single-syllable rhymes, *groove*, for instance, might be sufficiently lubricious to fill in the first line's blank). The reader here is thus the one sought later by Language Poetry: an active participant in the completion of the text and a necessary co-creator of its meaning. Marlowe's "passionate shepherd"— perhaps a courtly imposter, disguised like Brown's textual travesty— has already modeled such doubling by imagining himself looking idly down on the herding scene that ought (given the eclogue's title) to include him working.

Brown's poem amplifies other features of his source as well. Some scholars speculate that Elizabethan pronunciation would have rhymed *love* and *prove*, but for the modern reader they are more closely paired as eye-rhymes. The field of the poem's subsequent end-rhymes yields an invitation to sound the words alike, perhaps offering a formal allegory wherein the ideal of love, like the word *love*, must be wrestled with or deformed in order to bring it in line with its physical trials. By canceling "love," however, Brown makes the poem more phonically regular—hastening the reader more smoothly toward the punch line—while simultaneously engaging the source-text's solicitation of the reader's eye with his own text's ostentatious visual cipher.

That visuality is key. In a drama of spectatorship, the shepherd ushers his love to a stony seat from which they will "see" the pasture scene. Brown blocks the reader's view but thus underscores the visual aspect of reading. Seeking the prurient potential in both the poetic canon and his reader's mind, Brown matches Marlowe's scopophilia with a particular sort of voyeurism, enticing the reader to peer behind the curtain of the censoring screen while spotlighting a scene of eroticized viewing. In addition to the salacious connotations of voyeurism, Brown draws on cultural tropes linking bestiality and rusticity that go back at least to the early modern period of Marlowe's time. In fact,

Brown has hardly détourned an innocent verse against its own chaste message. The very occasion of Marlowe's poem is a sexual seduction, and the first stanza's opening scene details a suggestively corporeal topography of swells and crevices as part of its persuasive courtship rhetoric. Rather than brazenly eroticizing a chaste poem, Brown displaces its erotic mapping. His suggestiveness is abetted by the fact that "flocks"—flashing like a glimpse of the word forbidden by the censor's bar—provides a phonic mannequin for the vulgar word most likely to fill the gap in the last line of the sestet. Where a rude parody might explicitly include the word, Brown's technique implicates even the most innocent readers—anything indelicate has been added by them. Moreover, by hinting without stating outright, Brown's innuendoes ultimately draw their power from the fact that artful veiling is always more erotic than bare nakedness.[7]

NOTES

1 See, among others, F. A. Lydon, *Gems from the Poets* (London: Groombridge and Sons, 1860); S. C. Hall, *The Book of Gems from the Poets and Artists of Great Britain* (London: Bell & Daldy, 1868); and *Gems of National Poetry Compiled and Edited by Mrs.* [Laura] *Valentine* (London: Frederick Warne, 1880).

2 Bob Brown, *GEMS: A Censored Anthology* (Cagnes-Sur-Mer: Roving Eye Press, 1931), 17.

3 Mina Loy, *The Lost Lunar Bædeker*, ed. Roger Conover (New York: Farrar, Straus and Giroux, 1996), 53–68; Brown, *GEMS s*, 49–50.

4 See, for some examples among many, Tom Phillips, *A Humument* (London: Thames & Hudson, 1970–2016); Ronald Johnson, *Radi Os* (Berkeley: Sand Dollar, 1977); Stephen Ratcliff, *[Where Late the Sweet] Birds Sang* (Berkeley: O Books, 1989); Doris Cross, *Re-Works* (Santa Fe: Museum of Fine Arts New Mexico, 1993); Jen Bervin, *Nets* (Brooklyn, NY: Ugly Duckling Presse, 2004) and *The Desert* (New York: Granary Books, 2008); Jenny Holzer, *Redaction Paintings* (New York: Cheim and Read, 2007); Travis McDonald, *O Mission Repo* (Cambridge, MA: Fact-Simile, 2008); Janet Holmes, *MS of m y kin* (Swindon, UK: Shearsman, 2009); Erica Baum, *Dog Ear* (Brooklyn, NY: Ugly Duckling Presse, 2011); Srikanth Reddy, *Voyager* (Berkeley: University California Press, 2011); Yedda Morrison, *Darkness* (Los Angeles: Make Now, 2012); Hugo García Manriquez, *Anti-Humboldt* (Crown Heights, NY: Litmus, 2014); Philip Metres, *Sand Opera* (Farmingham, ME: Alice James, 2015); Niina Pollari, *Form N-400 Erasures* (New York: Tyrant, 2017); and Danny Snelson's brilliant reversal of the process in *Radios* (Los Angeles: Make Now, 2016).

5 See Valentine, *Gems*, 205. Marlowe's poem was published, with textual variants, under different titles and attributions.

6 Stephen Orgel, introduction to *Christopher Marlowe: The Complete Poems and Translations* (New York: Penguin, 2007), xxi; R. S. Forsythe, "*The Passionate Shepherd*; And English Poetry," *PMLA* 40:3 (September 1925): 741.

7 See Roland Barthes on the contradiction of striptease, which works to "désexualiser la femme dans le moment même où on la dénude [desexualize the woman at the very moment of nakedness]" (Roland Barthes, *Mythologies: Essais* [Paris: Seuil, 1957]: 137); cf. "l'endroit le plus érotique d'un corps n'est-il pas *là où le vêtement bâille?* [isn't the body most erotic when the garment gapes?]" (Roland Barthes, *Le plaisir du texte* [Paris: Seuil, 1973], 19).

Rodrigo Toscano

on **Genevieve Taggard, "Interior"**

(1935)

A middle class fortress in which to hide!
Draw down the curtain as if saying *No*,
While noon's ablaze, ablaze outside.
And outside people work and sweat
And the day clings by and the hard day ends.
And after you doze brush out your hair
And walk like a marmoset to and fro
And look in the mirror at middle-age
And sit and regard yourself stare and stare
And hate your life and your tiresome friends
And last night's bridge where you went in debt;
While all around you gathers the rage
Of cheated people
Will we hear your fret
In the rising noise of the streets? *Oh no!*

Source: *Proletarian Literature in the United States: An Anthology*, edited by
Granville Hicks, Joseph North, Michael Gold, Paul Peters, Isidor Schneider,
and Alan Calmer; with a critical introduction by Joseph Freeman (New
York: International Publishers, 1935). Reprinted with permission of Judith
Benét Richardson.

The practice and legacy of *Littérature engagée*—the idea of the artist's responsibility to society, especially as elucidated by Jean-Paul
Sartre, namely, that people existentially define themselves by con-
sciously engaging willed action—have, by now, quite a long and
traceable history. In 1942, in caves, fighting an imperialist Japanese

occupation, Mao Zedong penned his "Yenan Talks on Art and Litera-ture." In it, he laid out five basic challenges for the production of culture: The Problem of Class Stand (is one truly committed to "the masses"? in keeping with party spirit), The Problem of Attitude ("expose the duplicity and cruelty of the enemy"; be patient with the masses as they become conscious), The Problem of Audience ("is your art work for peasants, workers, or revolutionary cadres?"), The Problem of Work (cadres should conform their thinking to that of the struggling masses), and The Problem of Study ("artists must study Marxism-Leninism!").

But the *problem* with the Yenan plan for art and literature, as well as for its progenitors, such as the policies of RAPP (Russian Association of Proletarian Writers, 1925), was its reliance on "The Two-Line Struggle," a Maoist ideological staple (via Stalin). Basically, you're either *with* The Rev or you're *against* it. Properly "aligned" artists were thought of as being *interior* to the revolutionary process (good) and nonaligned artists as *exterior* to the process (bad). Although Genevieve Taggard's "Interior" is not carrying out "a task" of any spe-cifically declared "two-line struggle," the poem is still typical of many a class-goading (or class-harassing) poems that appeared in the *New Masses* magazine (1926–48), a Marxist forum directly influenced by the twists and turns of the U.S. Communist Party's "line."

The *lived* economic-cultural conditions of 1936 during the Great Depression are nearly unimaginable to the majority of contemporary Americans. A full 25 percent of the previously employed population was without work. Poverty reigned supreme. Finance Capital shat-tered the urn of Social Trust. Unions had scarcely become legal the year before. Something Big was needed to change reality, something Big was on the move to change reality: the labor movement. It is by this concomitance of social duress and elation over an upsurge of revolutionary action that "Interior" is forged. The poem's ideological target, though not explicitly stated, is bourgeois decadence. But to achieve the desired result of fighting and defeating this enemy, a sur-prising and effective twist in Taggard's tale emerges. Taggard transposes the interior/exterior dichotomy onto a stage where the domicile (a fortress with the curtain drawn down) is countered by an outside where "noon's ablaze," where "day clings by" as "people work and sweat." In this way, a kind of two-line struggle of direct agency is stressed. But it depends on people having free will and on people choosing their own reality. And there, the contradiction of employing Liberal Democratic core philosophy to Communist aims is itself "ablaze." What to do? Has Bourgeois Decadent made the first move here? Yes. At the beginning of the poem, Bourgeois Decadent acts out its No unto the surrounding social reality, and the resolute answer supplied by Genevieve Taggard (aligned artisan of the revolutionary upsurge) is: "Will we hear your fret / In the rising noise of the streets? *Oh no.*" The fight closes to a draw, it seems.

By now we can employ a fair amount of critical distance in examining any given charge of "Bourgeois Decadence." We can trace its genealogy. We can trace its DNA footprints in the present. We can even poetically break down a set of possible permutations concerning the two sides of the "two-line struggle" into instances of conscious (or unconscious) motivations for each side. We can lend these avatars some definition too!

On the one hand—as regards The Decadent:

"Bourgeois Decadence" —The Living Amnesia of Historical Bourgeois Ascendancy.

"Bourgeois Decadence"—The Living Conscious Revulsion to Revolutionary Ascendancy.

On the other hand—as regards The Revolutionary:

"Bourgeois Decadence" —A Perennial Preoccupation of Bourgeois Decadents.

"Bourgeois Decadence"—A Provisional Preoccupation of Revolutionary Decadents.

So that "commitment literature"—on the hunt for its apposite self—can be seen as one plot along a matrix of many possibilities of

Socially Significant Art. There is today a strong, and many believe healthy, tendency to exacerbate (or tease) the tensions among multiple modalities that make for a Socially Significant Art. For Taggard's generation, engaging notions of "commitment" (of human agency) was a Ground Zero of political inquiry. But today, a Concomitance of Commitment Literatures stands neither for nor against the modality of alignment literature, per se. Like Taggard's "marmoset" (her riff on Marx's "old mole"—the irrepressible burrowing of revolutionary potential), alignment literature strikes us as a perennial "walking to and fro," never quite aligned. The crucible of human agency remains barely legible. The urn's shards are chaotically scattered about. What's *not* a salvage operation? This also includes the vital questions that "Interior" is still asking us, quandaries that rocket us into a revolutionary *active* pause:

> How do we measure political agency?
> Are we *ever* in a post-movement poetics moment?
> If not, should we, in the main, be delineating concrete paths toward liberation?
> Are we *nodes* or *relays* of "humanity"?
> Are our well-intentioned steps along the path of culture-making enough?

And in light of these questions, an additional one: What indeed makes for an aesthetic "accomplishment"?

Rodrigo Toscano

Mark Nowak

on **Ruth Lechlitner, "Lines for an Abortionist's Office"**
(1936)

Close here thine eyes, O State:
These are thy guests who bring
To gods with appetites grown great
A votive offering.

Know that they dare defy
The words of law and priest—
(Better to let the unborn die
Than starve while others feast.)

The stricken flesh may be
Outraged, and heal; but mind
Pain-sharpened, may yet learn to see
Thee plain, O State. Be blind:

Accept love's fruit: be sleek
Fat and lip-sealed. (Forget
That Life, avenging pain, will speak!)
Thrust deep the long curette!

From Ruth Lechlitner, *Tomorrow's Phoenix* (New York: Alcestis Press, 1937).

Social critics and literary critics have, in recent years, returned to the Marxist concept of social reproduction to analyze both the social crises of capitalism and the ways in which the manifestations and implications of these crises have been inscribed in literary texts. Studies such as Tithi Bhattacharya's *Social Reproduction Theory: Remapping*

Class, Recentering Oppression, Amy De'Ath's "Reproduction," and *Feminism for the 99%: A Manifesto* (coauthored by Cinzia Arruzza, Tithi Bhattacharya, and Nancy Fraser) are just a few recent and significant texts in this area.[1]

When Karl Marx spoke of how the worker "reproduces" himself to return to work the next day to make cotton or linen or other commodities—the worker is always a male pronoun for Marx—the job of "childbearing and child-rearing, washing, cooking, cleaning, sex and emotional care," as Amy De'Ath notes, falls "to the category 'woman'" (399). Tithi Bhattacharya expands on this in her introduction to *Social Reproduction Theory*: "Capitalism, however, acknowledges productive labor for the market as the sole form of legitimate 'work,' while the tremendous amount of familial as well as communitarian work that goes on to sustain and reproduce the worker, or more specifically her labor power, is naturalized into nonexistence. Against this, social reproduction theorists perceive the relation between labor dispensed to produce commodities and labor dispensed to produce people as part of the systematic totality of capitalism" (2). Social reproduction theory emerges, as Bhattacharya writes, from the "silences in Marxism" to "show how 'the production of goods and services and the production of life are part of one integrated process'"; it questions "what it means to bind class struggle theoretically to the point of production alone, without considering the myriad social relations extending between workplaces, homes, schools, hospitals—a wider social whole" (3).

These sites, structures, and relationships—medical offices, homes, government offices, familial and sexual relationships—saturate Ruth Lechlitner's largely unknown poem "Lines for an Abortionist's Office," which appeared in her book *Tomorrow's Phoenix*, published by Alcestis Press in 1937 in a small edition of 550 signed copies. Lechlitner's opening line, "Close here thine eyes, O State," invokes and initiates her acerbic critique of the laws and doctrines of the official patriarchal government and the patriarchal Church that define and delimit women's lives. In *When Abortion Was a Crime*, Leslie Reagan details a range of new resistance practices that women employed to fight against the restrictive state in the mid-1930s: the creation of a Birth Control Club in New Jersey in 1936 that offered a type of abortion "insurance"; the American Birth Control League's expansion from fifty-five birth control clinics in the United States in 1930 to more than five hundred in 1938; and the expansion of services in Black communities such as the opening of a separate ward, the Abortion Service, at the Harlem Hospital in 1935 to care for mostly poor Black women "who came for emergency care following illegal abortions."[2]

The defiant second half of the second stanza of Lechlitner's poem inscribes the economic disparities between the rich and the poor, or what in today's parlance we would call "income inequality" (in the words of Bernie Sanders) or "the 99%" (in the words of Occupy Wall Street). These disparities have resulted in the poem's narrator being "Pain-sharpened" and ready to struggle against these injustices.

The personified "O State" returns in the first lines of the final stanza with sharp, percussive alliteration and consonance ("f" and "l" and "t") of "Accept love's fruit: be sleek / Fat and lip-sealed. (Forget," while the stanza's penultimate line portends protest ("will speak!"). Yet it's the poem's final line that most often jars readers. Alan Wald, writing in *Exiles from a Future Time*, reads it as "the disconcerting image of the abortionist's curette as the male phallus about to "thrust deep."[3] Yet I read the image through social reproduction theory as a more comprehensive scraping away at working women's options for birth control and family planning under the patriarchal capitalism that dominated the 1930s.

Lechlitner's antipatriarchal poem documents, unfortunately, not just an injustice from a previous century that has been overturned by resistance struggles. The abortionist's office continues to be a central site of social struggle. From protests during hearings over the confirmation of U.S. Supreme Court Justice Brett Kavanaugh, whose conservative vote could potentially shift the future of *Roe v. Wade* protections in the United States, to the massive abortion protests in

Poland and repressive new legislation in Angola, whose government recently made all abortions illegal and punishable by four to ten years of imprisonment, Lechlitner's poem, unfortunately, remains all too vital.[4] It reminds us that the predominantly patriarchal working-class poetry of the 1930s spoke solely to production struggles (the strike, the factory, the picket line) and additionally reminds us, as the authors of *Feminism for the 99%* write, that "struggle is both an opportunity and a school. It can transform those who participate in it, challenging our prior understandings of ourselves and reshaping our views of the world. Struggle can deepen our comprehension of our own oppression—what causes it, who benefits, and what must be done to overcome it. . . . It can broaden the shape of solidarity among the oppressed and sharpen our antagonism to the oppressors" (55).

Ruth Lechlitner's poem on the abortionist's office allows us to revisit one school of our struggles from the mid-1930s, and it reminds us that *class*, in all its connotations, is very much still in session.

NOTES

1 See Tithi Bhattacharya, *Social Reproduction Theory: Remapping Class, Recentering Oppression* (London: Pluto, 2017); Amy De'Ath, "Reproduction," in *The Bloomsbury Companion to Marx*, ed. Andrew Pendakis, Imre Szemana, and Jeff Diamanti (London: Bloomsbury Academic, 2019); and Cinzia Arruzza, Tithi Bhattacharya, and Nancy Fraser, *Feminism for the 99%: A Manifesto* (London: Verso Books, 2019).

2 Leslie J. Reagan, *When Abortion Was a Crime: Women, Medicine, and the Law in the United States, 1867–1973* (Berkeley: University of California Press, 1997), 133–36.

3 Alan Wald, *Exiles from a Future Time: The Forging of the Mid-Twentieth-Century Literary Left* (Chapel Hill: University of North Carolina Press, 2002), 238.

4 https://www.hrw.org/world-report/2018/country-chapters/angola.

Robert Fitterman

on **Mina Loy, "The Song of the Nightingale Is Like the Scent of Syringa"**

(c. 1944)

Nightingale singing—gale of Nanking

Sing—mystery

of Ming-dynasty

sing

ing

in Ming

Syringa

Myringa

Singer

Song-winged

sing-wind

syringa

ringer

Song-wing

sing long

syringa

lingerer

Mina Loy, "The Song of the Nightingale Is Like the Scent of Syringa," from *Lunar Baedeker and Time Tables* (Highlands, NC: Jonathan Williams Publisher, 1958). Copyright 1958 by Mina Loy. Reprinted with the permission of Roger L. Conover for the Estate of Mina Loy.

The trouble with being a sound poem. I open with this, reminded of E. M. Cioran's *The Trouble with Being Born,* and I'm also thinking about good "trouble," as in *difficulty*—the difficulty of teasing out meaning in a sound poem. In short, the trouble is this: sound poetry wants to be about sound, about the materiality of language, about the music that language can produce. There might be meaning derived from the soundscape, or the sounds might be the result of a preconceived strategy or theme, but the sound is always forefronted. And yet, when a sound poem directly points us to as much content as Mina Loy's "The Song of the Nightingale is Like the Scent of Syringa," then to grapple with the content-puzzle underneath the sonic patterns might also be part of the reader's experience. This is that trouble. Even though Loy encourages us to simply experience the poem as sound—in an interview, she states that "I'd only written these things for the sound"—she has carefully complicated that sound with a historical tragedy and subtle references to sensory perception tied to that tragedy. The political content of the poem might be referential, but the positioning to create sound poems, in a culture where content-based verse is the acceptable norm, carries its own political heft. Additionally, the fact that Loy was also a painter and actor and feminist (*Feminist Manifesto,* 1914) who bravely challenged the confines of creating in a single medium only doubles the trouble with being a sound poem. I think we can safely assume that Loy was aware of her resistance to literary conventions when she chose to write these sound poems.

The musicality of "The Song of the Nightingale is Like the Scent of Syringa" is composed with an unusual palette of sounds that reflect the song, or the chirp, of the nightingale bird: the prominent consonance of the *m, s, n,* and *g* sounds; the assonance of the *i* and the long *e* vowel sounds. Part of the trouble with being this particular sound poem can be partially unpacked by focusing on three uncommon words that triangulate the meaning: *Nanking, syringa,* and *myringa.* Nanking was the site of a horrific mass murder and mass rape of 300,000 Chinese by Japanese troops in 1937–38. This historical reference to a tragic event invites a politically engaged reading. The reference to Nanking appears early in the poem and casts a long shadow, or "sing-wind," throughout. The placement of the word "Nanking" interacts with "Ming-dynasty" on several levels: sonically, historically, culturally. The Ming dynasty represents the apex of a great cultural period in Chinese history; the Nanking tragedy represents a genocidal fall of China to Japanese troops. As such, the rhyme of *Nanking* and *Ming* suggests other trouble beyond the soundscape.

Further, the rhyming of "syringa" (a lilac flower) and "myringa" (the membrane of the eardrum) points readers to a triangulation in the poem where the song of the nightingale and the smell of the syringa flower fuse and register in the ear as sensory perception—through song and scent—of this Nanking human tragedy. Through the nightingale's song, these sounds reverberate in the eardrum (myringa), as does the rhyming between *syringa* and *myringa*. In a less obvious rhyme, Loy's placement of self in this scenario of the bird's song and the eardrum's perception is heard in her own name: we can easily recognize *Mina* in "myringa" as well as *my ring*. Also, in the word "syringa," we hear both *siren* and *syringe*—adjunct meanings that support this same triangulation of the bird's song, the political acts of horror, the reverberation in the eardrum. The nightingale's song resembles the song of the mythological siren (luring the poet); the nightingale's song also acts as a syringe, like a bee, pollinating scent and sound to the ear. And by placing her own name in concert with these sounds, Loy points to her own subjectivity in the abovementioned triangulation.

In a larger sonic sense, throughout the poem Loy also employs a constraint by having each line contain "ing." This *ing*-sound gives the poem its rapid movement and its reverberation in the eardrum, and even parallels the guttural *g*-sound that can be heard, frog-like, under the chirping sound of the nightingale, as heard in any field recording of a nightingale. This rapidity, and the overall short-line structure of the poem, not only echoes the nightingale's song but also mirrors—or even fabricates—the poet's perception of the Nanking horrors through the quick "gale" (or flurry) of sensory perceptions.

As with many sound poems, it's common for the reader to focus exclusively on the author's intention that the poem is predominantly about sound, that the content in a sound poem is often subordinate to the excessive attention to the soundscape. But in Loy's "The Song of the Nightingale is Like the Scent of Syringa," the complexity, or *trouble*, in the poem points to more specific meaning: how we perceive, through our senses, tragic histories. There are many ways to tie and untie such a poem. My intention here is not to reach any singular conclusion of meaning but to suggest that even though "The Song of the Nightingale is Like the Scent of Syringa" presents itself, foremost, as a sound poem, it also lends itself to a close reading of the natural world and the horror of political events, and how a poet subjectively perceives and processes both.

16

Davy Knittle

on **Allen Ginsberg, "A Supermarket in California"**
(1955)

What thoughts I have of you tonight, Walt Whitman, for I walked down the sidestreets under the trees with a headache self-conscious looking at the full moon.

In my hungry fatigue, and shopping for images, I went into the neon fruit supermarket, dreaming of your enumerations!

What peaches and what penumbras! Whole families shopping at night! Aisles full of husbands! Wives in the avocados, babies in the tomatoes!—and you, Garcia Lorca, what were you doing down by the watermelons?

I saw you, Walt Whitman, childless, lonely old grubber, poking among the meats in the refrigerator and eyeing the grocery boys.

I heard you asking questions of each: Who killed the pork chops? What price bananas? Are you my Angel?

I wandered in and out of the brilliant stacks of cans following you, and followed in my imagination by the store detective.

We strode down the open corridors together in our solitary fancy tasting artichokes, possessing every frozen delicacy, and never passing the cashier.

Where are we going, Walt Whitman? The doors close in an hour. Which way does your beard point tonight?

(I touch your book and dream of our odyssey in the supermarket and feel absurd.)

Will we walk all night through solitary streets? The trees add shade to shade, lights out in the houses, we'll both be lonely.

Will we stroll dreaming of the lost America of love past blue automobiles in driveways, home to our silent cottage?

Ah, dear father, graybeard, lonely old courage-teacher, what America did you have when Charon quit poling his ferry and you got out on a smoking bank and stood watching the boat disappear on the black waters of Lethe?

"A Supermarket in California" from *Collected Poems, 1947–1997* by Allen Ginsberg. Copyright © 2006 by the Allen Ginsberg Trust. Used by permission of HarperCollins Publishers.

———

The suburb and its commercial hubs—the supermarket and the shopping mall—were built en masse in the United States in the 1950s and 1960s to suit the desires of the "family shopper," the suburban housewife, who, in the normative model, was in charge of managing the home.[1] Midcentury U.S. supermarkets offered housewives "sensorial excitements," a break from the boredom and frustration of a life conscripted to housework, and fulfilled a desire that retailers "saw as a feminine longing for erotic excitement intensified by lives circumscribed by domestic norms."[2] In taking in the sights, sounds, and smells of the supermarket, the family shopper was offered an illusion of an outside (possibly a sexy one) to the domestic sphere.

Into a mid-1950s landscape of rapid suburbanization, car-oriented development across urban and suburban municipalities, the reification of the heteronormative family, and the privatization and devaluation of women's domestic labor enters queer, itinerant Allen Ginsberg, visiting the "neon fruit supermarket" to go "shopping for images."[3] Ginsberg claims and refigures the feminized labor of shopping by frequenting the supermarket as a form of social tourism. In Ginsberg's supermarket, the heteronormative family is part of the sensorium, rather than its audience. There are "babies in the tomatoes," "wives in the avocados," and "aisles full of husbands."[4] Anxious about the privatization of public sensory, sexual, and social life, Ginsberg visits the supermarket like the "family shopper" in order to see something, to have a sensory experience. But he also takes an informal census of what the United States is becoming in the wake of postwar mass suburbanization. He mourns the loss of a United States with a place for him, a way of living to which he might feel relevant.

In the place of a solely reproductive logic, Ginsberg establishes kinship with Walt Whitman as his aesthetic predecessor. Whitman is at once "childless" and Ginsberg's "dear father."[5] Referencing Whitman's loneliness, Ginsberg reflects on his own, as he seeks out Whitman more as witness to his loneliness than as protection against it. To summon Whitman, Ginsberg reaches across time, invoking a desire for what queer theorist Elizabeth Freeman refers to as a "stubborn lingering of pastness" that is "a hallmark of queer affect."[6] As queer and trans theorist Heather Love explains, "contemporary queer subjects are also isolated, lonely subjects, looking for other lonely people, just like them," a desire that frequently requires traveling out of the present and into the past.[7] Whitman's appearance in the asynchronous and expansive now of the poem draws out Ginsberg's own ghostliness as he feels both conspicuous and unnoticeable.

While families shop in the supermarket, Whitman and Ginsberg both profit from and are disenfranchised by their illegibility. They stride "down the open corridors together in our / solitary fancy tasting artichokes, possessing every frozen / delicacy, and never passing the cashier."[8] Ginsberg and Whitman's position outside a normative family model sets them outside of capital, free to eat and take commodities without paying for them. At the same time, Whitman is a grubber, both "a searcher among ruins" and a person looking for grub, for food, who is stealing, arousing suspicion, and being followed by the store detective.[9] Whitman the childless "grubber" illustrates that the externalities of the heteronormative family model, like those of capitalism, offer the possibility of a queer utopia while underscoring that, in a U.S. context, material resources are most available to those who are interpellated and participate in the social models sanctioned by the physical and economic infrastructure of suburban life.

After they've left the supermarket, in the poem's final sentences, Ginsberg asks Whitman a series of questions: "will we walk?" "will we stroll?" and finally, "what America did you have when Charon quit poling his ferry?"[10] Ginsberg, by summoning Whitman, looks for the origins of his own present in Whitman's United States. In asking Whitman about the United States of the past, Ginsberg speculates as to how he has arrived where he is now.

How, in other words, did we produce a physical landscape and set of sociocultural expectations with no purposeful consideration of the needs of queers, of "grubbers," of poets, of people outside of a white, middle-class, normative family model, of those who want to walk the streets at night? What, therefore, is the poem or the poet to the suburbs? And what is the suburb to the poet? How do we make sense of the suburb as a spatial form that in a U.S. context is both dominant and isolating? Suburban counties house the majority of people living in the United States and are growing faster than either urban or rural areas. The percent of U.S. residents living in the suburbs has more than doubled since Ginsberg issued his critique of suburbanization in "A Supermarket in California."[11] Ginsberg's defamiliarization of the suburbs and his questions about the future it offers to anyone and everyone estranged by or outside the normative family form matter more, in the flexible now of our reading, than ever.

NOTES

1 As Adam Mack argues of midcentury supermarkets, "they reinforced the notion that middle-class women should look to the excitements of the homemaker role itself—in this case, family shopper—and not to challenges to existing gender arrangements for contentment." Adam Mack, "'Speaking of Tomatoes': Supermarkets, the Senses, and Sexual Fantasy in Modern America," *Journal of Social History* 43:4 (2010): 818.

2 Ibid.

3 Allen Ginsberg, *Howl and Other Poems* (San Francisco: City Lights Books, 1959), 29.

4 Ibid.

5 Ibid., 29, 30.

6 Elizabeth Freeman, *Time Binds: Queer Temporalities, Queer Histories* (Durham, NC: Duke University Press, 2010), 8.

7 Heather Love, *Feeling Backward: Loss and the Politics of Queer History* (Cambridge, MA: Harvard University Press, 2007), 36.

8 Ginsberg, *Howl and Other Poems*, 29.

9 "Grubber, n." *OED Online* (Oxford University Press, December 2018). http://proxy .library.upenn.edu:2817/view/Entry/81938?redirectedFrom=grubber (accessed January 20, 2019).

10 Ginsberg, *Howl and Other Poems*, 30.

11 Kim Parker et al., "What Unites and Divides Urban, Suburban and Rural Communities," Pew Research Center, May 22, 2018, http://www.pewsocialtrends.org/2018 /05/22/demographic-and-economic-trends-in-urban-suburban-and-rural-com munities/ (accessed December 13, 2018).

17

Jake Marmer

on **Bob Kaufman, from "Jail Poems"**
(1960)

II

[...]
God, make me a sky on my glass ceiling. I need stars now,
To lead through this atmosphere of shrieks and private Hells,
Entrances and exits, in- out- up- down, the Civic seesaw.
Here—me—now—Hear—me—now—always here somehow.

III

In a universe of cells—who is not in jail? Jailers
In a world of hospitals—who is not sick? Doctors,
A golden sardine is swimming in my head.
O we know some things, man, about some things
Like jazz and jails and God.
Saturday is a good day to go to jail.

Sifting through Bob Kaufman's second poetry collection, his City Lights editors discovered a shred of brown wrapping paper with the phrase "GOLDEN SARDINE" scrawled on top of it. "Golden Sardine," wrote the editors on the book's back cover, "floated loose in a stream of tattered papers & visions." It floated to the top, turning into the poetry collection's title.

"Golden Sardine": incantatory and musical, a two-word near-rhyme. A dark joke because the sardine's gold is the grimy oil dripping from the fork's edge. Is there a fish less distinguished, in the whole Cannery Row? It is the opposite of the elusive and gentle wish-granting goldfish. Then again, to peer into a sardine can for revelations is the specialty of Bob Kaufman, San Francisco street-prophet poet. When he writes, in "Jail Poems," "A golden sardine is swimming in my head," he's talking about poetry, mythology, and visions flashing through his mind. To capture these, at the can's edge, using slang, music, and biblical imagery is Kaufman's particular kind of alchemy.

In "Benediction," a dirge to America's imploded ideals, Kaufman writes: "America, I forgive you ... I forgive you / Eating black children, I know your hunger . . . I forgive you / Burning Japanese babies defensively— / I realize how necessary it was. / Your ancestor had beautiful thoughts in his brain. / His descendants are experts in real estate." The accusatory tone, impossibly gory imagery, and dark sarcasm hearken back to the biblical prophets Jeremiah and Isaiah. And what would Kaufman say if he were alive in 2016, witnessing a "real estate expert" as the U.S. president? Kaufman's lines are uncannily prophetic but not magically so: they're the result of a profound understanding of the systems surrounding us. This is the poetic intuition, the most ancient sort. Like Allen Ginsberg said in an interview: "What prophecy actually is is not that you actually know that the bomb will fall in 1942. It's that you know and feel something that somebody knows and feels in a hundred years. And maybe articulate it in a hint—a concrete way that they can pick up on in a hundred years."

The prophetic tone—and ambition—was a common thread running through the works of otherwise vastly different poets in the Beat circle. When Kaufman writes, in "Jail Poems," "Oh we know some things, man, about some things / Like jazz and jails and God," the "we" here are his fellow poets and contemporaries—Ginsberg, Amiri Baraka, Diane di Prima, Michael McClure, and Philip Whalen, among others. Many of these poets had been arrested at one point or another, though Kaufman's record of thirty or more arrests became the stuff of legends. To know "God," to Kaufman, was to know jail—to descend into the heart of the injustice and absurdity of the world that surrounded him. "Saturday is a good day to go to jail" because it is the Sabbath, the sacred day of rest, and in Kaufman's testimony, the moment when injustice is made all the more absurd, all the more stark. But it is also a "good" day because it is an opportunity to enact the alternative. In Billy Woodberry's *And When I Die, I Won't Stay Dead*, a recent documentary about Kaufman, James Smethurst recalls the poet as the "uncompromising, most principled. Not the most extreme but the most principled in a sense that he made absolutely no concessions to bourgeois culture." In a letter to the *San Francisco Chronicle*, published in the back of the "Golden Sardine" collection, Kaufman himself writes: "Arriving back in San Francisco to be greeted by a blacklist and eviction, I am writing these lines to the responsible non-people. One thing is certain I am not white. Thank God for that. It makes everything else bearable." This is Kaufman's theology coming to fore.

And jazz? Certainly, one of the reasons Kaufman was so reluctant about publishing his work was his poetry's performative dimension. Silently scanning his poem on the page is not enough: the music of the poem comes alive when read out loud. See, for instance, "Here—me—now—hear—me—now—always here somehow." This is a mantra, made of three interrelated triplets. The first "here—me—now" does not sound like normative English. Each word within this triplet is its own fragment, its own exhalation and context—in a Dickinsonian kind of a way. The triplet is wrought and desperate, ripped up, inward-bound. It's a riff on the biblical *hineini*—"here I am," uttered, at their lives' peak moments, by Adam, Abraham, Moses. The phrase signifies spiritual readiness and is a response to the divine call. In Kaufman's case, however, there is no such beckoning from the divine. Instead, the immediately preceding lines recount the "atmosphere of shrieks and private Hells . . . the Civic seesaw." The poet's jumbled response comes in the absence of the call. It is a readiness to witness and put into words the unspeakable.

The second part of the triplet, "hear—me—now," is more directly liturgical, more grammatically proper. Here, in a slight melodic permutation, the phrase line turns from introspection to address. The second triplet's seeming earnestness, however, is a setup for the crash of the finale—"always here somehow." Liturgy turns into a resigned, dark joke, a diss. The "here" of the beginning of the line refers to a spiritual state; "here" at the end is the jail. Razor-sharp intensity of the "now" turns into the anticlimactic, purposeless "always . . . somehow." Kaufman is often funny, even in the darkest poems. But in "Jail Poems," the resignation is so strong, it saturates every bit of irony, as nearly every stanza demonstrates, though none as remarkably as the very last one: "Come, help flatten the raindrop."

"We know some things," writes Kaufman, thinking about his fellow Beats. "We know some things," he alludes to a long chain of the great poet-philosopher-inmates. Among them, "Socrates, still prisoner." And Cervantes, who invented his noble madman while jailed for unpaid debt, is another: "See the great American windmill, tilting at itself." Except that in Kaufman's interpretation, the Cervantes windmill, in its American incarnation, is itself the giant and the knight, at war with itself.

"We know some things" is, perhaps, an invitation extended to us, the poet's readers. Do we, reading Kaufman, know anything about jazz and jails and God? Do we have what it takes to truly witness Kaufman, "hard like jazz, glowing / In this plastic jungle, land of long night, chilled"?

18

Danny Snelson

on **Jackson Mac Low, "Call me Ishmael"**
(1960)

Circulation. And long long
Mind every
Interest Some how mind and every long

Coffin about little little
Money especially
I shore, having money about especially little

Cato a little little
Me extreme
I sail have me an extreme little

Cherish and left, left,
Myself extremest
It see hypos myself and extremest left,

City a land. Land.
Mouth; east,
Is spleen, hand mouth; an east, land.

From *Stanzas for Iris Lezak* (New York: Something Else Press, 1971). Used
with permission of Anne Tardos.

"Call me Ishwael"[1]

Jackson Mac Low spent the summer of 1960 devising strategies to
write poems on the subway route between his home in the Bronx and
his job(s) in Manhattan. He worked a number of positions at the time,
including "etymologist, writer of reference-book articles, copyeditor,

indexer, proofreader, and fact checker."[2] The poems that make up
Stanzas for Iris Lezak deploy these same detail-oriented labors
toward the disruption of the normative reading and writing practices
that govern professional life. Not unlike Melville's Bartleby, Mac Low
takes up the post of a knowledge worker who would simply "prefer
not to." His poems build new rules for reading in order to produce a
new method for writing. They are at their best when their own neatly
devised systems break down.

Perhaps the most famous of these poems, "Call me Ishmael," indexes
Mac Low's misreading of *Moby-Dick* (or, at least the first page thereof).
Like the sub-sub librarian who crafts the opening citations of Melville's
novel, Mac Low is known for his meticulous research and lexical precision. In this poem, we get a crystalline example of his groundbreak-
ing "chance-acrostic" poetic method. The method uses letters from an
index string to find corresponding words in another text to create a poem.
Here, for example, the iconic first line "C-a-l-l / m-e / I-s-h-m-a-e-l"
serves as the index that is spelled out by words with the same first
letter to generate five stanzas in 4-3-7 line arrangements. To produce
this, Mac Low simply starts over and over from the first page of the
book, looking for sequential words that begin with each corresponding index letter, retaining each word with its capitalization and trail-
ing punctuation as they're found in the text.[3]

Today, of course, it's easy to reenact Mac Low's "Call me Ishmael." A
quick Google search brings up the full text of *Moby-Dick*. You can test
it out yourself. Go ahead. Attentive readers/reenactors will notice
that the poem makes a striking number of errors.[4] Indeed, given the
range of Mac Low's textual practices—indexer, copyeditor, proofreader, computational precursor, anticipatory algorithmic agent—
one would expect that searching a single page for index letters would
pose no challenge at all.

In each instance, these "errors" should be seen as motivated poetic
decisions. Each intervention in the mechanics of the procedure
makes the poem more compelling for the reader. Rather than "pure

process," then, this is a poem written against the efficiency and precision of knowledge work. Indeed, I would propose that these errors, these decisions, *are* the poem. That its oft-stated procedural approach amplifies a refusal to proceed as instructed. That it performs an editorial poetics of deceptive diction.

With this in mind, rather than attempting to keep Mac Low on task with his procedure, I would extend an invitation to read by writing *with* Mac Low: to reperform his defective method as a way to read the poem. Or, even better, why not continue the process where Mac Low left off—with the agency to ignore the rules when it best suits the poem. In this spirit, here is one take on a "Part II" of "Call me Ishmael," using the same editorial procedure to pick up where Mac Low's stanzas conclude:

Coral and Look Look
My ever
I soul; hats my and ever Look

Commerce about like like
Myself experiment,
I such high myself about experiment, like

Cooled and leaning leaning
Meet; every
It strong himself meet; and every leaning

Crowds and looking looking
My enchanting
Is stepping his my and enchanting looking

Circumambulate a landsmen; landsmen;
Moral element
I street, her moral an element landsmen;

City a look! Look!
Me employs?
Involuntarily sea hours me an employs? Look![5]

1 "Call me Ishmael" was first published in 1968 in the twelfth issue of a little magazine called GRIST. In all the dozens of works that reference "Call me Ishmael"—
and in Mac Low's own books—precisely zero mention the poem's first publication
in GRIST. As I'm writing this, I like to imagine this neglected citation is due to one
excellent error in printing: in the third line of the poem, the word "mind" appears
as "wind." Generally, this wouldn't be an issue: errata happen all the time. However, in a system as rigid as Mac Low's, this small typographic variance has the
extraordinary effect of creating the chance-acrostic "I-s-h-w-a-e-l" in the opening stanza, which I can't help but misread as near-whale or whale-ish. Perhaps
the joke was too good to resist? This essay wishes to plug "Ishwael" back into the
poem, to attend to the poetics of "human error" in even the most mechanical procedures.

2 Jackson Mac Low, quoted in Joel Kuszai, "Jackson Mac Low (1922–2004)," Fifth
Estate 368-69 (Spring–Summer 2005) https://www.fifthestate.org/archive/368
-369-spring-summer-2005/jackson-mac-low-1922-2004/.

3 There is a subtle hilarity to this process, as anyone who has ever tried to pick
up a "great book" and promptly fallen asleep after the first page can tell you.

4 Lines 1 and 3 should read "ago—" instead of "and"; line 3 should read "In" instead
of "Interest"; line 7 should be "Can." instead of "Cato"; lines 8 and 9 should read "my"
instead of "me"—each with residual effects throughout the poem—and finally, on
a minor note, in lines 9 and 15, it seems that despite the flouting of grammatical
convention throughout the poem, Mac Low could not resist changing the article "a"
to "an" where necessary. By comparison, one might also produce a corrected version, as the poem should have been compiled had Mac Low followed his own rules
as a "strict algorithm." I've tried it and can attest that the result is not nearly as
good as the error-laden version you find printed in this volume!

5 In this poem, I skipped "ever." in the fourth stanza (to avoid a mid-poem period);
I dropped an "in" for the fourth stanza (to gain "involuntarily" in the final); I skipped
a "me" in the penultimate stanza (to get "moral element" instead); I cut "lath" (the
word is archaic and I wanted to get to "Look!" to conclude the poem); and finally, I
properly modified all indefinite articles. Feel free to revise at will.

19

Fred Wah

---

on **Robert Creeley, "I Know a Man"**
(1962)

As I sd to my
friend, because I am
always talking,—John, I

sd, which was not his
name, the darkness sur-
rounds us, what

can we do against
it, or else, shall we &
why not, buy a goddamn big car,

drive, he sd, for
christ's sake, look
out where yr going.

"I Know a Man" reprinted with permission of the family of Robert Creeley.

A Volkswagen is not a "goddamn big car." It's a beetle. And that was Creeley's car of choice for most of his driving life. I first met him and heard him read on February 16, 1962, at the University of British Columbia. He had been invited to the annual university arts festival by Warren Tallman, the kingpin professor behind our campus poet group known as TISH. We were excited to hear Creeley, one of our Black Mountain heroes, along with Robert Duncan and Charles Olson, featured in the recently published *New American Poetry, 1945–60*. He became central to our education as young poets in Vancouver in the early 1960s, and he and Warren cobbled together the 1963 Vancouver Poetry Conference. My wife, Pauline, and I bought our own Volkswagen and followed Creeley back to Albuquerque where I continued to learn about poetry from him. There, and through his years in Buffalo and Bolinas, he drove Volkswagen Beetles.

So now when I read "I Know a Man" I can't help but think of Creeley scrunched up in his little Volkswagen exclaiming to his friend John, "why not, buy a goddamn big car." But on Friday, February 16, 1962, I was eager to take in whatever he had to say and read about poetry. The poems he read that day were all from *For Love*, which was to be published the following month. To clarify the compositional context of his writing practice, he made extensive comments that shed some light on the intriguing possibilities of Olson's "Projective Verse"; we were hungry to know about "Projective Verse" and how this new approach to writing poetry actually worked. What he had to say about the act of writing that day was, for me, a memorable and provocative moment in learning how to write.

He definitely had cars on his mind. Early on in this 1962 reading, Creeley shares an anecdote about the possibilities of rhythm and the line that he had picked up from Olson:

> If you're saying something, the very fact that you are saying something is part of, say, a physiological or a complex of your whole body, your whole structure, that doesn't simply involve your intention alone and doesn't simply involve your attitude toward what you are saying, it involves the fact that you are saying it. So Olson, I think, usefully suggested that we might take this hint or this possibility in thinking of the problems of the line. . . . You can't fly with a car, you know that. You get into a car, you shut the door, you turn on the motor and you are not going to fly with it, nor can you usually drive across the bay on the water. Not unless you have unusual powers indeed. But equally so, if you want to think of cars only as cars.

He then outlines how a local Navajo used a car in a way entirely different from what we might expect and that poems could offer like-wise different intentions. William Carlos Williams, a poet Creeley admired, had described a poem as "machine made out of words"[1] and, as Creeley realizes, "You can live in them." Hearing his anecdote/ metaphor about the car minutes before I heard the poem "I Know a Man" set a resonant tone for that "goddamn big car." Listening to the commentary and then listening to the poem, before reading it on the page, helped open me to a physiological set of particulars that tend to override the usual visual/intellectual event of language in the head. So, as he explains, the "fact" of the language being said is the condition of the rhythm (and sound) "that may occur in the first few lines and then you pick up on what has happened and you then move from that." As he says a little later in the reading (recording), talking in a similar way about his poem "La Noche," "I want that particular stress to enforce and to emphasize the particular statement I'm interested in; the flat statement itself is really of not that interest." We could say the same thing about the anecdotal poem "I Know a Man." How it is said is what distinguishes it as a poem.

To me, as a then young poet, this was useful information indeed. What materials in language, in other words what particulars, might one pay attention to in composing a poem? So the poet is "persuaded . . . in the first few lines" to use certain rhythms and sounds and then "pick up on what has happened" ("look / out where yr going"). The first line alone offers some hints of how this works. The poem kicks off with that sound of "aah" in the first word and in the next few lines modulates through several variations of that sound (As, because, am, always, talking). The digraph "wh" is used in a similar way in the next two stanzas (which, was, what, we, we, why). Sounds and rhythm play off of one another throughout the poem, very much like music composition and jazz improvisation. Some of these particulars are used in repetition (sd, I, we). Like musical notes and phrases, these repetitions and echoes not only shape how the poem moves in its singular fashion but also emphasize what is being said.

Besides the percussive rhythmic stresses, both within the line but particularly at the line break, the poem explodes an otherwise conversational anecdote into an extreme of language into which a more complex and imaginative reflection ("the darkness sur- / rounds us, what / can we do against / it, or else, shall we & . . .") can be inserted. This is characteristic of Creeley's practice. By having the particulars of the words themselves propel the poem, syllable to syllable, he projects a fairly common and straightforward language into a unique experience of that language. Not "a goddamn big car" poetics but definitely a good way to drive a small poem.

NOTE

1 William Carlos Williams, introduction to *The Wedge*, in *Selected Essays of William Carlos Williams* (New York: New Directions, 1969), 256.

20

Marjorie Perloff

on **Frank O'Hara, "Poem (Khrushchev is coming on the right day!)"**
(1964)

Khrushchev is coming on the right day!
                                    the cool graced light
is pushed off the enormous glass piers by hard wind
and everything is tossing, hurrying on up
                               this country
has everything but *politesse*, a Puerto Rican cab driver says
and five different girls I see
                     look like Piedie Gimbel
with her blonde hair tossing too,
                        as she looked when I pushed
her little daughter on the swing on the lawn it was also windy

last night we went to a movie and came out,
                          Ionesco is greater
than Beckett, Vincent said, that's what I think, blueberry blintzes
and Khrushchev was probably being carped at
                     in Washington, no
                          politesse
Vincent tells me about his mother's trip to Sweden
                               Hans tells us
about his father's life in Sweden, it sounds like Grace Hartigan's
painting *Sweden*
               so I go home to bed and names drift through my
                                 head
Purgatorio Merchado, Gerhard Schwartz and Gaspar Gonzales,
       all unknown figures of the early morning as I go to work

where does the evil of the year go

> when September takes New York

and turns it into ozone stalagmites

> deposits of light

> so I get back up

make coffee, and read François Villon, his life, so dark

> New York seems blinding and my tie is blowing up the street

I wish it would blow off

> though it is cold and somewhat warms

> > my neck

as the train bears Khrushchev on to Pennsylvania Station

> and the light seems to be eternal

> and joy seems to be inexorable

> I am foolish enough always to find it in wind

Frank O'Hara, "Poem (Khrushchev is coming on the right day!)" from *Lunch Poems*. Copyright ©1964 by Frank O'Hara. Reprinted with the permission of The Permissions Company, LLC, on behalf of City Lights Books, www.citylights.com.

The opening line of this characteristically untitled poem is immediately arresting in its seeming absurdity. Why is a windy September morning (in fact, September 17, 1959), on which the poem's speaker is preoccupied with his personal relationships in his very particular art circle, the right (or wrong) day for Nikita Khrushchev to arrive in New York?

Frank O'Hara's great popularity surely has something to do with his ability to fuse public and private, to capture those moments of everyday life when we respond, overtly or just subliminally, to the "breaking news" of the day. Let's begin by remembering that Khrushchev, Stalin's successor, was the first Soviet head of state to visit the United States; his summit meeting with President Eisenhower in Washington and subsequent trip around the country dominated the news for two weeks, the Russian dictator being known for his shrewd assessments of his Cold War adversaries, even as he was mocked for his vulgarisms, buffoonish antics, and unpredictability. Khrushchev's subsequent arrival at Pennsylvania Station was greeted by sizable protests, and there was a circus air about the proceedings. Moreover, there was no right day for Khrushchev to arrive anywhere in the United States since, at any moment, he might turn on his hosts and go on the attack.

The politics of this historic Cold War moment seem to be wholly remote from the concerns of one busy poet-art curator, as detailed in this conversational and autobiographical lyric. O'Hara's speaker seems to be addressing a good friend, chuckling about his morning cab ride (where to his surprise the Puerto Rican driver says, "this country has everything but *politesse*)." He then recalls "last night" when he and Vincent (in real life, Frank's new lover, the dancer Vincent Warren) "went to a movie and came out," with the pun on "came out," he re-creates the little disagreement about Beckett and Ionesco and the subsequent conversation about travel and artists, and finally the sleepless night when "I get back up / make coffee, and read François Villon, his life, so dark." But the memory of the long night is brief: the last seven lines take us back into the poet's *present*, on an ordinary workday morning, even as "the train bears Khrushchev on to Pennsylvania Station."

And the poem ends, as it began, with the image of wind—the wind that, as in such precursor poems like Shelley's "Ode to the West Wind," functions as a symbol of life, creativity, energy, and the "joy" that "seems to be inexorable."

So again we may ask: What do the impersonal news headlines or radio bulletins—what does Khrushchev—have to do with the poet's personal narrative? In his "Personism: A Manifesto," O'Hara remarked that one day, while he was writing, "I was realizing that if I wanted to I could use the telephone instead of writing the poem, and so Personism was born." But despite this disclaimer, O'Hara's "I do this, I do that" poems are carefully structured. The Khrushchev lyric is framed as a process poem: its jagged lines, indented variously so as to make the page look like a visual construct, present not what is a finished meditation but rather a simulation of the process of consciousness even as it is taking place. But such a simulation (the poem as telephone conversation) is itself artful, and O'Hara's every word and image contribute to what is a very special soliloquy.

The key images wind and light, for starters, change in the course of the conversation. "The cool graced light" is the poet's ideal. It is the light of September, heralding the end of a hot Manhattan summer, and it is coupled with wind, stirring everything up in exhilarating ways: blonde hair is tossing, wind is pushing the little girl's swing, and later "my tie is blowing up the street." But the "cool graced light" starts to harden, turning, toward the end, "into ozone stalagmites / deposits of light." The blowing tie is no longer enough; Frank now wants it to "blow off"; and the light now "seems to be eternal"—an equivocal image for much as he wants light to *be* there, eternal light also suggests the permanence of death. "Joy seems to be inexorable," but, in the poem's last line, Frank admits that his search for the wind that brings joy may be "foolish." Perhaps, it is implied, this isn't the best idea. Perhaps the demand for "everything [to be] tossing" has its limits.

Now consider the use of proper names, one of O'Hara's signature devices. We don't have to know who all the people mentioned are in order to be drawn into the poet's very special world, but the first thing to note—and it cannot be a coincidence—is that all the names are foreign or exotic; dramatists Ionesco and Beckett, artist friends Purgatorio Merchado, Gerhard Schwartz, and Gaspar Gonzales, and then the French medieval poet François Villon. Grace Hartigan has made a painting called *Sweden*. And Vincent's friend is called Hans. Even Piedie Gimbel—a socialite friend?—has a resonant name, Gimbel's having been the rival of Macy's in 1950s New York. "Piedie" is familiar and cute, but it contains the French *pied* (foot). And its bearer is, after all, a Gimbel.

What do these names and what does O'Hara's anecdote about the post-movie conversation among friends reveal? Frank's sophisticated art circle goes in for European and avant-garde plays and movies, for *poètes maudits* like Villon, and for travel abroad: they even eat "blueberry blintzes," with their Russian derivation—but a Russia of the turn of the century when Jewish immigrants came en masse to New York. The Paris world of Beckett and Ionesco (whichever one you prefer!) is the antithesis of Khrushchev's dour and no-nonsense Soviet milieu; he is the "peasant" leader who despises *politesse*, but was he being "carped at" in Washington or was he doing the carping? It is a tense moment: however much you love the French avant-garde, the poem implies, the reality of the Cold War will keep intruding.

Is O'Hara's then a political poem? Yes and no. It is the antithesis of the didactic poem that tells us what to believe from a knowing perspective, that claims a corner on The Truth. Frank and his friends don't want to think about politics; note that they don't *talk* about politics at all. But the anxiety of the Cold War is always there, even if it affects no more than the traffic jam that delays Frank's cab to work. And further: what relates Frank's personal narrative to the Khrushchev plot is the emphasis on contingency and uncertainty. We don't know the outcome of the Eisenhower-Khrushchev Summit; we don't even know what Khrushchev's intentions are. The same contingency affects the other meeting, that of Frank and his friends in the café. He and Vincent suddenly disagree: are there consequences? Why is Frank later sleeping alone and why is sleep so hard to come by? In the end, joy is invoked but it only "seems to be inexorable." And we know how fragile joy is when, a moment earlier, Frank asks himself, "where does the evil of the year go / when September takes New York"? Notice that evil doesn't disappear; it just goes underground, masked as it is by the September light and wind.

What starts out as a comic and playful "personal poem" thus turns, in the end, slightly somber. But only *slightly*. O'Hara never takes himself too seriously; he can always laugh at his own arguments, as when he claims that the tie "blowing up the street" "somewhat warms my neck." It hardly sounds convincing, but it is fun to think of the warmth a little string tie might provide. Tomorrow, in any case, is another day: something surprising may well happen, perhaps in the O'Hara poem on the next page of the *Collected Poems*, which begins, "I cough a lot (sinus?) so I / get up and have some tea with cognac / it is dawn. / the light flows evenly along the lawn."

What has happened to the "cool graced light"? Never, O'Hara insists, take anything for granted! Or, as he put it in a 1964 essay on the sculptor David Smith: Don't be bored, don't be lazy, don't be trivial, and don't be proud. The slightest loss of attention leads to death.

21

Aldon Lynn Nielsen

on Langston Hughes, "Dinner Guest: Me"
(1965)

I know I am
The Negro Problem
Being wined and dined,
Answering the usual questions
That come to white mind
Which seeks demurely
To Probe in polite way
The why and wherewithal
Of darkness U.S.A.—
Wondering how things got this way
In current democratic night,
Murmuring gently
Over fraises du bois,
"I'm so ashamed of being white."

The lobster is delicious,
The wine divine,
And center of attention
At the damask table, mine.
To be a Problem on
Park Avenue at eight
Is not so bad.
Solutions to the Problem,
Of course, wait.

In 1970, Free Jazz artist Clifford Thornton recorded a session in Paris, released the following year on the America label under the title *The Panther and the Lash*. If Thornton's compositions and performances on such pieces as "Huey Is Free" found the brass player leaning more toward the *Panther* side of the then-recent Langston Hughes book title, works like "Tout Le Pouvoir Au Peuple" were clearly in accord with Hughes's imperatives and recalled the poet's transcontinental links to the Negritude of his Francophone friends. The Hughes volume had appeared just three years before the release of Thornton's vinyl record. At the time, *Kirkus Reviews* observed that Hughes's "style has not markedly changed, except that he has more or less dropped Negro dialect," then proceeded oddly to cite the poem "Motto" with its lines about digging all jive.[1] But *Kirkus* also cites "Dinner Guest: Me" as an instance of Hughes's address to "the plight of the American Negro," demonstrating not only that the reviewer was somewhat slow to pick up on the emergent language of the Black Arts (only a year later, James Brown's "Say It Loud, I'm Black and I'm Proud" ruled the airwaves) but also that *Kirkus* was somewhat missing the point.

Some confusion was probably inevitable. *The Panther and the Lash*, despite its au courant title, included poems written over a broad span of Hughes's career. In a note for the volume, the poet wrote: "There is no poem in *The Panther and the Lash* with which Langston Hughes does not have some direct or indirect personal and emotional connection."[2] Langston Hughes, it must be said, had a lifelong connection in the American reader's mind with mealtimes. There was that famous photo Hughes had posed for early in his career, dressed in his busboy's uniform and balancing a tray on his raised right hand, meant at least in part to memorialize his mythic "discovery" by Vachel Lindsay. It is true that Hughes had served Lindsay a portion of poetry that evening at the Wardman Park Hotel's dining room, and both Hughes and Lindsay had enough of an instinct for publicity to make the most of the meeting. But Hughes had already won prizes for his poetry, had published in the *Crisis* and elsewhere, been feted at the *Opportunity* banquet, had already connected with Carl Van Vechten, and had already been taken up by Knopf publishers. And if the most famous dinner associated with Hughes's early career was one at which he did not eat, that, too, was an early theme. By the time Hughes met Lindsay in Washington, D.C., he had already published "I, Too," where the poet writes of being sent to the kitchen when company comes. But tomorrow, the poem promises, "I'll be at the table."[3] Hughes must have made frequent use of the *Green Book* during his early decades of touring to lecture and give poetry readings. Just a few years after "I, Too," Hughes published "Advertisement for the Waldorf-Astoria" in *New Masses*, accompanied by artwork that made the poem resemble a fancy menu for the hotel where luncheon was not served by and did not serve Black people. With offerings that were truly mouth-watering (Gumbo Creole, Crabmeat in Cassolette, Brisket of Beef), the poem opens that exclusive hotel to the masses themselves, with sections dedicated to "hungry ones," "roomers," "evicted families," "Negroes," and, finally, "everybody." Looking forward to "Dinner Guest: Me," "Advertisement for the Waldorf-Astoria" satirically addresses White folks' love of Negroes: "You know, downtown folk are just / crazy about Paul Robeson! Maybe they'll like you, too."[4]

By the time Hughes came to write "Dinner Guest: Me," he was well out of the kitchen and was, indeed, often among the honorees. But then, he had been an honoree as far back as 1926, at least when those doing the honoring were Black like him. "Dinner Guest: Me" first appeared in a 1965 issue of *Negro Digest*, the venerable and widely read magazine that was soon to be rechristened *Black World*. The situation imagined in "Dinner Guest" is radically unlike Countee Cullen's "Incident" or Claude McKay's "If We Must Die," indicating how far we had come from that earlier era but also what strange fruit was on offer in a yet more militant time. As he had done in so many poems, Hughes here speaks not only for the masses but *as* an abstraction. He is "The Negro Problem" in his very person.

"I know I am," the poem begins, summoning a Torahnic tone ("I am that I am") while at the same time signing the self-assertiveness of the New Negro becoming the New Black. But then we cross the divide of enjambment. The persona is "The Negro Problem," capitalized, abstracted, and at the same time embodied, being wined and dined. "Darkness U.S.A." is the speaker's territory and provenance, his area of expertise and the reason for his invitation to the table. But, and this is what the reviewer for *Kirkus* seemed to miss, the darkness is all a matter of the "white mind" and its demure probing. The "plight of the Negro" is White people. One has to wonder how the diners can wonder "how things got this way / in current democratic night," but then that very wondering is itself a mode of evasion. *We can't be as bad as **those** White people, because we have invited the Problem here among us, invited him to explain himself.* And still, just as their guest is expected to stand for all Black people while withstanding this polite probing, the Whites at table feel somehow implicated: "I'm so ashamed of being White." Are they? Is *shame* the best that Blacks can expect from Whites? Is it even on the menu?

The time of this poem was also a time of such actual efforts at dinner table brotherhood. And it was, as this poem bears witness, a time for satirizing such ennobling efforts. In 1965, Tom Lehrer released his live album *That Was the Year That Was*, with its send-up of the kind of dinner Hughes wrote about. The song "National Brotherhood Week" acknowledges that the White folk hate the Black folk and the Black folk hate the Whites, but for one week, at one dinner, "Lena Horne and Sheriff Clark are dancing cheek to cheek," and "it's fun to eulogize the people you despise." Hughes, having been to many such dinners, appreciates the fine wine and lobster and the gentler murmurings of race over the servings of *fraises du bois*. That particular strawberry wasn't much grown commercially in the United States and didn't travel all that well. But, and this may be why this fruit finds its way into the poem, it is, like African Americans historically, a tough plant even when appearing delicate. A delicacy, we might say. Was Hughes also getting in a dig at the always somewhat haughty W. E. B. DuBois? Hard to say.

But as Problem Hughes sits at the damask table, in the place of honor on Park Avenue, he knows, even if *Kirkus* did not, that he is no problem to be solved and that the White question was yet far from being answered.

NOTES

1 *Kirkus Reviews*, July 1, 1967. https://www.kirkusreviews.com/book-reviews/a/langston-hughes-3/the-panther-and-the-lash/.

2 Arnold Rampersad, *The Life of Langston Hughes: Volume II, 1941–1967: I Dream a World* (New York: Oxford University Press, 1988), 410.

3 Langston Hughes, *The Collected Poems of Langston Hughes*, ed. Arnold Rampersad and David Roessel (New York: Alfred A. Knopf, 1994), 46.

4 Ibid., 145.

22

Sina Queyras

on **Sylvia Plath, "Lady Lazarus"**
(1965)

I have done it again.
One year in every ten
I manage it——

A sort of walking miracle, my skin
Bright as a Nazi lampshade,
My right foot

A paperweight,
My face a featureless, fine
Jew linen.

Peel off the napkin
O my enemy.
Do I terrify?——

The nose, the eye pits, the full set of teeth?
The sour breath
Will vanish in a day.

Soon, soon the flesh
The grave cave ate will be
At home on me

And I a smiling woman.
I am only thirty.
And like the cat I have nine times to die.

This is Number Three.
What a trash
To annihilate each decade.

What a million filaments.
The peanut-crunching crowd
Shoves in to see

Them unwrap me hand and foot——
The big strip tease.
Gentlemen, ladies

These are my hands
My knees.
I may be skin and bone,

Nevertheless, I am the same, identical woman.
The first time it happened I was ten.
It was an accident.

The second time I meant
To last it out and not come back at all.
I rocked shut

As a seashell.
They had to call and call
And pick the worms off me like sticky pearls.

Dying
Is an art, like everything else.
I do it exceptionally well.

I do it so it feels like hell.
I do it so it feels real.
I guess you could say I've a call.

It's easy enough to do it in a cell.
It's easy enough to do it and stay put.
It's the theatrical

Comeback in broad day
To the same place, the same face, the same brute
Amused shout:

"A miracle!"
That knocks me out.
There is a charge

For the eyeing of my scars, there is a charge
For the hearing of my heart——
It really goes.

And there is a charge, a very large charge
For a word or a touch
Or a bit of blood

Or a piece of my hair or my clothes.
So, so, Herr Doktor.
So, Herr Enemy.

I am your opus,
I am your valuable,
The pure gold baby

That melts to a shriek.
I turn and burn.
Do not think I underestimate your great concern.

Ash, ash—
You poke and stir.
Flesh, bone, there is nothing there——

A cake of soap,
A wedding ring,
A gold filling.

Herr God, Herr Lucifer
Beware
Beware.

Out of the ash
I rise with my red hair
And I eat men like air.

"Lady Lazarus" is one of the late October poems Sylvia Plath wrote in a burst, at Court Green, around the time of her thirtieth birthday. Like many of the poems in *Ariel*, this one is part rage, part self-talk. Biographer Anne Stevenson refers to it as "merciless self-projection": more "assault" than poetry.[1] "Lady Lazarus" is often read as an inevitable march toward the third, and final, suicide attempt. The lines "Dying / Is an art, like everything else. / I do it exceptionally well" seem to confirm this reading, as does the mention of the "third attempt" in the eighth stanza.

It is true that there had been two previous suicide attempts, and that Plath suffered from depression, but from the outset the tone in this poem is provocatively humorous—"I have done it again. / One year in every ten"—and filled with overstatement: "a sort of walking miracle . . . skin / Bright as a Nazi lampshade." Later the lines "peanut-crunching crowd / Shoves in to see" are delivered with a derisive laugh, as the speaker is unwrapped in "the big strip tease": a line that would come to describe a whole school of women's writing. That she is alive is "a miracle," yes, but why? Her own "life" knocks her out, but it is also a lark, she writes, echoing Virginia Woolf. "There is a charge / For the eyeing of my scars," she states, "there is a charge" for seeing her heart, "It really goes." This section seems to predict her own reception: the ghoulish dogs that Hughes describes trying to own a bit of the Plath legacy.

But are they trying to own? Or understand? Regarding the reference to enemy in the fourth tercet and "Herr Enemy" in the twenty-second, I point to a letter written to psychiatrist Ruth Beuscher on September 4, 1962, just over a month prior to writing "Lady Lazarus," where Plath states "any kind of caution or limit makes [Hughes] murderous," and later in the same paragraph she says this institution is prison: "the children should never have been born."[2]

These gendered power dynamics are palpable in Plath's poem: "I am your opus"; "I a smiling woman" "turn and burn." We can't help but try to fill in the life behind the mask. And it seems we readers were sensing correctly: in a letter dated September 22, Plath writes, "Ted beat

me up physically a couple of days before my miscarriage: the baby
I lost was due to be born on his birthday," and later "he tells me now
it was weakness that made him unable to tell me he didn't want children."[3] The rage, then, is not surprising: "Beware / Beware" she
writes, "out of the ash / I rise with my red hair / And I eat men like air."
While the poem ends with the speaker rising up, she is not yet out of
the fire: she still has to eat her way through the patriarchy. I read this
ending as a declaration of war. I read it as a will to live.

I wrote my version of "Lady Lazarus" in what was one of the coldest
winters in Montreal in many decades. Submerged in a converted
closet with two toddlers bouncing overhead I juggled my anger like
sticks of dynamite as the #metoo movement simmered.

> I like a direct hit as long as it's abstract. Come,
> Come into my pink bath, I am floating, my ambition is not pretty.
> My feeling is not a good colleague. I am not your affirmation machine:
>
> My unpredictability is epic. I am all up in my body. I shrivel for you,
> I undo all I have eaten, I pour myself into the ether and look, look.
> There is no shit having it all. Once the rains come there is no
>
> Having it all. You will or will not cut off your own head,
> You will or will not get through this coldest year of your
> Life, the season of your disagreement is a lengthy sentence.[4]

My first attempts were long lines that spilled over, loosely falling into
off-kilter couplets. I wanted to keep what I loved in Plath: the mid-
Atlantic syntactical swagger, the humor, but I suspected that *Ariel*
was as much a rejection of form as it was a declaration of war. I ran
"Lady Lazarus" through a randomizer over and over again to rid it of
any evidence of Plath's rhythms but also to try to find a connection
between her voice and mine:

> You men, you have it all and raw. They say
> The only gold left to pan is buried deep
> In shit. I will relish you right up inside me

And at my leisure. I will take the baby teeth and songs
Of happiness. I am no lady. I am scorching air.
You can eat my genius, rare.

I settled on tercets because there are many in *Ariel* ("Morning Song,"
"Elm," "Fever 103," "Gulliver," "Nick and the Candlestick," "Ariel") and
likely not a coincidence: those little tercets of "Lady Lazarus" tore the
veil off of lyric propriety. To my version I added a dose of joyful Stein-
ian resistance. Like Plath's my tercets thrive on anger and bask in
quick connections and sounds like knife wounds: "an umlaut in a grim
gown" or "Not a lucky cut. No lucky strut, you." There was also the
physical element "where your legs pivot I swan my neck limp." I
wanted to conjure up the way in which the difficulties of a new mother
trying to find her power might feel continually buffeted ("so gentle
where the will bent"): continually distracted by others' needs and
demands.

When I found out that Ted Hughes had cut and shaped *Ariel* into a
sequence that made Plath's suicide inevitable, it felt not only like an
act of self-protection on his part but also a final literary violence on
her "corpus." My poem enacts this violence. The speaker is continually
buffeted: she makes statements, feels shame and recrimination, she
is "threaded with old hurt" she will "shrivel for you," she is abject, she
tries to speak and causes shade, she is "off script," even her feminism
needs a good slap. She is also very aware: "I fell for a wolf don't think
I didn't know my bones would be gnawed." This self-awareness illustrates the ongoing cycle of what I think of as "aborted awakenings."

I cling to reports of Plath reading "Lady Lazarus" with the joy of a
woman released. I read the poem as victorious in the sense that while
Plath herself is not actually able to rise up out of the ash, her poems
do. In a letter to his sister Olwyn in 1962, Hughes described Plath as a
"death-ray." I suspect that what he was describing was not so much
her as *her ambition*. Her drive. Her desire for a parallel career. For
women, the price of a literary career has been far too high, far too
long. For Plath, the cost of that parallel career was her life.

NOTES

1 Anne Stevenson, *Bitter Fame: A Life of Sylvia Plath* (Boston: Houghton Mifflin, 1989), 269.

2 *Letters of Sylvia Plath*, vol. 2 (1956–1963), ed. Peter K. Steinberg and Karen V. Kukil (London: Faber & Faber, 2018), 816–17.

3 *Letters of Sylvia Plath*, 2:830.

4 Sina Queyras, *My Ariel* (Toronto: Coach House Books, 2017).

23

Herman Beavers

on **Gwendolyn Brooks, "Boy Breaking Glass"**
(1967)

To Marc Crawford
   from whom the commission

Whose broken window is a cry of art
(success, that winks aware
as elegance, as a treasonable faith)
is raw: is sonic: is old-eyed première.
Our beautiful flaw and terrible ornament.
Our barbarous and metal little man.

"I shall create! If not a note, a hole.
If not an overture, a desecration."

Full of pepper and light
and Salt and night and cargoes.

"Don't go down the plank
if you see there's no extension.
Each to his grief, each to
his loneliness and fidgety revenge.
Nobody knew where I was and now I am no longer there."

The only sanity is a cup of tea.
The music is in minors.

Each one other
is having different weather.

"It was you, it was you who threw away my name!
And this is everything I have for me."

Who has not Congress, lobster, love, luau,
the Regency Room, the Statue of Liberty,
runs. A sloppy amalgamation.
A mistake.
A cliff.
A hymn, a snare, and an exceeding sun.

From *Blacks* (Chicago: Third World Press, 1987). Reprinted by consent of
Brooks Permissions.

Critics of Gwendolyn Brooks's poems identify "Boy Breaking Glass"
as both a demonstration of how thoroughly she had mastered her
poetic craft and the reinvigoration of her political consciousness,
evidence that her sympathies had undergone a tectonic shift. Written
two years into the Black Arts Movement, Brooks's poem was initially
commissioned by Marc Crawford, the editor of a small literary magazine in Chicago called *Time Capsule*, who asked her to write a poem
that could speak to Chicago's Black youth, "surviving inequity[,] and
white power."[1] At a time when the thought leaders of the Black Arts
Movement were seeking to expand and extend the meaning of terms
like "art" and "poetics," moving them away from their meaning in the
Western canon, Brooks's poem works to bridge Modernist aesthetics
with a more radical, non-Western aesthetic sensibility.

What I would like to propose in this essay is that we can understand
Brooks's poem as an "audition" for the most visible figures in the
Black Arts Movement, most notably Amiri Baraka, Larry Neal, and
Haki Mahdhabuti, whom Brooks had met that spring at the Black
Writers Conference at Fisk University. Seen in this way, the poem's
hybridized and improvisational approach can be rationalized within
the context of a transitional, speculative form Brooks used to cast
aspersions on the "well-made" poem utilizing mainstream forms of
diction and syntax. Hence, Brooks's poem is a partial break from her

earlier poetics, resisting a total capitulation to the Black Arts Movement's penchant for free verse by utilizing conventional prosody to open the poem. Further, we can see Brooks's turn to open forms is accompanied by her refusal of the demotic language that was becoming a signature feature of African American poetry during this period.

Reading the poem's initial attack, one discerns at least three distinct possibilities for interpreting the poem's opening lines: the first reads the title as the first line of the poem, the second reads the title and dedication as interactive content, and the final possibility is the poem opens conventionally, meaning the title and dedication are not poetic content. The poem's rhetorical posture is simultaneously an effort to reimagine acts of artistic ascent while postulating aesthetic consent.

It should be noted that "Boy Breaking Glass" was not the first time Brooks had attempted to take up young people as poetic subject. One thinks here of "The Life of Lincoln West" or her 1959 poem "We Real Cool." Here, the wonderful compactness of the latter poem must be pondered in terms of the tone she employs, as in: "We / lurk late. We / strike straight." Perhaps the most prevalent reading is Brooks meant to elicit a sympathetic response. However, that sympathy occurs at a distance, subordinated to the poem's pessimism. Brooks's decision to utilize simple sentences of three words each communicates a sense of inevitability and, finally, resignation at the fate of seven boys whiling away the hours at the Golden Shovel. The name of their "hangout" notwithstanding, no gold awaits them at the end of their downward spiral into an early and tragic death, as if Brooks is content to stand apart from her subjects, observing as they describe their circumstances, content in the decision not to invest the lives of a group of young, Black, high school dropouts, hanging around a pool hall, with the ability to imagine other possibilities, to hint at their potential.[2] Recall that the speaker in "We Real Cool" is the one who gives voice to his bleak fortunes, who seems not to be imbued with an ability to dream of a life that does not involve sensation, thrill, and decline.[3]

By contrast, "Boy Breaking Glass" displays a number of features, both technical and thematic, that situate this poem at the proverbial crossroads. Where the compactness of "We Real Cool" is suggestive of how small and insignificant Black lives can become once they become inured to the downward spiral of tragic circumstance, "Boy Breaking Glass" eschews poetic motion via downward inertia in favor of quick, nearly random gestures whose larger objective is difficult to ascertain, in part because Brooks prevents the reader from drawing a direct bead on the poem's subject. Using language that is at once both specific and metaphorized, Brooks's rhetorical design relies on fragmented speech (which may also be occurring in locations at a remove from the broken window) and non sequitur, meaning the reader is perpetually off-balance. Scanning the poem, we note that its first ten lines are in blank verse (e.g., metrical, unrhymed) and iambic pentameter, which readers of Brooks's early poetry would recognize but which might have been considered by Black Arts Movement artists to be Brooks's final attempt to curry the favor of mainstream critics or as a sign that old habits die hard. But I submit that there is a more nuanced explanation for how she opens "Boy Breaking Glass." Brooks's conventional approach to prosody establishes contrapuntal tension, since the poem's first move is to frame the act of breaking a window as an artistic endeavor, not mere vandalism. Brooks's "audition" is one in which she tasked herself with gathering the speaker's thoughts while adopting Langston Hughes's technique of amplifying voices in the street.

Considered alongside those lines appearing in quotation marks we might opt to view the poem as oscillating between the young artist's voice and commentary about the underlying forces of the young Black artist's disillusionment. The dissonance she creates is meant, once again, to undermine the reader's belief in the primacy of the well-made poem.[4] Though Yusef Komunyakaa once argued the 1960s marked that time when Brooks was moving into a space of self-doubt and artistic decline, it might be more apt to see the poem for what it was: an effort to both impress and teach her new audience. But compared to poems like "We Real Cool," it is also a sign of Brooks's renewed commitment to foregrounding the voices of Black youth resisting white supremacy's repressive weight.

NOTES

1 Al Filreis et al., ModPo Week 5: "Brooks's 'Boy Breaking Glass,'" https://youtu.be /OIZ3Zq5Q6us, University of Pennsylvania, September 20, 2017.

2 Though I think it would be wrong to suggest that Brooks's sole aim is to communicate her disapproval, which would have meant speaking directly to us in the first person or using an omniscient speaker, the fact that her speaker cannot imagine a life apart from the one he and his fellows live can be traced to the fact that she either could not or elected not to imagine an alternative.

3 Seen in comparison to "The Life of Lincoln West," where the poet enters the mind of the young Lincoln in order to humanize him, thereby inviting the reader to empathize with his plight, "We Real Cool" exercises a level of restraint whose intention seems to be one of inhibiting the reader's ability to muster the warmth of compassion; the distance Brooks employs belies temperate emotionality. But this is what makes the later poem such an extraordinary departure.

4 Lines 17 and 18 assert, "The only sanity is a cup of tea. / The music is in minors," which are meant to serve as a descriptive gesture that names the discordance generated by the poem's constitutive parts. But it also dramatizes how the poem functions under the aegis of the blue note, which can create violently dissonant collisions (often at the microtonal level) of tonalities in the poem.

Gabriel Ojeda-Sagué

on **Barbara Guest, "20"**
(1968)

Sleep is 20
          remembering the
insignificant flamenco dancer
in Granada
          who became
important as you watched
the mountain ridge
          the dry hills

What an idiotic number!

Sleep is twenty

it certainly isn't twenty sheep
there weren't that many in the herd
under the cold crest of Sierra Nevada

It's more like 20 Madison Ave. buses
while I go droning away at my dream life
Each episode is important
that's what it is! Sequences—
I've got going a twenty-act drama
the theatre of the active
the critics are surely there
even the actors
even the flowers presented onstage
even the wild flowers
picked by the wife of the goatherd
each morning early (while I sleep)
under the snow cone
of Sierra Nevada

yellow caps like castanets
I reach into my bouquet
half-dreaming
and count twenty
yellow capped heads

flowers clicking twenty times
because they like to repeat themselves

as I do as does the morning
or the drama one hopes
will be acted many times

As even these dreams in similar
people's heads

20

castanets

"20" from *The Collected Poems of Barbara Guest* ©2008 by the Estate of
Barbara Guest. Published by Wesleyan University Press and reprinted
with permission.

"20" is a loop of foggy memories and dream scenes connected by
associative logic, beginning and ending with flamenco. Each of these
scenes, presented without context, exists somewhere between
memory and fabrication, and they are all linked by a specific particle
within each. The poem ends where it begins, endlessly repeating like
the cycle of sleep and morning ("the drama one hopes / will be acted
many times"). This is a poem about sequences but set in a context
where sequence does not occur with linearity or predictability. "20"
deals with the stubbornly random thoughts before falling asleep and
the logic of dream worlds by valuing the sometimes impossibly different nodes along the mind's movements, rather than attempting to
organize them in some traditional way.

Let's track the movements of the poem more explicitly. "20" begins with the memory of a flamenco dancer, connecting her importance to the "you" of the poem by her context: "the mountain ridge / the dry hills," specifically the Sierra Nevada mountain range in the Spanish province of Granada. The number 20 then focuses the speaker on a different aspect of the Sierra Nevada, a herd of sheep seen there. The sheep clearly connect to the flamenco dancer by their context, but their presence also functions as a jokey reference to counting sheep as a mental practice for falling asleep. "Counting sheep" is precisely the problem, as the half memory of the Sierra Nevada sheep fails to reach twenty.

This number is arbitrary, in that it could have been any other number ("what an idiotic number!"), but its presence in the poem is dominating. It hangs over each scene. Next, "20" brings us briefly to 20 buses on Madison Avenue, before we enter "the theatre of the active." The theater is linked to the Sierra Nevada as well, as the flowers presented onstage are the same as the flowers picked by the wife of a goatherd. The flowers, once inspected, are clicking like castanets. They are "capped [flower] heads" in a dream, bringing Guest to the inverse image of dreams in "similar / people's heads." The grammar of the final phrase is ambiguous, so that either the dreams in the heads or the heads themselves are like "20 / castanets." I lean toward thinking that the "20 / castanets" refers to the heads, since the flowers are described in similar terms, but frankly, it doesn't matter. The image of the castanet is flexible, but indelible, so that we know something is clicking, something is repeating. We know the association is solid.

A lightning-fast summary: the dreaming head goes to flamenco on the Sierra Nevada, the flowers of the Sierra Nevada, which are the flowers of the theater, each of which is a dreaming head, clicking. The loop from dreaming head to dreaming head, flamenco to flamenco, is complete.

I describe all of this simply to track the associative logic of the dream's seemingly disparate scenes. As the poem says, "each episode is important." We must understand the value of each scene, of each node along the course of thought, but we must also see it for its full "drama." I take the "twenty-act drama" in the "theatre of the active" to refer to this associative logic, the "drama" of moving ideas and referents. This drama is repetitive, "one hopes," in the same way as the cycle of morning and night, all the things that like to "repeat themselves."

This connection of association and repetition might start to answer the question *Why flamenco?* In flamenco, the castanet as controlled by the dancer defines the *compás* of the flamenco, the fundamental rhythmic structure of the piece that defines its type, quality, and lineage (*palo*). It may be instructive to think of the repetition of the "drama," the associative logic of the poem's scenes, and of the poem's own circularity as the *rhythm* of the poem. Though a small distinction, thinking of the associative logic of the poem as the rhythm of the poem might help us wrap our heads around the *why* of the poem's construction. It also reminds us that every poem is the simulation of association, the making of connections through form (reminding us, perhaps, of Eileen Myles's "I can / connect // any two / things" in the poem "Writing"). And *rhythm* as a term gets us also to *circadian rhythm*. I'm not trying to make a banal connection simply on a shared word, but I am trying to note that sleep has been figured as a rhythm of living. So, in a poem where musical rhythm is so present, the rhythm of sleep/wakefulness is useful to note, and I hope I've shown that both of these rhythms are microcosms for the greater rhythm of the poem's form.

I want to rest for a moment, to end, on a little phrase in the poem that I have already quoted but let sit unexamined: the "one hopes" of "the drama one hopes will be acted many times." I have already said that the repetition here is not just of the dream but of the morning, of another day, another "episode." This small but significant moment is a memento mori, a reminder that for an individual the morning may cease to repeat. There's a certain bit of sadness there. But it grounds, at least for me, a sense that repetition is the way of doing life. Association, circularity, the "drama," are not just a way of life, not just a technique one selects to live, but *the* way life actually happens. The natural, the alive, they are the products of pervasive, associative repetition. Guest is a poet who would never grimace at such an idea. She celebrates the associative because she knows it is the alive.

25

Tyrone Williams

on **Amiri Baraka, "Incident"**
(1969)

He came back and shot. He shot him. When he came
back, he shot, and he fell, stumbling, past the
shadow wood, down, shot, dying, dead, to full halt.

At the bottom, bleeding, shot dead. He died then, there
after the fall, the speeding bullet, tore his face
and blood sprayed fine over the killer and the grey light.

Pictures of the dead man, are everywhere. And his spirit
sucks up the light. But he died in darkness darker than
his soul and everything tumbled blindly with him dying

down the stairs.

We have no word

on the killer, except he came back, from somewhere
to do what he did. And shot only once into his victim's
stare, and left him quickly when the blood ran out. We know

the killer was skillful, quick, and silent, and that the victim
probably knew him. Other than that, aside from the caked
        sourness
of the dead man's expression, and the cool surprise in the fixture

of his hands and fingers, we know nothing.

Amiri Baraka's "Incident" appears in the third and last section, "Black Art: 1965–1966," of his first collected book of poems, *Black Magic: Poems, 1961–1967*. As critic Lynn Nwuneli reminds us, this poem, like all of Baraka's writing, must be understood, indeed, can only be understood, within the manifold of its various personal, social, cultural, and formal contexts. We might also note that Baraka's "Incident" alludes to Countee Cullen's famous poem "Incident," first published in 1925, and it precedes Natasha Trethewey's poem of the same title.[1] However, while Cullen's and Trethewey's "incidents" concern menacing acts of racism, Baraka's poem concerns actual and lethal intraracial violence.

"Incident" was, of course, written by LeRoi Jones, not Amiri Baraka. *Black Magic* in general, and the section (and poem) "Black Art" in particular, mark a crucial transitional phase from LeRoi Jones to Amiri Baraka. *Black Magic* is a record of his struggles to overcome his own middle-class background and orientation, his isolation from the experiences of "common" Black people, and his self-confessed apolitical aestheticism. In these poems he is no longer LeRoi Jones but he is also not yet Amiri Baraka. Hence, despite the exhortations, bombast, and anti-aesthetic ugliness of specific poems, ambivalence characterizes the book as a whole. And nowhere is this more apparent than in "Incident."

Jones's/Baraka's "Incident" is written as though it were a short story that Poe would have endorsed: short, dense, and psychologically disturbing. At the same time, it reads like a treatment for a film noir script: ambivalence is its central stance, an *homme fatale* its central character. Finally, the description of the killing reads, in part, like a police blotter. Baraka achieves all of these effects by drawing from his memories of radio dramas and films from the 1940s, 1950s, and early 1960s, reducing his characters to pronouns (he, him, we) and deploying repetition and redundancies of key words and phrases. The flattening of language, characterization, and description results in a mesmerizing monotone.

Comprised of five free-verse tercets and three single lines (two single lines separate the first three tercet stanzas from the next two tercet stanzas and a final single line), the poem opens with five of its
nine iterations of "he" and four of its six iterations of "shot" in the first
stanza alone. Likewise, the phrase "came back" appears twice in the
opening stanza and once thereafter, in stanza four, the same stanza
that contains the last two iterations of "he" and the last iteration of
"shot." The effect is twofold: we know *what* has happened, but we
don't know, and as it happens never know, *why* it happened. The last
clause of the poem affirms "our" ignorance: "we know nothing."
Between that closing laconic admission and the equally terse opening—"He came back."—the poem crawls forward, backs up, like a
car, over itself, adding details, some of which ("the speeding bullet,
tore his face / and blood sprayed fine over the killer and the grey
light") seem gratuitously graphic. Other details function like camera
shots from different angles. In the first stanza, "he fell, stumbling,
past the / shadow wood, down, shot, dying, dead, to full halt." The
very next stanza begins, "At the bottom, bleeding, shot dead." Details
zoom in—the killer "shot only once into his victim's / stare, and left
him quickly when the blood ran out."— and zoom out—"we know //
the killer was skillful, quick, and silent, and that the victim / probably
knew him." But all the other cinematic, journalistic, and law enforce-
ment tenets—who, where, when, why—are either absent or useless.
Who was involved? All we are told is that one "he" was the "killer"
(second and fourth stanzas) and the other "he" was the "victim"
(stanzas three and four). When did this happen? The only "timeline"
is the past tense of a verb, "He came back," repeated twice in the first
line and a half. Whence our killer? All we know is that "he came back,
from somewhere."

As the brutal harshness of the poem's last statement—"we know
nothing"—indicates, Baraka cannot quite maintain the poker-face
demeanor of the professional or a community inured to murder. LeRoi
Jones, poet and judge, makes an appearance at the end of "Incident."
"Our" know-nothing immunity to outrage, fear, disgust, and so forth is

part and parcel of our willingness to accept the dehumanization of men (stripped of their proper names, reduced to pronouns, etc.), good and bad, victims and killers. Jones includes himself in this condemnation because his "Incident" shares one feature with Cullen's "Incident": an objective description of a horrific event. The person Jones will soon become, Baraka, is indicated in those famous opening lines of the book's most infamous poem, "Black Art": "Poems are bullshit unless they are / teeth or trees or lemons piled / on a step." This accusing finger is pointed at Jones himself. His poems must take on the materiality of physical objects, poems that *be*, not (merely) *mean*. Both his and Cullen's "Incidents" sacrifice being to meaning, males (a boy, a man) to other males (a white man, a man with a gun), and no one—not Cullen's narrator, not Jones's "we"—appears upset, angry, frightened, and so on.

Just as Jones must transform himself into Baraka, so too each member of the community's "we" must transform him- or herself into new Black men and women. As he puts it in "For a lady i know," the poem that immediately follows "Incident," "Talk the talk I need / you, as you resurrect / your consciousness above / the street."

NOTE

1 While Cullen's poem is an aphoristic lyric that dramatizes a young Black boy's presumably first encounter with racism—he's called a nigger by a white man—Trethewey's "Incident" recounts a family story about a KKK cross-burning outside their house. Her poem appears in *Native Guard* (Boston: Houghton Mifflin, 2006).

26

Sarah Dowling

on **Lorine Niedecker, "Foreclosure"**
(1970)

Tell em to take my bare walls down
my cement abutments
their parties thereof
and clause of claws

Leave me the land
Scratch out: the land

May prose and property both die out
and leave me peace

Source: Lorine Niedecker, *Collected Works* (Berkeley: University of California Press, 2003). Permission granted by Bob Arnold, Literary Executor for the Estate of Lorine Niedecker.

A poem titled "Foreclosure" seems to speak to the twenty-first century's signature cruelties. As we know, some six million American homes have been foreclosed on—that is, they've been seized back from their owners by banks and mortgage lenders—over the past ten years. Despite the sharp immediacy of its title, though, this poem is not about the 2008 financial crisis. "Foreclosure," written sometime during the 1960s, speaks to the never-ending series of dispossessions that its author, Lorine Niedecker, suffered throughout her life before, during, and after the Great Depression. "Foreclosure" evokes that treasured American fantasy: ownership of one's own home, of a parcel of territory marked with a white picket fence. But this compressed, grief-stricken, and exhausted little poem shows what happens when the dream is snatched away. It shows what happens when the thief who steals your home and tosses you off your land is the law, an entity beyond reproach. This poem makes a radical statement: in mourning the loss of a home and a severed relationship to land, "Foreclosure" shows that dispossession is a foundational, if too often forgotten American experience. As a solution, and as a source of "peace," this poem calls for an end to property and to the cruel legal "prose" in which property's rules are enforced.

"Foreclosure" begins by drawing a contrast between two kinds of language: a specifically legal and contractual idiom, and the speaker's own vernacular. The title, of course, comes from mortgage law; the phrase "parties thereof" is a fragment of legalese; the term "abutments" is highly technical; and the unpoetic echo between "their" and "thereof" replicates the awkward repetitions of a legal document. Placed into collision with this technical language is the speaker's opening plea, "Tell em to take my bare walls down." Whom does the speaker address in this clear and unrefined appeal—the banks? The lenders? The reader? Calling out to a nebulous no one, in a language less Latinate than the law, the speaker conveys frustration. The riffing, quotational quality of her reaction to the law's predation lends the poem an element of humor, but Niedecker is vivid and specific in describing how the law operates. Rather than showing two equal "parties" to this contract, the image that concludes the first stanza, "clause of claws," asks readers to imagine the law, or a legal document, as a bird of prey. The law swoops in, snatching the "bare walls" and "cement abutments" from the speaker, their former owner. We are asked to imagine the speaker's "bare" vulnerability before these clawed clauses, which "scratch out," or erase, the shape of her dwelling, as well as her relationship to the land. The law struggles fiercely to get possession of—it *scratches for*—the one thing from which the speaker could "scratch out" a living. Following this attack, the speaker is left pleading for respite, for mercy, for "peace."

The speaker's repeated plea that the law not only "leave" her but leave her *something* can be read as a demand for a less cruel set of terms and for a different type of contract altogether. At first pass, the repetition of the word "leave" seems to refer to what remains after the foreclosure. However, to "leave" something is also to bequeath it in one's will. When the speaker begs, "Leave me the land," she asks that the law not take everything, that her relationship to the land remain unaffected by the foreclosure that will take her home. But then she revises her terms: the middle stanza is a negotiation, and the speaker asks that her interlocutor "Scratch out," or delete, "the land" from the contract. Rather than working within the system of property law, begging for scraps, Niedecker's speaker calls for its death and demands a bequest for herself. When property dies out, the poem implies, she can reconstitute her relationship to her home and to her land. The end of legal dispossession will provide the foundation for peace, a profoundly new kind of freedom.

We could say that this is a poem about what ends and what continues. Etymologically, the word "clause" comes from the Latin *clausula*, where it describes the close of a period, a formula, or a conclusion. The "clause of claws" enforcing the foreclosure redoubles and layers the connotations of dispossession and exclusion; it makes the violence of termination vivid. The repeated plea, "leave me," does the opposite: it emphasizes what survives, what remains, and what lasts beyond. It banishes the law from the speaker's presence, and it points to the things that the law cannot prevent the speaker from enjoying, to what escapes commodification as property. That this phrase is the only one repeated in the poem insists upon the existence of a future beyond foreclosure—*when* "prose and property both die out." It counterbalances the rapacious "clause of claws" and concludes the clanging, contractual off-rhymes with its inauguration of "peace," that is, of the silence that comes after the poem's end.

"Foreclosure" describes one moment—a moment where its speaker loses everything. But the poem makes clear that such moments pervade the reign of "prose and property." Obliquely, "Foreclosure" suggests that much of the history of the United States could be described as the taking down of "bare walls" and the scratching out of connections to land. The poem's seemingly contemporary title reminds us that the foreclosures taking place in our own time echo a long history of dispossession, beginning with the country's colonial foundations. There is nothing exceptional about foreclosure; it is of a piece with the governing system of property. There is something exceptional about "Foreclosure," though: this poem looks to a future beyond property and beyond predation. It insists upon the existence—and the necessity—of something else and something more. In the silence that follows the closing demand for "peace," we readers are asked to imagine what that might be.

27

Michael Davidson

on **Larry Eigner, "birds the"**
(1970)

birds the
    warmest blood in the world

        keeps hopping
          powerful breath a ground
           target while brooding

          the

         positions

man's
    growth precarious birth
      to soar in the mind

    so big to the earth

      whole parting

    active   wake
all the dimensions
a great head of

Source: Larry Eigner, *Calligraphy Typewriters: The Selected Poems of Larry Eigner*, ed. Curtis Faville and Robert Grenier (Tuscaloosa: University of Alabama Press, 2017). Courtesy of the Estate of Larry Eigner.

Our mandate in this collection of essays is to provide close readings of individual modern and postmodern poems, but this imperative is vexed from the outset. The very concept of a "close reading" of modern poetry is challenged by work that often defies explication, whether because its form is so disjunctive and fragmentary or because it lacks any discernable subject matter. Even the idea of an isolated, individual poem is complicated by the fact that many modernist poems occur in serial fashion, discrete elements linked together in much larger forms, from Wallace Stevens's *Notes Toward a Supreme Fiction* or Gertrude Stein's *Stanzas in Meditation* to more recent serial or conceptual poems. This fact is especially the case with the example I have chosen to discuss, an untitled poem from 1970 by Larry Eigner (1927–96). He was a central figure in postwar experimental poetry, often associated with the Black Mountain poetry movement and an important influence on subsequent language-writing. Eigner acquired cerebral palsy at birth and had little control over his bodily movements and speech. Typing was especially difficult for him since he only had control over his right index finger.

One might expect that Eigner's limited mobility would be a primary subject of his poetry, but in fact he seldom mentioned his disability. Thus a close reading of an Eigner poem might trace its linguistic and rhetorical features but would leave out his daily lived experience as a disabled person. How, then, to honor the poet's reticence about his physical condition while accounting for the disability that so informed his daily life? To paraphrase Wallace Stevens, how to account for the body that is not there and the body that is?

One answer would be to adopt a phenomenological perspective, to study the poet's particular way of seeing and understanding rather than the world that he represents. Instead of focusing on the poem's formal or rhetorical features, a disability reading would ask how those features embody a particular perspective of a person with limited mobility or sensory impairment. Eigner spent much of his life in a single room in his parents' house in Swampscott, Massachusetts, and his view was necessarily limited, yet he subjected the world seen from his window—birds, changing weather, clouds, cars, children— to minute inspection, seldom pausing to edit or qualify his observations. Each poem in his vast body of work was a snapshot of shifting attentions. His characteristic broken lineation, enjambment, and sudden shifts of focus provided a map of cognitive and perceptual acts.

Like birds that hop from one twig to another, Eigner's lines accomplish a similar busy movement, one image leading to another without transitions. His poetry is multistable, constantly shifting focus and perspective, leaving reference open to multiple readings, the "uncertain limits / of the simultaneous" as he says elsewhere. By leaving out relevant connectives, he correlates relationships between his physical body and natural growth, bird and man, birth and mortality.

The poem deals in various ways with precarity and vulnerability, "all the dimensions" that measure normal growth and inevitable decline. Perhaps influenced by a nature program on television or radio, Eigner begins by noting that birds have "the / warmest blood in the world," allowing them to be in constant motion against the threat of becoming a stationary "target." "While brooding" on the mortality of birds, he switches to human vulnerability, alluding to his own "precarious birth" in which a forceps injury during delivery led to his cerebral palsy. Precarity joins birds to humans, links material head to imagination ("to soar in the mind"). This mobile-like structure of the poem permits the two realms—avian and anthropomorphic—to reflect (on) each other. The poem is not "about" the onset of the poet's disability so much as the degree to which a different "head" permits identification with other species (birds) and spaces ("so big to the earth").

Readers might find Eigner's lineation confusing, perversely refusing to connect one to the next. The opening line, "birds the," doesn't make much sense until we read its enjambed continuation in the next line, "warmest blood in the world." This provides some clarity, but even here a good deal is left out: "Birds [who have] the warmest blood in the world" would be a possible subordinate clause, but it remains incomplete. The third line complicates things further by moving from the plural noun, "birds," to a singular verb, "keeps hopping." What we would ordinarily characterize as a grammatical error becomes, in Eigner's usage, a verbal equivalent of the poet's perception, moving quickly from the general category ("birds") to a specific bird seen, perhaps, out of his window. And this shifting perceptual awareness continues as he reflects on how the bird's constant motion is essential for its survival.

This reflection on mortality leads Eigner to move in a more philosophical direction as he shifts the focus from birds to human frailty. I initially said that *Eigner* was "brooding," but of course he could be deploying another meaning of the verb, referring to the bird's protection or incubation of eggs in the nest. This second reading of "brooding" suggests that the bird's quick movement allows it to *become* a moving target in order to protect its young. Whether "brooding" refers to an intellectual activity (to reflect darkly) or a species necessity (to incubate and protect), both describe the twin "positions" that connect mind to body, birth to growth. Eigner's birth was, indeed, "precarious" because his large head made delivery difficult, damaging certain nerves and causing his palsy. Yet precarity of birth and growth remain a preoccupation of the poem, embodied in the reflection on birds that we have been witnessing. It is as if he is saying that precarity allows him "to soar in the mind," turning disability into capability. The mind's ability to soar, like Shelley's Skylark, is connected with the "great head" that is the source of his disability yet also the source of his poetry.

The poem's final lines, in their disjunctive movement, attempt to characterize "all the dimensions" or all of the associations with a "great head": the poet's physical head, the head as seat of mind, the part of the body that is "active" and "awake" and that permits, perhaps even the phrase "a great head of steam," to complete the image of bodily energy and integrity. What makes this an interesting example of disability poetics is not by any specific reference to cerebral palsy but its embodiment of perceptual acts instantaneously and without reflective commentary. Like the bird's busy movement to protect life, Eigner seeks to connect that warm blood and quick breathing with his own mortality. For a poet who often watched and wrote about birds from his wheelchair through a window, his limited perspective ceased to be limited; he danced, to paraphrase Charles Olson, "sitting down."

28

Christie Williamson

on **Tom Leonard, "Jist Ti Let Yi No"**
(c. 1974)

(from the American of Carlos Williams)

ahv drank
thi speshlz
that wurrin
thi frij

n thit
yiwurr probbli
hodn back
furthi pahrti

awright
they wur great
thaht stroang
that cawld

"Jist Ti Let Yi No" reprinted with permission of Sonya Leonard.

"Jist Ti Let Yi No" is a poem by the Glaswegian poet Tom Leonard (1944–2018). It is a translation of "This Is Just to Say," a famous poem by the American poet William Carlos Willams (1883–1963). In this essay I hope to bring the language of Leonard's poem (more) alive to non-Glaswegian audiences, to examine where Leonard's poem does and doesn't deviate from the original and to look at the impacts these deviations have.

"This Is Just to Say" is classic Tom Leonard territory. The Williams poem claims for poetic tradition the everyday language of a kitchen note. Tom Leonard's poem extends that democratization by rendering the by then classic text into phonetic urban Scots. Both advance poetry through using everyday situations and everyday language. It marks him out as an experimental writer, and distances his work from more traditional Scots language writers who would tend to frown on orthographies like "frij" and "probbli." Instead of questing for "correct" orthographies, Tom Leonard was fascinated with the relationships between power, language, sound, and meaning.

While it may be more "spoken" and less "written," the title of Leonard's poem carries a near identical meaning to the title of the Williams poem "This Is Just to Say." Still, certain differences reward exploration. In the Williams title, the meaning is carried through three main words—This, Just, and Say. The title is a key part of the poem's success. It becomes part of the text of the poem, and it directs the reader's focus on "This." It tells us that something, "This," is being said. It also places emphasis on the word "Just"—which doesn't only mean only, it also means fair, correct, equitable. Just. Whether or not the eating of the plums is just, Williams contends that his confession of the act is.

Tom Leonard's title, on the other hand, has four load-bearing words— Jist, Let, Yi, and No. The claim to justice implied in the Williams title is subordinated— "Jist" jist means jist, as in only. I find the deviation from the Williams original perfectly fascinating in the other three words. Tom Leonard was passionate about empowerment, about the relationship between accepted standards in language and authority in power. He gives space to "Yi," to you, to the reader—especially the Glaswegian reader. And his relationship to the Glaswegian reader is one of empowerment, facilitation. Finally, he Lets Yi "No." On a surface level, this means to know, to have knowledge of. He is also letting the addressee of the poem "No" drink the speshlz.

Leonard's position on language and authority is reiterated in the attribution of his poem "from" Williams. He chooses to call the language "American," not English or American English, and he also refers to Williams by both his middle and surname. Leonard's attribution to the

"American" strikes me as a way of stating that Carlos Williams owns his own language. It's also a measure of the esteem in which Leonard holds him—people who lose their forenames tend to be cultural touchstones. Think Shakespeare, Milton, Burns, MacDiarmid. Or García Lorca.

It also marks the poem as a translation, and a translation into what you could call a specialist idiom. The language of "Jist Ti Let Yi No" is a very urban, Glaswegian working-class speech, which is rarely written down, and never written down quite like Tom Leonard writes it down. Classic "Leonardisms" in this short poem include "speshlz," a very specific word for cans of "heavy," a brown, malty beer, one leading example of which is brewed in the East End of Glasgow, "hodn" for "holding" and "n" for "and."

In the first verse, the language of "Jist Ti Let Yi No" mirrors "This Is Just to Say" more directly than in the title. Upper case is dispensed with, "I have eaten / the plums" becomes contracted to "ahv drank / the speshlz." Similarly, "were in" is contracted to "wurrin." Other than that the Glaswegian employed is identical to the original New Jerseyan text. Except, of course, that simply isn't the case. The speaker in the Williams poem eats plums; the speaker in the Leonard poem drinks beer. Turning the plums into beer does a number of things. First and most importantly, it's funny. Just like "This Is Just to Say," "Jist Ti Let Yi No" is a light-hearted poem that works by making the reader or hearer laugh, or at the very least smile. Humor (often much darker than this) is a key feature of Leonard's oeuvre.

I'm also tempted to read a statement about poetry, about language, about culture. Whereas the Williams speaker has "eaten," the Leonard speaker has "drank." Both involve essential ingestion through the mouth and throat. We eat food, solids, and from this action the Williams materializes. By turning the plums into beer, Tom Leonard's poem speaks to fluidities of language and of poetry. By making a Depression-era New Jersey poem resonate in the context of 1960s Glasgow he teaches an essential lesson of change and constancy.

Finally, the speshlz and the plums are comparable in that both are modest luxuries. Williams's speaker hasn't eaten the steak, nobody's going to starve, but they will have a much less pleasurable breakfast. Likewise in Glasgow nobody's missing a bottle of champagne or whisky. But both the plums and the speshlz are for someone else, are little oases of pleasure (no longer) waiting to cheer the lives of their rightful owners.

The other key deviation from the Carlos Williams text is the first line of the final verse. Whilst the family doctor in New Jersey begs forgiveness (Forgive me / they were delicious) for the desecration of his wife's breakfast, Tom Leonard simply intones the multipurpose "awright," before both delight in the pleasure they derived from the stolen goods. "Awright" is a word which can be used in many ways by the discerning Glaswegian. It is a greeting, an indication of or a request for agreement. It is all these things and more, but it certainly is not much if any kind of apology. The two Penn Sound recordings exhibit very different "awrights." The "stand alone" recording is a much more heightened performance, and you can hear the poet smiling with self-approval at his conquest. The recording from a more extended reading is much more muted. Either way, neither constitutes any kind of remorse—what's done is done, and you will be okay with it. I think this may be a comment on the sincerity of Carlos Williams's pleas for forgiveness in the original poem, and is also characteristic of a poet and polemicist of fierce integrity who would rather fall out with everyone around him than say something he didn't believe.

29

Laynie Browne

on **Bernadette Mayer, "Invasion of the Body Snatchers"**
(1976)

Moon out and no snow yet, November first
The first anniversary of our wedding and
The day before election day, 1976, yesterday
Was Halloween, next Friday I have an appointment
With the dentist and the following Tuesday is
Lewis's thirty-second birthday, exactly one week
After that Marie will be eleven months old.
The day before yesterday we turned the clocks back
One hour which made it seem like every day
Will have an extra hour in it, not only of darkness
But of just plain time, the time I used to spend
Skipping lunch is longer, the time for dinner
Is too early now, the time for sunset comes too soon
The time between dinner and Marie's bedtime is too long
When it's time to go to bed there's still a few hours left
To read, I'm dreaming twice as much as before
I spend all my new time lying in bed thinking.
Last night I saw "Invasion of the Body Snatchers"
And tonight when I came into my room to go to work
I found an old seedpod on the floor by my desk.
In the movie if you see one of these it's time to die.
It's time to write some letters, good cold air
Comes in my window, it wakes me up, we had a bottle
Of champagne and Marie went to sleep without crying
It's time to read *Fielding's Guide to European Travel*
And the *Alice Toklas Cookbook* again, a few books by
        John McPhee
Our new American Heritage anniversary dictionary,
The Adventures of a Mathematician by Stanislas Ulam

And *The Wild Boy of Aveyron* by a behaviorist psychologist
About a boy brought up by wolves

"Invasion of the Body Snatchers" is reprinted with permission of Bernadette Mayer.

──────────────

How do we understand ourselves as beings constructed of time? Mayer
investigates time throughout her writing, for example, in the exploration
of nine months as gestational in her book *The Desires of Mothers to
Please Others in Letters* and in the study of a day in her book *Midwinter
Day*. The poem "Invasion of the Body Snatchers" is a brief and harrowing meditation on the impossible yet persistent temptation to manipu-
late time, and ultimately on notions of ephemerality and all of the generative processes that enliven and baffle between birth and death.
Mayer's poetry often resides within the quotidian in concert with the
global and questions of personhood. She consistently defies convention and redefines assumptions about women's work and worth.

We understand time by being in body and on this planet. Looking
up at the night sky has always been one method for simultaneously
marking time and placing oneself in relation with the unknowable.
"Invasion of the Body Snatchers" insists on holding both perspectives
together in one seamless continuum. The poem begins with the moon,
thus time begins in the dark, unconscious space of dreaming, in the
intimate space of home, and in the space between bodies. In this context time is relational, elastic, and dynamic.

The poem is written on November 1, the Day of the Dead, associated
with remembrance of ancestors. What does Mayer choose to remember? She is determined to create a poem brimming with categories
of time and activities that fill not only our days and nights but also
our archives of the present and documents of our thinking and movements. In the poem we navigate the temporal through marking events.
The poem lists categories of time, such as holidays (Halloween),

appointments (dentist), occasions (anniversaries and birthdays), and dates for public hope or disappointment (elections). The poem also chronicles the trials of moving fluidly within the rhythm of a single day. How does time behave? Why do the minutes slow before bedtime when one is a parent of young children? Why is there never enough time to make dinner? How might we double our time to dream, to love, to read, to ponder gifts and plights? Is it possible to rest or to work without interruption? Might we adorn "plain time"? Why does some time hang heavy and despondent while other time dissipates with a rapidity we find alarming?

Mayer's attempts to defy time despite mortality are energizing. What are our actions relating to time? We turn back our clocks but this does not help. If seeing a seedpod signals death in the film *Invasion of the Body Snatchers*, it also signals something new and, I'd argue, brighter in Mayer's poem than in the film. Mortality "time to die" is of course one root of our obsession with time. Yet what is a seedpod if not also regenerative? If the film *Invasion of the Body Snatchers* is an allegory against conformity, in Mayer's poem we can read not only death but also the recurrence and the dispersal of reproductive powers, the future, and the beauty of ephemerality. A woman gives birth and a former self expires. A mother is born. And isn't the life of a poet a death or elevation of ordinary sense and a birth of something we cannot name, beyond the poems? Does Mayer, as a poet and mother, have access to a new medium of time, one that is nonnegotiable yet acts as a curious and at times spectacular catalyst? Mayer is a foremother of a resiliency that cannot be stolen by any form whether it be alien, animal, or vegetable.

As parents we lose some autonomy or individual freedom. At the same time the domestic portrait exists in many registers. Playful caretaking leads to polymorphous being. Instead of, or in addition to, dying the poet continues to write. The poet tells us, post-seedpod, of an abundance of sources of sustenance, many related to language.

How does the poet fill time? In the poem she watches a film, she writes letters, she notes "good cold air / Comes in my window." She breathes. She wakes. She reads. The poem simultaneously laughs through the exhaustion entailed in parenting (a form of death similar to loss of agency reflected in the film) and counters the dark rebirth through her generative powers. Mayer is both deeply affected and indefatigable. She continues, despite death, into the alchemy of cooking, the celebration of occasional and seasonal events, humor coupled with frustration, love, and literature.

It seems no accident that a poem beginning with the moon ends with reference to a boy brought up by wolves, which suggests a different notion of time, not exclusive to humans but open to other animals and modes of intelligence. A feral child calls into question the problems of socialization. What is convention and who is free? Persistent defiance of expected attitudes and outcomes exists throughout Mayer's work. What else supplants our awareness and self-knowledge? How do aspects of civilization suppress being present or awake to our bodies and environment? Mayer does not romanticize a feral existence, but she does wonder about the lunacy of human convention. After all, no other animal has caused so much harm to our planet. In a way we have all been removed from our senses, and our lack of connection to our own transient nature is certainly part of the problem. How does time behave? How is time a character? How is time a problematic human invention? Isn't time the thief in Mayer's poem? In her poem physical and temporal constraints are subjects of both lament and fascination. Mayer's poem encourages us to enter into an infinitely exploding series of moments simultaneously inside and immune to the ravages of time. A poem written on the Day of the Dead asserts: if our literary antecedents and ancestors are with us, they are alive. The poem asks: what do we know about death and its sequels? Even though we cannot find adequate answers we must go on to cook dinner. We will not cease to seek pleasure. We are all invited into and implicated in the poem. If invasion is to copacetic what conformity is to wildness then seeing a seedpod is in equal measures both devastating and sublime.

30

Charles Bernstein

on **Lyn Hejinian, from *My Life***
(1980)

What is the   A dog bark, the engine of
meaning hung   a truck, an airplane hidden
from that depend   by the trees and rooftops.
My mother's childhood seemed a kind of holy melodrama. She ate her pudding in a pattern, carving a rim around the circumference of the pudding, working her way inward toward the center, scooping with the spoon, to see how far she could separate the pudding from the edge of the bowl before the center collapsed, spreading the pudding out again, lower, back to the edge of the bowl. You could tell that it was improvisational because at that point they closed their eyes. A pause, a rose, something on paper. Solitude was the essential companion. The branches of the redwood trees hung in a fog whose moisture they absorbed. Lasting, "what might be," its present a future, like the life of a child. The greatest solitudes are quickly strewn with rubbish. All night the radio covered the fall of a child in the valley down an abandoned well-fitting, a clammy narrow pipe 56 feet deep, in which he was wedged, recorded, and died. Stanza there. The synchronous, which I have characterized as spatial, is accurate to reality but it has been debased. Daisy's plenty pebbles in the gravel drive. It is a tartan not a plaid. There was some disparity between my grandfather's reserve, the result of shyness and disdain, and his sense that a man's natural importance was characterized by bulk, by the great depth of his footprint in the sand—in other words, a successful man was no lightweight. A flock of guard

geese are pecking in a cold rain, become formal behind the obvious flower's bloom. The room, in fact, was used as a closet as well, for as one sat at the telephone table, one faced a row of my grandparents' overcoats, raincoats, and hats, which were hung from a line of heavy, polished wooden hooks. The fog burned off and I went for a walk alone, then was lost between the grapevines, unable to return, until they set a mast, a pole, into the ground and hung a colored flag that I could see from anywhere around. A glass snail was set among real camellias in a glass bowl upon the table. Pure duration, a compound plenum in which nothing is repeated. Photographed in a blue pinafore. The way Dorothy Wordsworth, often, I think, went out to "get" a sight. But language is restless. They say there has been too much roughhousing. The heat waves wobbled over the highway—on either side were flat brown fields tilted slightly toward the horizon—and in the distance ahead of the car small blue ponds lay in our path, evaporating suddenly, as if in a single piece, at the instant prior to our splashing in. I saw a line of rocks topped by a foghorn protecting the little harbor from the tide. Fruit peels and the heels of bread were left to get moldy. But then we'd need, what, a bird, to eat the fleas from the rug. When what happens is not intentional, one can't ascribe meaning to it, and unless what happens is necessary, one can't expect it to occur again. Because children will spill food, one needs a dog. Rubber books for bathtubs. Coast laps. One had merely to turn around in order to see it. Elbows off the table. The portrait, a photograph, had been made so that my grandmother was looking just over the head of the observer, into a little distance, not so far as to be a space into which she might seem to be staring, but at some definite object, some noun, just behind one. Waffle man everywhere. She had come upon a set of expressions ("peachy" being one of them and "nuts to you" another) which exactly suited her, and so, though the expressions went out of everyone else's vocabulary, even years later, when everyone else was saying "far out" or "that's nowhere," she continued to have a "perfectly peachy time" on her vacations. This was Melody Ranch, daring and resourceful. As for we who "love to be astonished," we might go to the zoo and see the famous hippo named "Bubbles." The sidesaddle was impossible, and yet I've seen it used successfully, even stunningly, the woman's full skirts spread like a wing as the horse jumped a hurdle and they galloped on. Lasting, ferries, later, trolleys, from Berkeley to the Bridge. This is one of those things which continues, and hence seems important, and so ever what one says over and over again. Soggy sky, which then dries out, lifting slightly turning white—and then banks toward the West. If I see fishing boats that's the first thing I think, Insane, in common parlance.

Reprinted with permission of the author and Wesleyan University Press.

———————

I've always been confused by the difference between the beautiful and the sublime. I mean if something is really beautiful, isn't it also sublime? Well, I see already I'm getting off on the wrong foot. And what do feet have to do with poetry anyway?

There's more to a poem than blue cheese!

This is meant to be a guide for reading one section of Lyn Hejinian's iconic *My Life*. I say iconic because there's no work from the 1970s or 1980s that better shows the possibility of serially ordered, disjunct (*not* junk) sentences than *My Life*. The poem reads like a series of non sequiturs except that it all ties together, the way a series of at first unrelated clues starts to add up in a detective story. In *My Life*, the palpable sense of connection among the non sequiturs (*that's no non sequitur, that's my life!*) is aided and abetted not only by the striking repetition of phrases throughout the book but also by a relatively simple device that Hejinian invented for the poem. The first edition of *My Life* was published in 1980 by Burning Deck, when Hejinian was 37. This version consisted of 37 sections, each with 37 sentences. In the

1987 edition, published by Sun and Moon, the poem was expanded to 45 sections of 45 sentences, reflecting Hejinian's age at the time.

Each section of *My Life* is set off by a keynote phrase, taken from another part of the poem. "What is the meaning hung from that depend" is the keynote of the section under consideration here. *So much depends*, William Carlos William famously writes, *upon a red wheelbarrow*. Depends is the mark not of subordination but consanguinity, as in, we're all in this together. The sentences in *My Life* are codependent but in a good way. None of them can stand on their own, but the ensemble shimmers.

What comes next? In my life, at least, I don't know what comes next. One afternoon it rains and then before you can call it a day I'm overcome by the sun. But it's really snowing, and I hear a piercing sound coming from under the rafters. Or the circuit breaker blows but it's not because I had the toaster and coffee maker on at the same time.

Just because something don't follow don't mean it don't come next, do it?

The sentence-to-sentence disjunction in *My Life* is not arbitrary but weighted, one moment to another, to create a constellation—a music of changing parts—that illumines the patterns of life lived, as reflected/refracted in/as writing. *My Life* is a crossover poem, a signal work of radically inventive poetry that is readable as memoir and autobiography.

Each sentence of *My Life* is beautiful because of the music made with the sequence of words (the turning of the phrases) but also because of a wistfulness verging on sentimentality (but never dwelling in it). That is to say, the beauty of the individual sentences is grounded in the exquisite valences of Hejinian's observations and sensibility.

You can see what I mean by looking at any sentence in the poem. The most memorable line in *My Life* is "A pause, a rose, something on paper." It comes up 18 times in the poem and its meaning changes with each new context. "A pause" suggests the space between moments, the lacunae between the sentences, the sense of life as an unfolding series. A pause is a line. "A rose" brings to mind Gertrude Stein's "rose is a rose is a rose"; here, as in Stein, not a symbol, not *the* Rose, but a given instance flowering in its specificity—arising anew with each mention: memory's air/heir of Eros. "Something on paper" is the book in our hands, or our mind's eye—perhaps echoing Williams again, "no ideas but in things."

"As for we who 'love to be astonished'" is another emblematic phrase from *My Life* that, like "A pause," also appears in this passage—and 24 other times in the poem. Here it is being astonished at the zoo seeing "Bubbles" the hippo, a childhood memory of amazement. In another instance, the phrase on its own, a pivot for the book, registering that each crystalline moment jogs the aesthetic sense, where love leads. The shock of each new sentence: stoned into sentience. But mostly astonishment is yoked to quotidian events and observations that hardly seem out of the ordinary. In *My Life*, the ordinary is astonishing.

The section at hand begins with a sentence without a verb, that is, a fragment, three phrases without explicit connection: "A dog bark, the engine of a truck, an airplane hidden by the trees and rooftops." The phrases are metonyms and the string of three is metonymic of the structure of this long poem-in-prose. Metaphors and similes work by comparison, as in *my love is like a rose*, the beauty of the rose is compared to the beauty of the one loved, where, moreover, "rose" is not "a" rose, for example, the one decomposing in the street, but the symbol of beauty. Metonymy works differently: it's a part, a fragment, that evokes—perhaps *triggers* is more vivid—something else, something with which it has no metaphoric relation. An object—a keepsake—given to you by a parent, lover, or friend may evoke—every time you see or touch it—your relation to that person, but it is not a metaphor for the person or for the relation. *A dog bark* might involuntarily bring to mind a moment in childhood when you were suddenly left by yourself and you associate that moment with the bark of a neighbor's dog, for this was the first time you noticed it. A metonymic shard pierces the present with something absent or lost. *My Life* is an elegy, just as my life is shot through with the piercing light of what is *nevermore*.

Every word is a metonymic echo chamber. When I am writing I am Quasimodo, ringing one bell in counterrhythm to the next. The poem is my cathedral.

People sometimes think fragments and disjunction underscore a lack of relation. In *My Life*, the metonymic structure creates unconscious, intuitive, *felt* connections, which can be more intense than logical or plot-driven ones. *My Life* may not have plot but it's crackling with narrative.

Each sentence is beautiful. The work as a whole is sublime.

31

Al Filreis

on **Cid Corman, "It isnt for want"**
(1982)

It isnt for want
of something to say—
something to tell you—

something you should know—
but to detain you—
keep you from going—

feeling myself here
as long as *you* are—
as long as you *are.*

"It isnt for want" is reprinted with permission of Bob Arnold, Literary
Executor for the Estate of Cid Corman.

I revere this tiny poem because it is not at all about content. Who
needs content when you have the urgency of human connection?
Surely the basic situation of every poem is a convergence somehow
of the writer writing (or uttering) and the reader reading (or listener
hearing). Most poets imply this. Corman in hundreds of poems made
such convergence explicit. We are called upon as a "you." When in
1999 I heard Corman's frail baritone say "It isnt for want" (by telephone
from Japan, piped in through speakers in a room at the Kelly Writers
House in Philadelphia), I was moved to tears because I was certain
he was speaking to me—calling out to me to stay with him. I have
memorized this poem; a week doesn't pass when it's not in my head,

even on my lips. Thus an absence (he is, alas, long gone by now) is made again and again into a presence.

Where exactly does the convergence between poet and us take place? In the poem, of course, which is always for Corman thus a living space (his term for this is "livingdying"). And when does the convergence happen? *Just then*, whenever "then" might be: past, in both the theoretical and practical readerly present, and, boldly, in anticipation of a future in which poet has departed but reader has encounters with something once written—a special "moment's notice," to use Nathaniel Mackey's term (via jazz) for the improvisational combination of writerly and readerly subjects. Corman believed that the recipient of his pithy arrangements of words was as much a subject as was the author of them.

Here is what I think Corman is saying:

> Whatever this poem is about, it has little to do with a lack of topics I like to discuss (for there are so many things indeed I could discuss), nor with such topics that I could convey to you, or indeed a topic that you in particular need to know, as a warning to you or carrying the implication that you lack information that I possess. No, this poem is not a public service announcement—indeed, the very opposite. The poem exists precisely as its speaker exists, merely to keep you in the new here-ness invented for it. Insofar as you stay in the poem, you will feel the me-as-speaker in the space my words make between us. So long as you are "detain[ed]" by the poem, you exist for me and only thus do I exist at all.

Although Corman's speaker implies a sureness about content (it's *not* "something you *should* know"), there is still pathetic desperation here. Like some modernist, metapoetic Ancient Mariner, he keenly longs to behold you, to keep you from straying beyond his story. If you stray, the here in which the poetic self obtains will dissipate, as will his subject.

"It isnt for want" has been plausibly read as a love poem ("you" is the beloved other). But that interpretation only intensifies the codependence in a writer-reader relationship. If "you" is a lover, the lover nonetheless *receives* the sentiment. Corman once commended an utterance of Wallace Stevens as follows: "Poetry is not a literary activity: it is a vital activity."[1] Vitality predates and also presupposes any poem. The poetic qualities of "It isnt for want" serve aesthetic purposes secondarily; primarily, the poem must be poetically compelling in order to dissuade readers "from going."

Cid Corman (1924–2004) lived for decades in a kind of poetic and political self-exile in Kyoto, Japan. In later years especially, he lived a life of precarity. His returns to the United States were infrequent. He was physically cut off from most readers and colleagues, but he bombarded us (I among them) with letters and eventually with email messages and wrote thousands of poems. He thought of poems as "slightly-off reflections" and he felt "beset" by them. It seemed that he couldn't quite let them escape him, but then again he was obsessed with wanting to share them. This radical tension was the main reason why so many are metapoems like "It isnt for want." The struggle with his own "slightly-off reflections"—the process by which the struggle enables a new poem *about* that struggle—is Corman's major theme. Here is how he described the creative problem in 1986, and note that even here he is talking to a readerly "you":

> I'm only telling you of my experience, which it is your privilege
> to dismiss or despise or be intrigued by. Or maybe sooner or
> later all three. But the slightly-off reflections continue to beset
> me. I cant quite let go of them, almost as if something—some-
> thing perhaps entirely within me—were trying to get something
> across to me, as if there were some attention I was being asked
> to look "into."[2]

As in "It isnt for want," there is a "get[ing] something across." But whether it is "to me" or to you is confused, as is who is asking him to "look 'into'" the problem of how and what to attend. Vital rather than merely poetic, it is an existential problem.

Here is one of Corman's many metapoems:

> Did I ever
> exist? Ask the
> poetry. If
>
> no answer is
> there for you—I
> have none either.[3]

It is another instance of writerly "livingdying." And another:

> They tell me to
> go away—get
> lost. And here you
>
> are feeling me.
> I feel hopeless
> and you know why.[4]

Hopelessness is paradoxically—yet positively—this poet's reason for being. By this point, at the end of such a poem, you *do* know exactly why you haven't yet gone away.

NOTES

1 Quoted in Cid Corman, *At Their Word: Essays on the Arts of Language* (Santa Barbara, CA: Black Sparrow Press, 1978), 2:108.

2 Cid Corman, *Where Were We Now: Essays & Postscriptum* (Seattle: Broken Moon Press, 1991), 17.

3 Cid Corman, *Of* (Culver City, CA: Lapis Press, 1990), 719.

4 Ibid., 729.

32

Adam Fitzgerald

on **John Ashbery, "Just Walking Around"**
(1984)

What name do I have for you?
Certainly there is no name for you
In the sense that the stars have names
That somehow fit them. Just walking around,

An object of curiosity to some,
But you are too preoccupied
By the secret smudge in the back of your soul
To say much and wander around,

Smiling to yourself and others.
It gets to be kind of lonely
But at the same time off-putting.
Counterproductive, as you realize once again

That the longest way is the most efficient way,
The one that looped among islands, and
You always seemed to be traveling in a circle.
And now that the end is near

The segments of the trip swing open like an orange.
There is light in there and mystery and food.
Come see it. Come not for me but it.
But if I am still there, grant that we may see each other.

"Just Walking Around" is one of those cruisy poems whose specific meanings we are supposed to be able to pin down with a tiny of pair of tweezers for leg or wing like some dippy entomologist. Of course, the vague morass of the lyric tilts toward love poetry (Love Poetry), addressed as it is from one forlorn speaker to Ashbery's obscurant You. Though suffused with a mood of lyric beauty, "Just Walking Around" is a poem as happily irresponsible with precise or direct statement as anything in *Tennis Court Oath* or *Flow Chart*. Yet here is that very pleasing "middle voice" John developed and could have gone on writing inside of for a thousand years. Gone is the too-recondite diction, the whippersnapper herculean syntax. Instead, a gush of unapologetic pathos.

"What name do I have for you?" The word "you," the most beautiful word usage in all of Ashbery's many-thousand-worded works, is so beautiful in part because of its tufted resistance to floating off like dandelion fuzz. That is, unlike nearly all of his other wet-paint verbalisms, the inflating/deflating images and screwball allusions. The indestructibility of "you"—often aloof, anonymous, suspended like some slightly menacing divinity—is the secret/non-secret anchor, I'd argue, in so many of John's poems. ("And I am lost without you," as he says in another love lyric, admitting that "being lost" and loss, like "you," are the poet's central projects.)

Here, we're treated to a particular dousing (dowsing) in Metaphysical Poetics 101, which, by the way, was one of his favorite undergraduate courses—where he was introduced to Donne, Vaughn, Traherne, and, crucially, Marvell for the first time. I suppose they meant so much to him because they too were oddball, intimate yet alien, almost prissily fastidious, a kind of hyperelegance of compressed winks, nods, and oh boy tons of music. The music of "Just Walking Around" is a poem that fluctuates in this tender game of catch, alternating between statement and counterstatement. What name? Well, no name. Curious to others, yet self-preoccupied. Not saying much! . . . yet smiling to everyone. Wandering every which where; at the same time, sooo lonely (off-putting, even).

No poet has ever articulated the inarticulate music of dissociation as truly as John Ashbery did—a tone at once playful, melancholic, and fugue-like. Rereading the poem, it's curious to me that my memory is wrong. The poem *isn't* about the speaker's feelings, at least not on the surface. It's all rather a ten-car-pile-on about this or that projection, discerned affect concerning the loved object. The speaker is only observing the observer, like Jimmy Stewart tailing Kim Novak in that epic scene from *Vertigo*. I'm getting some strong whiffs of the Sonnets—not Shakespeare's phrasing exactly but the presence of that sweet (cruel) Young Man, a figure caught in the thicket of incandescent yet wasted possibility. And isn't this curious object, this sealed speaker, just like John's own poems? So preoccupied and trafficking in secret soul-smudges that we can't help but ascribe and assign all sorts of shadow dramas and concocted undertows. We're in love with them. We too seek their wayward efficiency of making shit up as we go.

But perhaps this "you" doesn't fit so simply into the role of lover as I'm positing. Unless the "you" does fit as lover, but not just lover-as-lover, but lover as stranger, friend, self, reader, poet, the poem itself finally. If that's a hermeneutical cheap trick, so be it. Even so, "Just Walking Around" quite enjoys its queer tour of getting lost and traveling in circles even as it parodies old-hat sturdy Elizabethan declarative synthesis. Yet the poem is genuinely courtly, regal, in the way that many Ashbery poems start dappy and daffy until it's time toward the very close, Rachmaninov cascading glissandos firing up, to surrender into the arms of such unlikely yet oddly earnest sentimentalisms. We've become dizzy and stupid with newly won avowal.

Now let me quote the poem's most beautiful lines:

> The segments of the trip swing open like an orange.
> There is light in there and mystery and food.
> Come see it. Come not for me but it.
> But if I am still there, grant that we may see each other.

I think, if I can say so, that this type of effortless lyricism didn't come naturally at first to John Ashbery. It's doing something I associate with the surreal Play Doh–like effusions of E. E. Cummings—a poet John and I both cherished despising. Here there's a kind of parable-like, Old Testament gracefulness that I quite enjoy. The poem has been prospecting after its stranger-cum-lover, like John walking around Paris for almost a decade, meeting up in those delicious street urinals, or sneaking into some dingy theater that plays old American flicks. The poem has waxed poetical, backing itself up into some lovely image out of Rilke with those looping islands and existential circles that probably, in fact, owes something to Hölderlin's final fragments, another favorite of Ashbery's.

In the final passive thrust, there's an almost Wordsworthian piety of simple statement. An accumulation of flat yet unflappable nouns: trip, orange, light, mystery, food. Evocatively, the key verbs are *swing* and *come* and *grant*. It's so moving that this poet who didn't really believe in the afterlife, and tried most of the time not to believe in death, allows in the last quatrain for this fantasy of a chance reunion with a muse that probably never existed in the first place, at least as any single real person. There's a benevolence to this closing. I think of the end of *Dr. Strangelove*'s montage of atomic clouds while "We'll Meet Again" croons along so sweetly. Well, I guess Ashbery's version would forgo any hint of apocalyptic warfare. And that has so much to do with John's deliberate ignorance as yet a very worldly poet. You know, irresponsible, sweet, hiding in plain sight, accepting a befuddlement that's really low-key despair, ceaselessly beseeching.

33

Stephen Collis

on **Susan Howe, from *My Emily Dickinson***
(1985)

> Dickinson was expert in standing in corners, expert in secret
> listening and silent understanding. Bristling with Yankee energy,
> chained to an increasingly demanding agoraphobia, she moved
> through that particular mole of nature in her—she studied
> Terror. Adopted parataxis and rupture to tell the feverish haste,
> the loss, to warn of storm approaching—Brute force, mechanism.
> Cassandra was a woman. All power, including the power of Love,
> all nature, including the nature of Time, is utterly unstable.

Susan Howe, *My Emily Dickinson* (Berkeley: North Atlantic Books, 1985),
116.

Every time we return to a beloved author we read them anew. On this
occasion rereading Susan Howe I see *time* everywhere—not *space*,
which the parataxis of her study on Emily Dickinson scatters about
every page, but the stuttering out of temporal order. *My Emily Dickinson*
always was a book about futurity—about how Dickinson fashioned
the new from the old, and how Howe in turn took up that now-old-new
and, finding its overflowing and unrealized potential, renewed it.

Howe writes sentences that one feels one could spend a lifetime
unraveling. They resist our easy understanding. They do this by
refusing to relinquish their potentiality, by refusing to be singular,
definite, by refusing to let us go, and move on, as readers. I believe
in this method: *when writing about writing we must entangle not
unwind*. Not reduce but expand. Not close down but open out. Not
resolve but join in irresolution. This is the truth I take from Howe,
for whom every other writer presents a wilderness to get lost in.

Let others build the road, we would—ramble and roam. Radical undecidability (which Howe tracks through Dickinson) means things double, mirror, have shadow forms, reverse and turn upside down, are posited and retracted all at once—"indeterminacy involves all of life," she writes most recently in *Debths* (2017). It's this indeterminate *all* that Howe found pathways to in Dickinson and Stein.

Noting the refusal of these two female precursors to "conform" to literary tradition and the institutions that support it, Howe marks a horizon she herself would walk toward. "In prose and in poetry," Howe writes of Dickinson, "she explored the implications of breaking the law just short of breaking off communication."[1] It is this line between literary law and lawlessness with which Howe productively entangles herself. But what is this "law"?

> I'll institute an "Action"—
> I'll vindicate the law—
> Jove! Choose your counsel—
> I retain "Shaw"!

Dickinson's early and playful poem ("I had some things that I called mine") imagining a "property" dispute between the poem's speaker, God, and a "rival" claimant (the church?) encodes some serious mischief. Saturated with the language of her own father's legal practice, Dickinson's speaker would "institute an 'Action'"—which no woman could, legally, in her day. She also rushes sideways out of temporal and grammatical order in this, the closing stanza, as the carefully scripted steps of the legal procedure—from retaining legal counsel to instituting an action to vindication—come crashing down in a storm of simultaneous and enthusiastic dashes.

Howe correctly places the investigation of "patriarchal authority" at the center of Dickinson's and Stein's projects: "Who polices questions of grammar, parts of speech, connection and connotation? Whose order is shut inside the structure of a sentence?"[2] But this "law," as the law of grammar and connection, is also a temporal law—a law governing the flow of time, across which Dickinson "cut" and Stein sought to undo by instituting a "continuous present." As Lisa Ruddick writes, in *Reading Gertrude Stein: Body, Text, Gnosis*, glossing Stein's "space of time that is always filled with moving": "The father may own linear time, but the continuous present defies the closures of linear time by setting everything in motion."[3]

All at once in motion, hesitating to progress to conclusion. Hesitation here is not a sign of "weakness" or "passivity" but of resistance—to a grammatical-temporal order that prioritized the accumulation of "wins" in progressing through hierarchical states of increase. We could entangle ourselves further and further in proliferating connections here, from Thoreau's Concord River current (never the same river twice) to Charles Olson, writing to fellow poet Robert Duncan of the synchronous and simultaneous: "time is a concrete continuum which the poet alone—I insist—alone practices the bending of."[4]

Howe—everywhere in *My Emily Dickinson*—practices this temporal and grammatical "bending." Her point is to establish the terms of female literary tradition and inheritance—which cannot be the same as the patriarchal "law" of time that decrees that one great Man follows another great Man, perhaps overthrowing his predecessor in an agonistic Bloomian contest. Howe prioritizes a Dickinson as bricoleur, taking the "scraps" of her "female learning" and combining them with "voracious and 'unladylike' outside reading, and [using] the combination" (like the combination of a lock)—innovation has always been unlocked by a new and unexpected combination. She "built a new poetic form"—"backward through history into aboriginal anagogy." Anagogy: a climb or ascent—but here for Howe following Dickinson, a movement down and up (simultaneously) the ladder of history. All this to construct "a new grammar grounded in humility and hesitation"—which is a new grammar of literary history too, where "My precursor attracts me to my future."[5]

This is key. The female poet, Howe argues, hesitates, and goes back before any forward movement begins—again and again in a continuous present of circling composition—potentially leading us all away from "aggressive industrial expansion and brutal Empire building."[6] Howe as any practicing poet practices the bending of time to find her way to new expression. Throughout *My Emily Dickinson* this is the point: Howe's way forward is back to Dickinson's way forward is back to—and so on in continuous presence—

> Adopted parataxis and rupture to tell the feverish haste, the
> loss, to warn of storm approaching—Brute force, mechanism.
> Cassandra was a woman. All power, including the power of
> Love, all nature, including the nature of Time, is utterly unstable[7]

What Howe's project does is rescue Dickinson from her "pastness," her status as "posthumous" author, poet whose poetry only appeared once the poet had irrevocably "passed away." For Howe, Dickinson marks a futurity she yet writes toward. To write her way to a future Dickinson, Howe "practices the bending of" language's "forward progress [which she] disrupted reversed."[8] She also—at the same time—makes a specifically female poetic tradition *inheritable*— bending broken laws into new wilderness methodologies.

NOTES

1 Susan Howe, *My Emily Dickinson* (Berkeley: North Atlantic Books, 1985), 11–12.

2 Ibid., 11.

3 Lisa Ruddick, *Reading Gertrude Stein: Body, Text, Gnosis* (Ithaca, NY: Cornell University Press, 1990), 86.

4 Charles Olson, *An Open Map: The Correspondence of Robert Duncan and Charles Olson*, ed. Robert J. Bertholf and Dale M. Smith (Albuquerque: University of New Mexico Press, 2017), 43.

5 Howe, *My Emily Dickinson*, 21.

6 Ibid., 21.

7 Ibid., 116.

8 Ibid., 24.

34

Nick Montfort

on **Rosmarie Waldrop, "A Shorter American Memory of the Declaration of Independence"**
(1988)

We holler these trysts to be self-exiled that all manatees are credited equi-distant, that they are endured by their Creditor with cervical unanswerable rims. that among these are lightning, lice, and the pushcart of harakiri. That to seduce these rims, graces are insulated among manatees, descanting their juvenile pragmatism from the consistency of the graced. That whenever any formula of grace becomes detained of these endives, it is the rim of the peppery to aluminize or to abominate it. and to insulate Newtonian grace. leaching its fountain pen on such printed matter and orienting its pragmatism in such formula, as to them shall seize most lilac to effuse their sage and harakiri.

This poem is highly amusing and yet not quite completely nonsensical. Those of us from the United States, even if we have short memories, can't help but recognize its syntax. Although many words have been substituted, an interesting type of sense can still be activated, at least by a generous reader of the sort I am.

In the first sentence there is some yelling that seems to cause people to stop their assignations. Just a bit further into this sentence, I can't help but envision an evenly spaced lattice of necklaced sea cows, beset by electrical strikes, an infestation of the little hair they have, and suicide. Through fortune and favor, things improve for these creatures and, as some sort of culinary and herbaceous activity occurs, the mark of ink is made on paper, seeping into it. That's what I figure, anyway.

To begin at the beginning, this text was composed in an unusual way and, even more strongly than it asks for the sort of interpretation I just provided, asks the reader to think about how it was composed. Just from looking at the poem itself, a reader can reverse engineer some of the compositional process: the framework for the text is drawn from the preamble to the Declaration of Independence[1]— Waldrop doesn't wait for the beat to drop to let us know this; it's in the title. However, words have been substituted, and that substitution has been done systematically.

The extraordinary verbal juxtapositions in "Shorter American Memory of the Declaration of Independence" no doubt arise from a very straightforward application of what has become, in recent decades, a standard method of textual transformation. This originates as Jean Lescure's "S+7" technique (or, in English, N+7), first discussed during Oulipo's February 1961 meeting.[2]

Describing the Oulipo in the context of modern and contemporary poetry is a bit like a writer for *Rolling Stone* taking a moment to introduce the Velvet Underground. Nevertheless: the Oulipo (Ouvroir de littérature potentielle), founded in 1960, is a Paris-based group, largely of writers and mathematicians, devoted to the exploration of "potential literature." While many of the members wrote extraordinary and successful literary works—cofounder Raymond Queneau, Italo Calvino, Harry Mathews, Georges Perec, and Jacques Roubaud, just to name a few—the group's purpose is not the development of literature but of constraints and procedures that delineate spaces and dimensions within which literature can exist. This they did richly; this they continue to do. N+7 is an example of a procedure for literature-making rather than a work of literature.

Succinctly, a writer using the N+7 procedure selects a source text and, for each noun in that text, finds that noun in a dictionary, or simply in a lexicon or list of nouns. After locating the word, the writer skips ahead to the seventh noun beyond that one. Using N+7 and my *Merriam-Webster's Collegiate Dictionary*, eleventh edition, I would replace the word "aardvark," whenever I found it in a source text, with "abacus." Or, as Harry Mathews explains, "the priority governing the procurer known as N+7 is respected by replacing each nub in a given theme with another found by counting seven nubs down in a previously chosen liberator."[3]

One need not restrict oneself to changing the nouns. It's possible to use a generalized version of this technique and change *all* the open-class words,[4] shifting each one ahead by a similar amount. As far as I can tell, this is what Waldrop did in composing this poem.[5]

Waldrop's compositional process adopts an originally French technique, but a very general one that applies to any language with a written form, a phonetic and ordered alphabet, and of course at least one dictionary or word list. What we are considering is an English-language poem. It is also rather obviously an American poem. (Waldrop, who is a German-born American, doesn't even wait for any of the poems' titles to announce this; the title of her book is *Shorter American Memory*.) The nationality of the poet and the origin of the source text, however, are not the only things that make this an American poem. The very first word replacement, in which *hold* becomes *holler*, brings in an American dialectical word. The poem shouts its American essence at it from the very beginning.

The highly abstract and formal "Newtonian grace" meets, in this poem, the leaching of "its fountain pen on such printed matter" in an extremely material moment. This conjunction is quite appropriate for someone like Waldrop, who writes formal poems using formal procedures and, with her husband, runs the letterpress publisher Burning Deck, involving very material interactions with language as well. So, maybe there is something to the specifics of the unusual vocabulary that emerges, even if that lattice of manatees doesn't seem the most meaningful. There are, after all, more fish in the sea for us to try to catch as readers.

If the American "holler" rings true to you, or if you see the conjunction of formal and material in the Newtonian fountain pen, it could be that constrained writing leads somewhere. Even if one takes an abstract and mathematical approach when composing a poem, it's not only the selection of a source text, and not only the procedure, but also the lexicon used and the underlying language itself that can result in a poem that resonates within our culture and society.

NOTES

1 United States National Archives, "Declaration of Independence: A Transcription" (reviewed December 18, 2018), https://www.archives.gov/founding-docs/declaration-transcript.

2 Jacques Bens, *OuLiPo, 1960–1963* (Paris: Christian Bourgois, 1980), 34.

3 Harry Matthews and Alastair Brotchie, eds., *Oulipo Compendium* (Los Angeles: Make Now Press, 2005), 91.

4 For instance, nouns, verbs, adjectives, adverbs. One way to understand the distinction between open- and closed-class words is that people can add new open-class words fairly easily: blog, hater, chillax. The set of closed-class words, which includes prepositions, articles, determiners, and conjugations, is much more fixed within a language over long spans of time.

5 An attentive reader may notice that "manatee" comes before "men" alphabetically. However, the dictionary entry under which the irregular plural word "men" is found is "man," and in any large dictionary there will be several words between "man" and "manatee," such as "management," "manager," "manakin," and "man-at-arms," not to mention several more obscure and obsolete ones.

35

Eileen Myles

on **James Schuyler, "Six Something"**
(1990)

On June 5th, '90:
closed shops
and well-washed
bluelessness, and
across the street
a man finishes
his polishing. I
count seedlings:
always counting,
cars, trees, not
infinitudes of
leaves. The Veterans
Building hides all
the Empire State Building
excepting
its antennae
rising in stages
first woven then
slim out of thick
to an ultimate
needle taper pricking
the day: its
point a test
of clarity. And
where is God
in all this?
Asleep? Resting?
and if so, from
what? Eternity

is tireless
surely, like:
rest now forever
blessed tired heart,
wakening otherwise
in bell-like blue.

"Six Something" from *Collected Poems* by James Schuyler. Copyright © 1993 by The Estate of James Schuyler. Reprinted by permission of Farrar, Straus and Giroux.

The poem's outside, its title is precise and vague. It's thrown up its hands and invited you in. The something is the exact moment of the poem, the what it's tracking. It's Jimmy's last poem. (One of them.) The something is almost the part he'll fill in later. A blank on the page, a word that holds that. It's fuzzy. Imagine a fuzzy calendar. That's this.

Weirdly once in he nails it. June 5, '90 and then the wide-open mouth of a colon exhaling all the rest. "Shops" rhymes with "washed," this poem is flooded with well-placed rhymes, plotted by eeee sounds like a needle pricking something throughout. It's inflation and defla- tion. The poem is pre-drone, but it's up—starting *down* but heading up. It's important that the man across the street is finished with his polishing. This poem from the top is done. It's a Sunday feel. Jimmy's like the guy. His work is to count. Impossible shit—seedlings, cars (a more feasible object) but NOT infinities of leaves. I mean a not is having it both ways. Computers deny negatives and so perhaps do poets. If it's in there it's in there, not or not. The only reason to not count infinities of leaves is to leave all of the abundant foliage in the world in the vague ecstatic pile which he does by not counting them, but honoring them. They're not. But they are. It flickers. The veterans building is also a dull flirt "hiding all." Sorta closeted. For me, defi- nitely a gay joke. And behind it: New York's most well-known cock: the empire state building. Lovingly stroked into existence. Is he knitting it or has it gotten down to business, no nonsense: slim. Like a slim Jim? Now Jimmy's pun: its point a test of clarity. What is the point of a tall building except what it is. It's a tautology. To be a test of clarity is . . . ? I guess by jamming it into the sky you can see it. That would be a test of both I bet. This profound visibility tall buildings give us. It's how we see in the city. Out of the blue he asked the first of three questions. God (Gawd) like the washing and the shops evokes a bodily sensation. While "he's" gone, we can't see him.

That's a masculine father for sure. Dad's asleep, dad's resting. Which could cover a multitude of badnesses. We just can't see him now. But we feel him. We think about him. Why now? It's like he, the poet, woke up at the end of the poem and asks where am I? A reassuring something swarms in saying the opposite thing. Opposite of what? About everything, and framed in that busy eee sound: "Eternity is tireless surely" and then we get a very Schuyler-like *like*, which is to say he doesn't do metaphor but refers to the body of things we say. He allows *it* to speak. You know like the coolest epitaph you ever heard like one half of the universe saying to its other, or to itself, flipping their spots eternally:

> rest now forever
> blessed tired heart,
> wakening otherwhere
> in bell-like blue.

Doesn't Emily Dickinson's gravestone say something about where she's going. Or, no: "called back." Like presuming the other place [known here] in this one. It's bold and kind to imagine an "other-where," a magical childlike fairy-tale place written BY an adult for a child, thereby being both, holding both spots, here and there, then and now and having it all ways, that bell-like blue, heaven would be a beautiful ringing sound you can see and hear as one. As if the day once pricked exploded silently into that. I'll go . . .

36

Simone White

on **Erica Hunt, "the voice of no"**
(1996)

No need to be contrary, I put on a face.
No use for muscle, the workers stand on line for hours.
No need to read, 24 hours of the shopping channel.
No fire, we have the illusion of doing what we want.

Is that any way to talk with your tongue pressed against glass?
The tv set is barking this Sunday morning off
when we acquire an instant memory,
and round language, where the ends justify the ends.
We rummage among the many
unplugged connections

looking for that darn
fraction of a percent of the landscape
you say it is possible to live in,
who will miss
it when we divide up
the sun, devour the
young rather than
give up our good seats.
The postcards
are bought out,
the lp is skipping
and anyway
rescue is sure to be slow.
In place of a raft
we paddle
ladders past the
litter of drifting bodies.

Source: *Arcade* (Berkeley: Kelsey Street Press, 1996). Reprinted with permission of Erica Hunt.

One finds oneself writing after the death of Toni Morrison on August 5, 2019—as one found oneself after the death of Baraka—writing in an atmosphere of hush, writing in the corner, almost cowering, unsure how to move; what Morrison's power held at bay advances to fill the vacuum of her departure.

Just because you're paranoid doesn't mean they're not after you.

Cue Erica Hunt's "the voice of no." Really, cue it up.[1] "Listen to this lady" (the project of reconstructing the art role of radical black womanhood continually begins and continues) bellow, as into a megaphone, in the poem's stately opening 4-line stanza, which is perhaps too stately, overdetermined in the figurative pose of anaphora (anaphora, from the Greek, bring back, repeat):

> *No need to be contrary, I put on a face.*
> *No use for muscle, the workers stand on line for hours.*
> *No need to read, 24 hours of the shopping channel.*
> *No fine, we have the illusion of doing what we want.*

Questions proliferate rather quickly. First and perhaps most pressing, how is this rather joyless kind of talking poetic talking? What kind of voice attaches to such language to render it speech? Whose speech, then, is this? Why are they giving a speech? Also pressing, why does this speech feel threatening?

In her 1988 lecture "Notes for an Oppositional Poetics," Hunt proposed that "conventional poetics might be construed as the way ideology, 'master narratives,' are threaded into the text," while, by contrast, "an expanded sense of poetics" loosens the connection between writing and experience so that writing need not mimic practices of social organization, never-not hierarchical. *Free* writing (my term not hers), Hunt claims, need not be some identifiable body's true account of moving through time; it need not be personal, in the sense that it is derived from one person's experience, at all.

In this light, the first lines of "the voice of no" embark upon, via prosodic embodiment, an exploration of "conventional" poetic values at the generic level of verse, that is, rhythmic balance brought about through regularity of stress or sound matching/rhyme, scrutability and extreme plasticity of signification of word-sign employment, so that text and reader enter an unstable, pitched forward/about to fall over orthodoxy. *No need to be contrary, I put on a face.* This *speech* involves us in a performance of compliance or complicity that announces itself as performance and invites liberal assent to a certain postmodern self-understanding (heads nod, I, uh huh, uh huh), then alienates—"the workers stand on line" where? where are workers on line except in the poems of Philip Levine?—then demands the reader's self-implication in the specific sin of media-commerce addiction. The invented voice is government-y; it's trick-POlice; it's so outwardly defined that it's "nature" can only be ascertained by attention to the literal: NO.

No fine, we have the illusion of doing what we want.

No fine. [I am] no[t] fine? We have. How was this we engendered? We have illusion. Oh. :(We no doing what we want.

Fast, Hunt's poem lifts into uncertain, anagrammatic positionality, a kind of poetic dystopia. Initially, the substitution of poetic dystopia for actual social hell is the only refuge this poem leaves to the highest capital P Poetic value—metaphor.

Such a beginning might—does—propose an alternative, if not utopian, order. In the second section, the language of the poem shifts dramatically. From the dependent clause:comma:independent clause sentence-unit of each of the poem's first four lines, the eye and ear must adjust to a highly figurative, visually and grammatically and conceptually serpentine situation/situatedness:

> *Is that any way to talk with your tongue pressed against*
> *glass?*

Face all smashed against the tv screen or shop window, sounding *mrrrrlllllllaaaaacgghhhh*—a rhetorical question insofar as the rhetoric is one of shaming. Look at yourself: ridiculous. The face to which the poem's first line refers is revealed to be a kind of bewitched mask that conceals a struggling and contorted face, whose effectively garroted mouth is unable to connect with the will to be a speaking subject.

The surreal follows the odd and the apocalyptic follows the surreal in the remainder of the poem. "The voice of no" was first published in Hunt's 1996 book *Arcade*, before *The Matrix* (1999), before images of Hurricane Katrina's devastation of New Orleans forever altered the meaning of risen waters (and black people marooned, fleeing or failing to escape death by natural disaster) in the mind's eye, before the Occupy and Black Lives Matter movements, and it could not have contemplated any of those events.

Yet it prophesies.

> . . . *instant memory*
> *and round language, where the ends justify the ends.*
>
> *We rummage among the many*
> *unplugged connections*
>
> *looking for that darn*
> *fraction of a percent of the landscape*
> *you say it is possible to live in,*

Notice how enjambment allows adjectives and prepositions to linger on the edge of print. "Off," "in," "up," "out," "past" disorient in a landscape ultimately defined by the watery surface of a warming earth upon which "we paddle / ladders past the / litter of drifting bodies."

Is Erica Hunt paranoid? NO. Her work, Tyrone Williams writes, is "motivated . . . by a progressive politics that deploys avant-garde forms and methods to uproot politically retrogressive values,"[2] values that have predictably murderous consequences.

In 1988, preparing the text of "Notes for an Oppositional Poetics," Erica Hunt turned to Toni Morrison's *Beloved*, that year's recipient of the Pulitzer Prize for fiction, to illustrate how daring, intentional, oppositional writing interrupts the reader's complicity. Hunt, a new mother at the time and deeply disturbed by *Beloved*'s early invocation of infanticide, pressed on to consider how "the use of [the] supernatural approximates white Americans' conventional belief, even obliviousness to the most rudimentary accounts of slavery and its legacy."

They are after you, this strange, extraordinary, and timeless poem declares. They have always been after you.

NOTES

1 https://media.sas.upenn.edu/pennsound/authors/Hunt/Close-Lstening/Hunt-Erica_10_Voice-of-No_WPS1_NY_6-20-05.mp3.

2 Tyrone Williams, "A B=L=A=C=K=W=O=M=A=N Poetics: Erica Hunt's Prose Poetry," *ON Contemporary Practice*, 148, https://static1.squarespace.com/static/52010d47e4b0eefc5e9e9bf0/t/5286be01e4b0ae423465f8cb/1384562177410/Tyrone+Williams+on+Erica+Hunt.pdf.

37

Mónica de la Torre

on **Erica Baum, from *Card Catalogues***
(1997)

"Déjà vu" from *Card Catalogues*, used with permission of Erica Baum.

Five Takes on Erica Baum's *Card Catalogues*

1. Erica Baum's images/found poems give you the sense that you've seen what they picture before. Granted, that sense of déjà vu is precisely part of photography's magic. This might be one of the reasons why a work from her series of gelatin silver prints, *Card Catalogues* (1997), has lodged itself in my mind with the persistence of an idée fixe. It's as though the two-word found poem—a miraculous apparition, really, if you think of all the possible subject headers Baum could have come upon—had a hidden message for me to decode. Picture a close-up black-and-white photograph of a library catalogue card with the subject header "Déjà Vu" typewritten on the top margin. A period at the end of the phrase turns the subject header into a sentence or a line of poetry preceded and followed by thin beautiful lines made by the graying edges of the other cards in the catalogue.

2. Déjà vu: a sight seen, the sense of reliving of a past experience, a version of "been there done that," and that's precisely the point. Baum's art consistently taps into the poetics of analogue print technologies that have become, or are in the process of becoming, obsolete. I can't help but find significance in the fact that even the Wikipedia entry for the particular technology that Baum trained her large-format view camera on here brings up the sense of sight: "The card catalog was *a familiar sight* to library users for generations, but it has been effectively replaced by the online public access catalog" (emphasis added). There's poetic justice in the fact that, in the perpetual present of Baum's images, the passage of time becomes permanently halted, except when it comes to reading the words in them. Given that reading is an optical activity that inevitably involves duration, here we hit a particularly stimulating snag that troubles medium and is at the core of Baum's project of presenting ambiguous works that are images to be read as much as poems to be seen in all their instant glory. Seeing and reading are collapsed into the frame, their corresponding temporalities in tension with one another, animating the image and giving us

viewers the sensation of having just encountered this card and of being about to continue browsing.

3. I keep wanting the noun "brow" and the verb "to browse" to share an etymological origin. How could they *not* be related? I mention this because of the humor in the image, which we owe to the fact that, as Baum pointed out, the acute and grave accents visibly placed by hand over the *e* and the *a* in "Déjà vu" look like thick eyebrows above eye-looking letters framing a *j* whose shape resembles a nose. Writing technologies are collapsed here, where there is also another reduplication: not only is the sight before us that of an object we've seen before—a card in a library catalogue—itself, in turn, containing a phrase that designates the sense of recognition of having seen something already. What is more, the sight before us graphically mirrors a viewer in the act of seeing it, the first being the artist herself.

4. *Untitled (Déjà vu)* is not the only self-reflective image/found poem in Baum's series but it is perhaps the most concise. Another is *Untitled (Pupil)*, a celebration of the mirrored workings of the eye and camera lens and the eye's exquisite motility. Words dance in this composition that, like *Untitled (Déjà vu)*, stimulates both retinal and conceptual engagement with it:

Pupil (Eye)
Pupil (Eye)
Pupil (Eye).
Pupil (Eye)

Notice that I've omitted the horizontal lines indicating the edge of each card on which the words are typed. Also omitted are the smudges on the cards, evidence of their decaying physicality. The words' material support is one that cannot be quoted, only described, or pointed to through photography thanks to the medium's indexicality. Perspective is such that the font in the poem's last line looks about one point larger than the others, and hence viewers are inscribed in the piece, our position before it impressed upon the object. That the last line belongs to a card corresponding to an earlier

entry in the catalogue—because the order in which we see the subject headers is reversed—speaks to the incommensurability between
text and object. And yet, even if we considered *Untitled (Pupil)* a page
poem only, it would speak volumes about the way in which the eye, in
the process of decoding a poem's signals that include punctuation
and blank spaces, relays rhythm.

4. This brings us to concrete poetry as articulated by the Brazilian
Noigandres group. Much in the "Pilot Plan for Concrete Poetry" of 1958
applies to Baum's works at the intersection of image and text: "Tension
of things-words in space-time." The degree of literariness in the *Card
Catalogue* poems almost approaches zero, yet their critical and
semantic possibilities unfold in tandem with prolonged physical or
mental contemplation. They portray "objects in and of themselves" and
are "not an interpreter of exterior objects and/or more or less subjective feelings." And yes, there is "thorough realism" too. Yet the comparisons stop when I read the following line in the manifesto: "Against a
poetry of expression, subjective and hedonistic." Baum's works are not
programmatic. They are nothing if not pleasurable, and her choices
intuitive and playful. They're not against expression, even if they don't
seem invested in expressing much other than the giddiness and surprise caused by her uncanny finds, and that's already a lot!

5. I am reminded of Jack Spicer's claim in *After Lorca* that a "really
perfect poem has an infinitely small vocabulary" and of his desire to
"point to the real, disclose it, to make a poem that has no sound in it
but the pointing of a finger."[1] Was it a telepathic spirit that prompted
the chance encounter leading to *Untitled (Fingerprints)*? It reads:

> Finger-prints.
> (The) finger.

Where the finger points to itself in the phrase's parenthesis inexpli-
cably placed by hand.

NOTE

1 Jack Spicer, *After Lorca* (New York: New York Review Books, 2021), p. 24.

erica kaufman

on **Joan Retallack, "Not a Cage"**
(1998)

Scientific inquiry, seen in a very broad perspective may
see Foot 1957, also Wetermarck 1906, Ch. XIII
To man (sic) the world is twofold, in accordance with
that witness is now or in the future
It wasn't until the waitress brought her Benedictine and she
Villandry, "Les Douves" par Azay le Rideau
mine. Yours, CYNTHIA.
Not a building, this earth, not a cage,
The artist: disciple, abundant, multiple, restless
a forgery: Opus Ioannes Bellini
We named you I thought the earth
is possible I could not tell
to make live and conscious history in common
and wake you find yourself among
and wake up deep in the fruit
Did you get the money we sent?
I smell fire
AT FULL VOLUME. STAGE DARK]
1. Russia, 1927
God, say your prayers.
You were begotten in a vague war
sidelong into your brain.
In Letter Three & Four (as earlier) the narrator is
North Dakota Portugal Moorhead, Minnesota
The lights go down, the curtain opens: the first thing we
gun, Veronica wrote, the end.
'Wittgenstein'
Tomorrow she would be in America.
Over forty years ago

a tense, cunningly moving tale by the Hunga-
Then he moved on and I went close behind.
Interviewers: What drew a woman from Ohio
to study in Tübingen? American Readers
with this issue former subscribers to Marxist Perspectives
The shadow of the coup continues to hover over Spain
In the ordinary way of summer
girls were still singing
like a saguaro cactus from which any desert wayfarer can draw
as is Mr. Fox, but in literature
Twenty five years have gone by
Ya se dijeron las cosas mas oscuras
The most obscure things have already been said

Joan Retallack, "Not a Cage," in *How to Do Things with Words* (Los Angeles:
Sun & Moon Press, 1998). Reprinted with permission of Joan Retallack.

"How can we communicate the importance of opening spaces in the
imagination where persons can reach beyond where they are?" asks
educational philosopher Maxine Greene. This question follows a
description of how poems "transform" and "call on us to move beyond
where we are,"[1] emphasizing the poem's unique ability to use language
to awaken a sense of possibility. Greene, echoing John Dewey, sees
the poem (work of art) as able to "re-orient" readers through the
experience we have of grappling with "modes of apprehending
nature that at first are strange to us."[2] Similarly, Joan Retallack's
"Not a Cage" asks the reader to be open to a reading experience that
reorients, one that surpasses the "combination of chance and intuitive composition" from which the poem evolved.[3] "Not a Cage"
emerged from beginnings and endings of books Retallack was "culling
from [her] library," a list of sentences transcribed on a "yellow pad."
This roster of lifted language gained new life by way of Retallack's
recombination; although she "didn't change any words or orders of

words within the units," the phrases inevitably take on new meanings because of the language chosen to surround them—language that does not flow in a predictable, grammatically normative way. As the lines speak to each other through proximity, the reader is driven to be fully present in (and through) the act of reading, an experience created and re-created by writer and reader.

"Scientific inquiry, seen in a very broad perspective may" is the opening line of "Not a Cage," one that surprises and situates the reader. The tone of these words is formal, academic, philosophical, scientific. The line ends with "may"—a word that signifies possibility and is grammatically used to supplement or help other verbs. It's a strange line break and becomes stranger when followed with "see Foot 1957, also Wetermarck 1906, Ch. XII," a total swerve into bibliographical speech. This line reads as an interjection, a reference, an inside joke, a literal footnote. Yet the poem moves forward without mandating that the reader look anything up.[4] In these first two lines, we see already the way the poem brings new attention to its recycled lines, new ways of reading and interacting with source texts.

For the contemporary reader accustomed to the quick access and instant answers the web can provide, there is the temptation to look up each line, to piece together the list of books culled from Retallack's library. But to do this would be to stymie one's imagination instead of opening up space for new "geometries of attention" to take shape. The poem's title supports this; it offers the space for lines to be released from the cage of their original texts. The poem continues: "Not a building, this earth, not a cage, / The artist: disciple, abundant, multiple, restless." The title phrase joins a chorus of negations. It is a metapoetic moment; the text seems to be telling us what it is "not." Then the line breaks. We meet "the artist" who is described by a list of competing adjectives (a "disciple" is not often thought of as "abundant").

In "Uncaged Words," Joan Retallack writes, "What Cage's poetry gives us through its use of defamiliarizing artifice and chance operations is a complex intersection of what poet and wor/l/d cant avoid saying to/with/among three or more others."[5] Retallack's writing on John Cage describes the intentionality behind "Not a Cage"—to uproot and defamiliarize the reading process so that one's attention is redirected anew. We push ourselves to try to make our own paths from line to line, as our eyes notice enjambments closely, and then what is at stake is the discovery of new kinds of sense-making. One might describe this experience as "mak[ing] live and conscious history in common" ("Not a Cage"), the idea that content is alive and transient, and "conscious history" becomes something to be made.

As "Not a Cage" continues to propel us forward, we are repeatedly introduced to the known turned strange: "You were begotten in a vague war / sidelong into your brain" evolves into "the narrator is / North Dakota Portugal Moorhead, Minnesota." Each "you" in the text seems to introduce a new interlocutor; here we have the one who got away "into your brain." There is also the "you" who is narrator as well as geographical place without commas. It seems as though the procedural impulse here is tied to close reading, asking the reader to actively participate in the "*new*sense" to be made through active engagement with language. This sentiment appears again in the last two lines—"Ya se dijeron las cosas mas oscuras / The most obscure things have already been said." If this is true, then the rest is up to the imagination.

Retallack's *Procedural Elegies/Western Civ Cont'd/*[6] begins with several definitions: "Procedure. The action or fact of proceeding or issuing from a source. A methodical way of determining how to begin, how to go on, and sometimes—antecedent to elegy—how to end." If procedure signifies an endeavor with roots, then the poem that arises through procedure represents a combination of intentionality, indeterminacy, and "a dicey collaboration of intellect and imagination."[7]

NOTES

1 Maxine Greene, "In Search of Critical Pedagogy," *Harvard Educational Review* 56:4 (November 1986): 429–30.

2 John Dewey, *Art as Experience* (New York: Wideview/Perigee, 1934), 334.

3 See PoemTalk #53, https://jacket2.org/podcasts/obscure-things-have-already
-been-said-poemtalk-53.

4 I think it is significant to note that Retallack wrote this poem (in 1990) years before Google Books existed, before the Internet was the hub to the kinds of quick
answers it has become. Locating the source of this footnote or the text it refers to
would not have been easily electronically feasible when the poem was first published.

5 Joan Retallack, *The Poethical Wager* (Berkeley: University of California Press,
2003), 240.

6 "Not a Cage" appears (republished) in *Procedural Elegies/Western Civ Cont'd/*
(New York: Roof Books, 2010).

7 Retallack, *The Poethical Wager*, 5.

erica kaufman

39

Lyn Hejinian

on **Lydia Davis, "A Mown Lawn"**
(2001)

She hated a *mown lawn*. Maybe that was because *mow* was the reverse of *wom*, the beginning of the name of what she was—a *woman*. A *mown lawn* had a sad sound to it, like a *long moan*. From her, a *mown lawn* made a *long moan*. *Lawn* had some of the letters of *man*, though the reverse of *man* would be *Nam*, a bad war. A *raw war*. *Lawn* also contained the letters of *law*. In fact, *lawn* was a contraction of *lawman*. Certainly *lawman* could and did *mow* a *lawn*. *Law and order* could be seen as starting from *lawn order*, valued by so many Americans. *More lawn* could be made using a *lawn mower*. A *lawn mower* did make *more lawn*. *More lawn* was a contraction of *more lawmen*. Did *more lawn* in America make *more lawmen* in America? Did *more lawn* make *more Nam*? *More mown lawn* made *more long moan*, from her. Or a *lawn mourn*. So often, she said, Americans wanted *more mown lawn*. All of America might be one *long mown lawn*. A *lawn* not *mown* grows *long*, she said: better a *long lawn*. Better a *long lawn* and a *mole*. Let the *lawman* have the *mown lawn* she said. Or the *moron*, the *lawn moron*.

"She hated a mown lawn." With that simple declarative sentence, Lydia Davis bluntly begins an untitled, short (twenty-three-sentence) prose poem that is at once a study of open-throated vowel tones (open As and Os) and a feminist lament, raging at the negating disempowerment of women and nature. "She hated a *mown lawn.* Maybe that was because *mow* was the reverse of *wom*, the beginning of the name of what she was—a *woman.*"

The obsessiveness with which the speaker mulls words over and turns words around can at first seem comical (*"Law and order* could be seen as starting from *lawn order*, valued by so many Americans"), and certainly wit is here. But it is wit, not laughter, and delivered with irony. The poem's protagonist, "she," is pissed off and unhappy. The surface of comic sonic plenitude ripples uneasily over a landscape that was probably doomed to practices of negation from the moment it became acculturated as "America." It is of "America" that Davis sings her lament; the word "America" appears three times, the word "American" twice, in this relatively short poem. The lament, mean-while, is delivered more in the manner of Joan Rivers (or her reincar-nation as "The Marvelous Mrs. Maisel" on the contemporary Amazon Video series of that name) than in that of William Carlos Williams in "The Widow's Lament," though some echo of it may be present in Davis's poem. The identity of the central figure in the Davis work is presented as a "she," but the poem is essentially an interior mono-logue, and this is the case likewise in "The Widow's Lament," whose speaker, too, is a woman.

> Sorrow is my own yard
> where the new grass
> flames as it has flamed
> often before but not
> with the cold fire
> that closes round me this year.

Thus begins the Williams poem. The expression of grief, even anguish, with which it begins is sustained throughout the entirety of the poem, and the speaker never removes herself from the landscape that remains the site of her pain. That landscape is only a very small bit of "America"— a "yard"—but its being identified with "sorrow" assures that, whatever its physical dimensions, it has enormous emotional magnitude.

As we know, Williams was the author of a collection of essays titled *In the American Grain*, its title indirectly but clearly alluding to Walt Whitman's foundational American poem, *Leaves of Grass*. With the fifth line of the original 1855 version of that work, Whitman establishes its central symbolic image: "I lean and loafe at my ease . . . . observing a spear of summer grass." And this, in turn, invokes the landscape of *The Prairie*, the novel with which James Fenimore Cooper's enormously popular *Leatherstocking Tales* concludes. Published twenty-eight years before the first edition of *Leaves of Grass*, *The Prairie* depicts the great American grasslands as a fecund but untamable terrain. Now an old man, Natty Bumppo, the novel's main character, has moved west so as to escape the sound of men felling trees in the eastern American forests, though ironically, in the second chapter of the book, the two young men of the small group of "emigrants" whom he has encountered on the prairie as dusk is approaching and shown to a suitable campsite immediately set about felling the trees standing nearby. "As tree after tree came whistling down, he cast his eyes upward, at the vacancies they left in the heavens, with a melancholy gaze."[1] Something of that melancholy can be heard in the third sentence of Davis's poem: "A *mown lawn* had a sad sound to it, like a *long moan*."

I've situated Davis's poem in a context intended to suggest that, at least to some degree, it invokes some canonical encounters in American literary history between man and grass, man and prairie. There are many others—including, of course, Robert Frost's "Mowing," with its lyric musings by a man with a scythe happily striking down the tall grass in an Edenic meadow (the speaker notes that he "scared a bright green snake" in the course of his mowing), making hay while the sun shines. Davis's poem groans at the thought of all this denudation. "From her, a *mown lawn* made a *long moan*."

The poem bewails the American proclivity for mowing nature down and downing American womanhood in the process. She makes use of the long-standing trope that has persistently gendered nature, especially that of the American landscape, as female. In an array of literary works from the eighteenth and nineteenth centuries, America is metamorphized either as maternal or as virginal (with her "virgin forests," "virgin prairies"), sometimes nourishing, sometimes sexual, and sometimes both: "The mountain being cloven asunder, she presents to your eye, through the cleft, a small catch of smooth blue horizon, at an infinite distance in the plain country, inviting you, as it were, from the riot and tumult roaring around, to pass through the breach and participate of the calm below." So wrote Thomas Jefferson in his *Notes on the State of Virginia*.[2]

Much could be said about the feminized—indeed vaginalized—mountain of Jefferson's description, and something in relation to it could be made of the moaning expressed quite literally in Davis's poem. But in my reading of the moaning O that dominates the sonic space of the poem, its most important, though not most obvious, effect is that of negation. It enunciates an ongoing zeroing, carried out by suppression (law) and ruination (war and rapacity). In place of copses, there are cops; in place of prairies, there are lawns; in place of woman, there's woe: mown and moaned down.

NOTES

1 James Fenimore Cooper, *The Leatherstocking Tales* (New York: Library of America, 1985), 1:898.

2 Thomas Jefferson, *Notes on the State of Virginia* (Chapel Hill: University of North Carolina Press, 1955), 19, as quoted in Annette Kolodny, *The Lay of the Land: Metaphor as Experience and History in American Life and Letters* (Chapel Hill: University of North Carolina Press, 1975), 28.

Elizabeth Willis

on **Rae Armantrout, "The Way"**
(2001)

Card in pew pocket
announces,
"I am here."

I made only one statement
because of a bad winter.

Grease is the word; grease
is the way

I am feeling.
Real life emergencies or

flubbing behind the scenes.

As a child,
I was abandoned

in a story
made of trees.

Here's the small
gasp

of this clearing
come "upon" "again"

Rae Armantrout, "The Way," in *Veil: New and Selected Poems* (Middletown, CT: Wesleyan University Press, 2001). Reprinted with permission of the author and Wesleyan University Press.

What do you know and how do you know it? What is the difference between who you are, what you say, and the way you are feeling? How does meaning feel—and feeling mean? These are some of the questions underlying Rae Armantrout's "The Way." In fact, concerns about the *way* we know—our technologies of knowing—resurface throughout Armantrout's work.

The poem's mysteries and ambiguities begin with its title, which seems to promise something instructive: a manual, methodology, or map to some real or imaginary place, though the poem's route toward meaning is anything but direct. The first line has the clipped syntax of a shot called in a game of pool: "Card in pew pocket." No verb, just the declared fact of an object and its triangulated location.

The setting snaps into focus with the third word: if the pocket belongs to a pew, we're in church, a place that often claims to show "the way." Both setting and title suggest a signpost from the King James Bible: "I am the way, the truth, and the life" (John 14:6). But like an arrow bleeding through from the other side of a map—or Friday's footprint in *Robinson Crusoe*—the message is as disorienting as it is reassuring. A return to the Bible for direction only makes more slippery our grasp of the invisible "I" in the card's message:

> "Here am I." (Exodus 3:4)
> "I Am that I Am." (Exodus 3:15)

The first of these voices is Moses responding to the call of an angel; the second is God answering Moses. This echolocation between divine and earthly voices occurs throughout the poem. If at any point in "The Way" you're uncertain who is speaking, you are not alone. In fact, being "not alone"—especially in one's disorientation, bemusement, and abandonment—may be the central message of the poem.

The writer is with you in all these moments, just on the other side of the page, whether in her own "real life emergencies" or "flubbing behind the scenes," deciphering and re-presenting the mysteries of sense-making, as she goes. We know where we are by the ways we are lost and found, the ways we reflect, and are reflected by, others.

The second stanza sounds to me like a ventriloquized explanation of what precedes it: an unnamed person imagining the reality behind the text they are reading. Can a "bad winter" result in putting even God at such a loss for words that the most they can say is that they exist?

Through this leap of faith or doubt, we arrive at the poem's other primary reference, the theme song to the musical *Grease*: "Grease is the word; grease / is the way // I am feeling." But even here, biblical echoes continue: "In the beginning was the Word, and the Word was with God, and the Word was God" (John 1:1).

While the coexistence of these two voices—God and Broadway— suggests a contrast between sacred and profane speech acts, both texts are concerned with the relation between the divine/spiritual and the earthly/embodied. The meeting of opposites in *Grease*— in which the drama circulates around the attraction, repulsion, and eventual union of churchgoing Sandy and daredevil Danny—could be read as an enactment of the same opposing philosophical, aesthetic, and ontological tensions that some find themselves sorting out in a place of worship.

A tune, a verse, a phrase may be caught in the ear and reemerge at the strangest times. Think of something else! In a moment of quiet, the mind's noise, endlessly processing. Like the sentence on the card, *Grease*'s title song delivers the vocal residue of someone who is no longer before us but who has left behind a pattern we carry with us, like it or not. Something reaching through the empty space of its own architecture. A deus ex machina.

How far is the poem from Moses's formative encounter with the voice emanating from a burning bush in Exodus, a scene from which Moses extracts a deal with God? And is Jesus, a.k.a. "the Way," not a figural embodiment of the merger of human and divine, mortal and immortal in and of itself? Is "grease" the word or is God the Word? Is *Grease* the word of God or just the way one is feeling? What is grease anyway but the slippery medium by which a mechanism moves things from one place to another? Are the words that move us the grease or the backstage pulley—or both?

The relation between voice and context, between content and setting, is contractual. Every printed story or poem, every book, exists because a tree has been made into paper. So there is an ethical contract between writers and forests. In that sense, every text exists in a "clearing" that enables enlightenment.

The child "abandoned" in a story is found in the poem in ways that rhyme with the poet's own experience of coming into language through books that shape her imaginative landscape. This earthly child likewise has her divine double: Jesus too was a child who was abandoned—or, as he ultimately put it, "forsaken"—in a story made of trees. That is, in a book whose human drama begins with a tree of knowledge and ends in the carrying of a cross on which the central figure is left to die.

Whether or not the ghost in the machine of the poem is holy is not our concern, nor is it, I suspect, Armantrout's. What language does with us—the ways it works in us—*is*. In that sense, poetry offers a belief system of its own that is not about bringing us toward a prescribed set of meanings but toward the multiple possibilities that already exist all around us. The poem's final gasp may be one of delight or terror, but it is certainly a mark of recognition. One comes "upon" this place "again" in an account that has not been closed by a final period.

41

Sharon Mesmer

on **Michael Magee, from "Pledge"**

(2001)

1

I plug elegance
two thief rag
off-Dionysus tastes of America
in tune theory public
four widgets hands
one day shun
on dirge odd
ring the busy bell
with lip hurting
and just this
for all

2

hype ledge a lesion
to deaf egg
oft die you nightly stains of a miracle
and too deep repugnant
for withered spans
wan etching
unnerved dog
inapplicable
with liver tea
and just this
for all

13

my friend Steven
tofutti bag
over mitt lighted stinks of a measuring cup
and tutoring Bobby
for fifty clams
one eggplant
undercooked
and uneatable
with liverwurst
and just this
for all

16

I planned a neat myth
today's rags
ugly unified fates never heard a ya
& ten & three colonies
or fifty nifty states
coronation
underground
indemythical
palabricity
and just this
for all

From Michael Magee, "Pledge," in *Morning Constitutional* (Philadelphia: Spencer Books, 2001). Reprinted with permission of the author.

———

Did you ever see (or have you seen footage of) Jimi Hendrix playing "The Star-Spangled Banner" at Woodstock? If not, stop reading this and look it up on YouTube. Notice how his version of the national anthem alternates between lyrical eloquence and dissonance, paralleling 1969's cultural politics of hope and despair, peace and chaos. Notice the way he uses the whammy bar to mimic the sound of bombs falling, bursting in air—eight years earlier he'd been a paratrooper in the 101st Airborne Division. Notice how (at 2:35) he references "Reveille," the bugle call played to wake military personnel at sunrise. Throughout his entire performance you'll no doubt hear lyricism in his shredding, as well as anger, disappointment, affection, and ridicule.

Michael Magee's 16-part poem "Pledge," which mimics and comments on the American Pledge of Allegiance, does much the same thing. In 1998, Magee was working with the concept of "homophonic translation"—a phrase, line, or a longer text "translated" into another language using only the *sounds* of the words, not their real meanings, usually for humorous effect.

"I sort of liked the idea of speakers who had forgotten the words to the Pledge," Magee told me, "but not the sounds. That the compulsory nature of the words would vanish and there would just be music. And maybe some jokes."

As you can see in the four sections excerpted here, the off-rhymes (and almost-no-rhymes) that parallel the end words in the Pledge provide the jokes:

> *I pledge allegiance*
>> I plug elegance
>> hype ledge a lesion
>> my friend Steven
>> I planned a neat myth
> *to the flag*
>> two thief rag
>> to deaf egg
>> tofutti bag
>> today's rags

of the United States of America
    off-Dionysus tastes of America
    oft die you nightly stains of a miracle
    over mitt lighted stinks of a measuring cup
    ugly unified fates never heard a ya
and to the republic
    in tune theory public
    and too deep repugnant
    and tutoring Bobby
    & ten & three colonies
for which it stands
    four widgets hands
    for withered spans
    for fifty clams
    or fifty nifty states
one nation
    one day shun
    wan etching
    one eggplant
    coronation
under God
    on dirge odd
    unnerved dog
    undercooked
    underground
indivisible
    ring the busy bell
    inapplicable
    and uneatable
    indemythical
with liberty
    with lip hurting
    with liver tea
    with liverwurst
    palabricity

> *and justice for all*
>> and just this for all
>> and just this for all
>> and just this for all
>> and just this for all

Like the variational qualities and structures of music—the motifs and themes that create memorable melodies ("hooks")—Magee's poem runs us through different ways of hearing the Pledge via repeating sound, rhyme, and off-rhyme motifs. While repetition, or restatement, of motifs and themes is an integral part of music, creating the consistent, satisfying, and memorable melody lines that stay with us, those same features can be annoying. Theodor Adorno, the German philosopher, sociologist, psychologist, and composer, found the repetition in most contemporary popular music to be infantile, even psychotic, and if you've ever experienced earworms, you'll probably agree. Magee is taking the infantile to a new level here, while at the same time letting us in on the joke by deploying the familiar "variations on" device of modernist poetry—think of Kenneth Koch's "Variations on a Theme by William Carlos Williams"—to its infantile and almost psychotically logical extreme.

Ideas of allegiance, patriotism, and democracy morph and evolve throughout—and finally devolve. Allegiance is elegance, and a lesion; the flag is a rag, an egg, a tofutti bag, and a rag again; the idea of "one nation" becomes a wan etching, one eggplant; liberty is a lip hurting, liver tea, liverwurst, and palabricity, which isn't a word at all (go ahead, Google it; the results contain only references to this poem). In the midst of all that non-sense are some actual references to the United States, its history, mythology, foundational philosophy, and "mission":

> — I planned a neat myth
> — ugly unified fates never heard a ya
> — & ten & three colonies
> — for fifty claims / or fifty nifty states

By the end, the poem devolves into "just this for all"—prescient, considering our current deteriorating political situation. While plenty of poems address in serious language ideas of democratic collapse, dictatorial rise, and the horror of war—"July 1914" (Akhmatova), "Dover Beach" (Arnold), "Easter, 1916" (Yeats)—Magee's poem addresses these issues by replicating the disintegration via the hom-onymic phrasings that themselves devolve. Witness the process the name "United States of America" undergoes: "off-Dionysus tastes" makes me think of a bottle of wine that's gone off and now tastes like vinegar; "oft die you nightly stains of a miracle" sounds like a curse upon the nocturnal emission that the poet believes the country has become; "over mitt lighted stinks of a measuring cup" might be a cooking disaster (local, domestic, fiery); and "ugly unified fates never heard a ya" suggests a final pronouncement on the American "democratic" experiment which, of course, could only happen along-side the genocide of the country's original inhabitants. "I planned a neat myth," occurring at the beginning of the poem, foreshadows (via the air-headed "neat") the collapse of the half-baked cooking disas-ter of an idea. The beliefs of the poet are as dissonant and layered as Hendrix's take on the national anthem.

But there is eloquence in the dissonance: If you didn't know the words to the Pledge, you might think you were hearing it—but you *do* know the words, so you may pick up on the grace with which Magee translates the disintegration of things into language. You'll surely recognize lyricism in the poet's version of shredding, as well as anger, disappointment, affection, and ridicule. Magee's sense of humor is the whammy bar, but instead of sounds of bombs bursting, what you're hearing is—hopefully—laughter. And a whole lot of other things the poet most certainly intended, like being comfortable in uncertainties, mysteries, doubts, without any irritable reaching after fact and reason. Negative capability *should* be this lyrical.

42

Rachel Zolf

on **Eileen Myles, "Snakes"**
(2001)

> for Kathe Izzo

I was 6 and
I lost my snake.

The table shook
I can do better
than this
and shambled
to the kitchen
to the scene
of the crime

I was green
I put my sneaker
down, little shoe

I felt the cold
metal tap
my calf

moo and everything
began to change.
I am 6
turned into lightning
wrote on the night

At 6, I was feathers
scales, I fell into
the slime of it, lit

You think you are six,
it yelled. I am face
to face with a frog
a woman alone
in bed. The square
of the window
persists. I am 6.

The phone rings
It's my sister
blamm I dropped
a plate. Sorry.

Now the clouds slide
by afraid, awake
my feet are cold
but I'm fearless

I am 6.

Under here
with bottle caps
and stars
adults and low
moans, busses

slamming on brakes
I am 6

the cake is lit
it's round
the children
sing. I will never
return. We are
so small.

My husband turns
his fevered

face. I put
the medicine
down. Click.
I am 6.

The movie rolls on.
Tramping feet,
music blaring
at the end of
the war. I
am frightened
hold my hand

The round face
of the woman
upstairs, moving
the faucets, strips
of vegetable

slithering down,
her reptile child
will never
return. The telephone
rings. It's me.
I'm six.

Eileen Myles, "Snakes," in *Skies* (Los Angeles: Black Sparrow Books, 2001).
Reprinted with permission of the author.

I hate snakes. I used to have these dreams, maybe visions, of a slithering mass of snakes at the foot of my bed curling round my feet,
sucking, nipping at my toes, tentacling along the tender inside skin
of my legs. I even wrote a poem about them in my first book, "poking
pointy faces at my too-small pussy, pressing / cold dank underbellies

to belly, sucking too / tightly tender nipples, hissing, forked tongues / flickering in my ears, stuffed tiny quiet throat (tastes like earth)." I hate snakes. My brother used to hide behind the door with a garter snake in a paper bag, then toss the bag at me when I came into the room. My mom once had three huge milk snakes living under her fridge and they slithered in front of me and I almost shit my pants. I couldn't even look at a snake in a magazine. I hate snakes.

But I don't hate Eileen's "Snakes." I love its slippery elusiveness, its surprising torques, its enactment of all-over-the-place six. Now, I'm supposed to perform a close reading of Eileen's poem, but I have a bit of an aversion to doing close readings, think they can close off open reading experiences of open poems like "Snakes." So to get to my 1,000 words and 350 bucks I think I'll muse alongside the poem kind of like (but nowhere near as sophisticated as) Eileen muses about life and art and sex and dogs and memory in their loose and layered, incisive and erudite "second-generation New York School" (that means edgier than the first) poems, autofiction, and essays. I mean, what do you expect me to do, hand you one reading of this dense, involuted, and elliptical poem that you can put in your back pocket or purse or safe and feel assured about?

Fuck that.

Really, what would you do with, say, a psychoanalytic reading of the poem? Suck on it? That kind of reading jumps out with the first lines: "I was 6 and / I lost my snake." The AFAB (assigned female at birth) poet (I mean persona) finds themself smack at the end of Freud's phallic psychosexual stage. Just as they are coming into (i.e., "individuating") a more fully developed sense of "self" (which supposedly happens around age six), they realize with a primal-sceney shocked start that they don't actually own/have/sprout a penis (um, snake) and all its special powers. The poet's persona is psychically castrated, hence all the loss and dread that follow: the crime, the slime, the fear, the shame, the woman alone in bed, the silent mother and lost reptile child, everything changing, never to return. I or you or we could do a similar reading of the dream or vision that opened this piece. But do I or you or we really desire that?

Why not just give in to the id and instinctively enjoy the poem and all its queer swerves. Like the way the speaker plays with time and positionality, how they seem to be an adult remembering being six ("little shoe" . . . "so small"), but the poem reads like they actually are six and having a lot of fun falling "into / the slime of it, lit." The poem *is* six, with all its wonky juxtapositions, which I guess we could also call paratactic, even though parataxis as a rhetorical term is sort of misused by critics of experimental poetry, but I digress. I love "I felt the cold / metal tap / my calf // moo," the enjambment from snake and body to cow and moo producing a surreal associative thrill. I love the torque to "my husband," definitely unexpected from a child or the very out queer Eileen (I mean persona). My mind goes to queer kinship and the AIDS crisis, how perhaps the speaker snaking along this memory montage as "the movie rolls on" swerves to a more recent experience of taking care of a sick friend. Maybe they got married for health care, who knows.

But for me the most interesting aspect of reading "Snakes" today in 2019 (the poem was first published in 1998) is thinking about its use of pronouns and plurality. I don't mean to dwell on the biographical, but I can't help noticing that Eileen's Twitter bio reads "I am they." They go by they now, as a lot of us do, as gender conventions and distinctions fall away and pluralize. When I read "I am they" next to "I am 6," something particular happens, something social. They (and the yelling "it" in the poem's seventh stanza) is a third-person pronoun that, according to philosopher Roberto Esposito, "is situated precisely at the point of intersection between no one and anyone."[1] Genderqueer poet Cheena Marie Lo claims, "They is neutral while at the same time being a marker, they is neither and both."[2] They slips between singular and plural in a not dissimilar way to how I and we slip in A. A. Milne's famous book of kids' poetry, *Now We Are Six*, the first-person singular and plural positions accompanying Christopher Robin, Winnie the Pooh, and Piglet on their adventures as a threesome that could also be read as three parts of a being. In "Snakes," the I/it/they is also a we, you, us, "Tramping feet, / music blaring / at the end of / the war." Eileen's poem is six and so are we. Eileen's poem is frightened and asks us to hold hands. Eileen's poem inhabits multiple durations and positions. The poem isn't called "Snake," it's "Snakes." The telephone rings at the end and the speaker isn't a single voice, they is six, they're plural and expansive, not just 6 but six. "I was" or "I am" becomes a condensed "I'm" paradoxically allowed to proliferate. "We are / so small" and big, together, now. In the Milne book, the words "I am Six" don't appear until the last page, in a poem called "The End." The poem ends with "So I think I'll be six now for ever and ever."[3] Sounds like an excellent plan. And one of many possible clever readings of "Snakes."

NOTES

1 Roberto Esposito, *Third Person: Politics of Life and Philosophy of the Impersonal*, trans. Zakiya Hanafi (Cambridge: Polity Press, 2012), 107.

2 Cheena Marie Lo, *Ephemera and Atmospheres* (Brooklyn: Belladonna, 2014), 5.

3 A. A. Milne, "The End," in *Now We Are Six* (1927; repr., London: Methuen, 1977), 102.

Edwin Torres

on **Anne Waldman, "Rogue State"**

(2002)

I'm in a rogue state, honey
Getting unpredictable & strange
Just a rogue state itching to
Test my harridan verbalistic (bardic) range

R's for the radical ecologist on the fringe
O is the opportunity to make First War powers cringe
G is the genius hacker under alien skin
U better watch out,
Ever Female Activist's akin

I'm in a rogue state papa Ashcroft
Don't tell me what to do
Your rules aren't my rules
Cause I'm the Lady of Misrule

Wild card they call me
Imperious, sultry, dark
Loose cannon on the gunwale
This literary canon's got a subversive quark

National Missile Defense System
Got nothing on me
I can pierce through the genome project
With a cyborg's vitality

Gated communities tremble
I'm coming through the door
Rogue state's a state won't humble
Call her witch call her a whore

I'm in a rogue state Bushie
Don't tell me what to do
Your rules aren't my rules
Cause I'm the Lady of Misrule

This version of "Rogue State" (sometimes improvised in performance)
was published in *The Room of Never Grieve* (Minneapolis: Coffee House
Press, 2003). Used by permission of the author.

The *rogue state* being celebrated in this poem is a defiantly female
being, bursting past gender, appearing in the guise of mobility. If
poem is path / poet is pathfinder.

In this performance, Anne Waldman embodies the mobile state,
empirically fluid, to create a hyperbolic freedom-creature as "a Lady
of Misrule," using internal combustions of softness and hardness,
a mercurial remora. If you allow your ears to observe, you will find
subtextual syncopations underlying your delirium—indeed, a body
rendered by vocality is a rogue state to occupy. Here, Waldman is
presenting us with an offering: to challenge convention by inhabiting
the dynamic of our listening, our internal states. She identifies female
archetypes, "Call her witch call her whore," to propel their exorcism,
out of the poem into the Rogue State.

Anne Waldman's poetry is a trigger for activation, an intraspecies
pass—to enter, from one, to other—and the question becomes
whether the receiving audience is ready to travel, whether you *allow*
that much ability *into* your liberty. Orality inhabits a core question:
Can we give ourselves that much freedom to connect with our innate
phenomena, our own infinite possibility for transformative direction?

From an interview for the anthology *Beats at Naropa* (Coffee House
Press, 2009), coedited with Laura Wright, Waldman talks about the
Beats' lineage: "Many of us in the sixties were feeding on the energy
of the New American Poetry outrider lineages. I felt a personal alle-

giance to the ethos, to the quality of mind. Of poetics investigation, to the moment-to-moment playfulness, the daily-ness, the tracking of the mind and experience, plus being awake to the minute particulars to daily existence of thought and dream and location." And here, the messenger attempts to define the interjection of *mobility* with *species*. When is the poem lifted off the page, as "poetic" as the poem *defined* by the page?

> the audience is in receptor's mode awaiting discovery
> > the animal delivers
> the audience is in position for judgment
> > the animal undermines delivery
> the audience signifies membership
> > the animal signifies speed

This is the phenomenological territory occupied by the *ur-poet* . . . the mobile creature at home between homes, between planes of meta-physical embodiments—where the organism is rooted to its evolu-tion—where the poet, as "subversive quark," transforms with every cadence.

> The humanist strain [is] the legacy of a style of 1960s poetry reading . . . mainstreamed through the Beats and their imita-tors. It's characterized by what at first glance looks like faith in the power of "presence" . . . its belief in the possibilities of aesthetic or personal coherence, and the power of poems to enact themselves and all their incongruous energies fully, faithfully, and at once.[1]

Waldman's performance is not confined to "a style of Beat reading"; the poet becomes the poem through the sensory activation that per-meates definition. To my ears, the "at-once" presence of "Rogue State" is in the naturally fluctuating timbre of voice, championing *rule-breaking* as a natural ability that occupies a *felt sense*,[2] an inte-rior landscape with its own sonic ability. To trigger a body's natural patterning toward a familiar path is to trigger the natural voice toward the *unheard pitch*, one that reaches with a deeper resonance than the *perfect note*. In an interweaving of Hindu and ancient principles, Waldman finds the creation we inhabit by owning the fleshy parts, the creature we become, our natural Prakritic state, "wild card, they call me."

> Today, feminists around the world continue to use ideas of non-self and interdependence to argue that Buddhist philosophy is a bastion for women's liberation in multiple social and spiritual spheres.[3]

Waldman's higher resolve is to create union while remaining female, thereby redefining *energy* as a mobile gender, "to test my Harridan Bardic range." Beyond feminism or any-ism, the center of Waldman's performance here is to shift, in breath/pitch/lyric, among parallel dualities; a fast-speaking Beyond-ism, not to be confused with the Russian Futurist *Beyonsense* that was steeped in proletarian utopias seeking language beyond mere human understanding.

Here, outliers of trance states delineate the precious telepathy divined as process, the heterogeneity of a body inhabited by motion, which then allows circumnavigating across intrapersonal planes—this is where free jazz enters the essay. Explaining a run by Bird by being the run, or the bird, like Ornette Coleman flourishing on a stop-start note, where "gated communities tremble." Where do you put your faith in, as you hold tight along the scrawl? *Glissando Motorandi*; to travel *the parallel*, where infinite varieties off the main tangent open arousals of other tangents. What, disguised as availability, becomes stability, before ability, ignites mobility? How confident are you in your liberty, in allowing *the unknown* its ability to match your continual evolution?

Ornette says, "My music is not interested in any one person/nature/thing but just in the concept of existing"; when is the poem not sung or seen but lived? Coleman's composition with the London Symphony Orchestra, "Skies of America," works as perfect accompaniment to Waldman's "Rogue State" performance, specifically the track "The Artist in America,"[4] which, to this writer's ear, sounds like an ekphrasis translation of "Rogue State," as rendered by orchestra with vocals by saxophone.

Like most things Waldman, this poem leads to beginnings, to Sanskrit. *Rasa* is a Sanskrit word for an experiential essence or nectar.[5] Bharata, the third-century BCE Sanskrit aesthetician, further defines *Rasa* as "a realization of one's own consciousness as colored by emotion." The term was formulated for drama and later adapted to poetry. *Rasa*, in the strict sense of the word, is the soul of poetry.

▨ Could there be an essence to the state of being rogue? Primordial wisdoms of energetics within principal dynamics of *Rasa* can be revealed in many ways; the mission is to explore the partnerships you recognize—the audience, the message, the absolute—how our bodies play on so-called male/female energies, and what categories of interference we claim to allow us survival, "Don't tell me what to do, / Your rules aren't my rules."

The receiver's state realigns with the messenger's state—that continual rebirthing of consciousness, a rogue state to embody. Anne Waldman's *traveling* through the origin of the poem is the *arrival* of the origin. The intonation of the mobile creature is heard, continually reborn, transcending ability with mobility.

NOTES

1 Raphael Allison, *Bodies on the Line: Performance and the Sixties Poetry Reading* (Iowa City: University of Iowa Press, 2014), xiii.

2 Philosopher Eugene Gendlin originated the concept of a bodily "felt sense" as a path to healing in his book *Focusing* (New York: Bantam Books, 1981), 47–117.

3 Amy Holmes-Tagchungdarpa, "Can Women Become Leaders in the Buddhist Tradition?" 2015, https://berkleycenter.georgetown.edu/forum/can-women-become-leaders-in-the-buddhist-tradition.

4 "The Artist in America," audio of Ornette Coleman with London Symphony Orchestra, https://www.youtube.com/watch?v=hUDcls1pnd0.

5 "Rasa is something experienced by the audience. Neither object, nor emotion, nor concept . . . the immediate experience, gestation of life, pure joy, relishes its own essence as it communes with the 'other'-actor or poet. Rasa can transport one to a transcendental level, a merging with the absolute. There is no Western equivalent for this widely discussed Sanskrit term." Edward Hirsch, *A Poet's Glossary* (Boston: Houghton Mifflin Harcourt, 2014), 512–13.

Amber Rose Johnson

on **Harryette Mullen, "Elliptical"**
(2002)

> They just can't seem to ... They should try harder to ... They
> ought to be more ... We all wish they weren't so ... They
> never ... They always ... Sometimes they ... Once in a while
> they ... However it is obvious that they ... Their overall ten-
> dency has been ... The consequences of which have been ...
> They don't appear to understand that ... If only they would make
> an effort to ... But we know how difficult it is for them to ...
> Many of them remain unaware of ... Some who should know
> better simply refuse to ... Of course, their perspective has been
> limited by ... On the other hand, they obviously feel entitled
> to ... Certainly we can't forget that they ... Nor can it be denied
> that they ... We know that this has had an enormous impact on
> their ... Nevertheless their behavior strikes us as ... Our
> interactions unfortunately have been ...

"Elliptical" from *Sleeping with the Dictionary* (Berkeley: University of California Press, 2002). Used with permission of the author and the University of California Press.

198
———

In her poem "Elliptical," Harryette Mullen churns calcified lines from
social scripts through experimental procedures that reveal the deep
entrenchment of intolerance, judgment, and fear of others embedded
in American English. Easily recognizable, though smothered in
detached and impersonal tones, the lines that populate the poem
could have been plucked from a Human Resources report or ethno-
graphic evaluation just as easily as they could have been overheard
on a crowded train or caught passing through office hallways. The

poem taunts us with the beginning phrases of a series of sentences strung together by trails of ellipses; it toys with our internal readiness to complete the lines evidencing biases and stereotypes that are exhaustingly familiar. By employing found language in a form that instigates an interactive reading experience, "Elliptical" is aligned with Mullen's oeuvre that explores "the reciprocity between language and culture," calling her readers to interrogate with her how we use this language to differentiate between ourselves and each other.[1]

"Elliptical" comes from Mullen's 2002 collection, *Sleeping with the Dictionary*, wherein the unabridged dictionary plays the role of her mischievous co-conspirator, her verbose accomplice, and, as she describes in the collection's title poem, her "silver-tongued companion, whose lips / are ready to read [her] shining gloss."[2] Mullen's skillful lexical play can turn from humorous to hazardous as it disorders both the words and their ideological foundations, which Hortense Spillers describes in her influential writings on "American Grammar" as grossly underwritten by histories of immeasurable violence, exclusion, and dehumanization.[3]

Deploying procedures of redaction, Mullen withdraws the parts of each line that could anchor the accusations and assumptions in any specific context. Free from situational particularity, the opening phrases of each line spin off and into one another, illuminating myriad prejudices that persist invariably to differing conditions. In the lines "They just can't seem to . . ." and "We all wish they weren't so . . ." the collective speakers reduce the group under scrutiny to a flattened, singular inadequacy—first, in their behaviors (what they can't seem *to do*), then in their fundamental ways of being (what *they are* that they *should not be*). The overtly patronizing tone of "But we know how difficult it is for them to . . ." and "Of course, their perspective has been limited by . . ." offers no sincere concern for whatever real conditions may contribute to the group's behavior, precisely because the group's voice and perspective are completely absent.

The collective "we" of the poem claims that the inferiority of the ostra-cized group's "tendencies" are "obvious," making the "consequences" appear inevitable. This argument, that the subjective value of a set of behaviors is "obvious," is propped up by long histories of people in power justifying their use of various degrees of discrimination with the belief that the differences between us are indicators of natural or divinely delineated social hierarchies. Using this argument, the speak-ers attempt to evacuate their responsibility and dodge accountability for their influence and control over the "consequences" at hand. It does not matter if they "make an effort." It does not matter what their "per-spective has been limited by," nor the conditions that have "had an enormous impact" on them. These riddles of justifications are merely distractions; the undisclosed details matter less than the assumption of an irrefutable and irreconcilable chasm between "us" and "them."

By suspending the second half of each line, Mullen composes an irregular repetition and internal echo that makes the recognition of the poem's discursive pattern inevitable. The situational specifics, which may otherwise be considered the most crucial elements of this imagined statement, are, in fact, the excess. In conversation with Barbara Henning about the poem, Mullen says the division could be of any denomination: "it could be race, gender, age, class, religion, nationality, or anything else that divides us."[4] The premise of the divi-sion is not the focus. The poem shines a spotlight instead on the per-vasive *logic* of division and the ease of its transferability.

The circulation of this language is not without consequence. The apa-thetic tone of the text is reminiscent of various kinds of institutional docu-mentation, bringing into view the stakes of this thinking: the power to expel or exclude others—from employment security, citizenship, legal rights, medical resources, and so forth—and thus to maintain inequitable material conditions that contribute to the vulnerability and dispossession fronted by those who have been historically disenfranchised. This cap-italist world depends upon us/them, citizen/alien, human/nonhuman dichotomies, and the stakes of these die-hard divisions are incredibly urgent. For some, it can mean an exclusion from the right to life.

Strung together by relentless ellipses, the fragments circle and ensnare one another. The ellipses themselves suggest a kind of accumulated exhaustion with the prevalence of this hierarchical thinking, a fatigue from battling what feels inescapable about this ingrained logic. The withdrawn elements hail the reader's imagination and we become collaborators in the meaning-making of the poem, activating its political intentions with our reflexive, internal responses. These responses vary according to our unique intersectional positioning within lived social arrangements, and as such, the poem prompts our own interrogation of where we stand within these kinds of divisions and how we have been conditioned to either perpetuate this logic or work against its insidious impulses.

The metaphorical play of the title, "Elliptical," turns on the structural similarities between a machine that can be pushed and spun but remain in the same place and the indurate ideas that underwrite American English and produce a lived reality that can feel at once cyclical and stagnant. Against a collective exhaustion from spinning our wheels trying to make sense of these nonsensical social norms that mark difference as a measure of value, Mullen's poem strips down this pervasive grammar and challenges us to confront what is absent. More than the second half of each line, what is missing is our capacity to recognize the constructedness of power hierarchies and to acknowledge our shared humanity and our essential dependency on each other for our future.

NOTES

1 Harryette Mullen, *The Cracks Between What We Are and What We Are Supposed to Be: Essays and Interviews* (Tuscaloosa: University of Alabama Press, 2012), 6.

2 Harryette Mullen, *Sleeping with the Dictionary* (Berkeley: University of California Press, 2002), 67.

3 Hortense Spillers, "Mama's Baby, Papa's Maybe: An American Grammar Book," *Diacritics* 17:2 (1987): 67.

4 Barbara Henning and Harryette Mullen, *Looking Up Harryette Mullen: Interviews on Sleeping with the Dictionary and Other Works* (New York: Belladonna Press, 2011), 42.

45

Jena Osman

on **Caroline Bergvall, "VIA"**

(2003)

Nel mezzo del cammin di nostra vita
mi ritrovai per una selva oscura
che la diritta via era smarrita

The Divine Comedy – Pt. 1 Inferno – Canto I – (1–3)

1. Along the journey of our life half way
   I found myself again in a dark wood
   wherein the straight road no longer lay
         (Dale, 1996)

2. At the midpoint in the journey of our life
   I found myself astray in a dark wood
   For the straight path had vanished.
         (Creagh and Hollander, 1989)

3. HALF over the wayfaring of our life,
   Since missed the right way, through a night-dark wood
   Struggling, I found myself.
         (Musgrave, 1893)

4. Half way along the road we have to go,
   I found myself obscured in a great forest,
   Bewildered, and I knew I had lost the way.
         (Sisson, 1980)

5. Halfway along the journey of our life
   I woke in wonder in a sunless wood
   For I had wandered from the narrow way
         (Zappulla, 1998)

6. HALFWAY on our life's journey, in a wood,
   From the right path I found myself astray.
         (Heaney, 1993)

7. Halfway through our trek in life
    I found myself in this dark wood,
    miles away from the right road.
        (Ellis, 1994)
8. Half-way upon the journey of our life,
    I found myself within a gloomy wood,
    By reason that the path direct was lost.
        (Pollock, 1854)
9. HALF-WAY upon the journey of our life
    I roused to find myself within a forest
    In darkness, for the straight way had been lost.
        (Johnson, 1915)
10. In middle of the journey of our days
    I found that I was in a darksome wood,
    the right road lost and vanished in the maze
        (Sibbald, 1884)
11. In midway of the journey of our life
    I found myself within a darkling wood,
    Because the rightful pathway had been lost.
        (Rossetti, 1865)
12. In our life's journey at its midway stage
    I found myself within a wood obscure
    Where the right path which guided me was lost
        (Johnston, 1867)
13. In the middle of the journey
    of our life
    I came to myself
    In a dark forest
    The straightforward way
    Misplaced.
        (Schwerner, 2000)
14. In the middle of the journey of our life I came to
    myself in a dark wood, for the straight road was lost
        (Durling, 1996)

15. In the middle of the journey of our life I came to myself
     within a dark wood where the straight road was lost
               (Sinclair, 1939)

16. In the middle of the journey of our life
     I found myself astray in a dark wood
     where the straight road had been lost sight of.
               (Heaney, 1993)

17. IN the middle of the journey of our life, I found myself in a
     dark wood; for the straight way was lost.
               (John A Carlyle, 1844)

18. In the mid-journey of our mortal life,
     I wandered far into a darksome wood,
     Where the true road no longer might be seen.
               (Chaplin, 1913)

19. In the midtime of life I found myself
     Within a dusky wood; my way was lost.
               (Shaw, 1914)

20. In the midway of this our mortal life,
     I found me in a gloomy wood, astray,
     Gone from the path direct:
               (Cary, 1805)

21. Just halfway through this journey of our life
     I reawoke to find myself inside
     a dark wood, way off-course, the right road lost
               (Phillips, 1983)

22. Midway along the highroad of our days,
     I found myself within a shadowy wood,
     Where the straight path was lost in tangled ways.
               (Wheeler, 1911)

23. Midway along the journey of our life
     I woke to find myself in some dark woods,
     for I had wandered off from the straight path.
               (Musa, 1971)

24. Midway along the span of our life's road
    I woke to a dark wood unfathomable
    Where not a vestige of the right way shewed.
        (Foster, 1961)
25. Midway in our life's journey I went astray
    from the straight road & woke to find myself
    alone in a dark wood
        (Ciardi, 1996)
26. Midway in the journey of our life I found myself in a
    dark wood, for the straight road was lost.
        (Singleton, 1970)
27. MIDWAY life's journey I was made aware
    That I had strayed into a dark forest,
    And the right path appeared not anywhere.
        (Binyon, 1933)
28. Midway on our life's journey, I found myself
    In dark woods, the right road lost.
        (Pinsky, 1994)
29. Midway on the journey of our life I found myself within
    a darksome wood, for the right way was lost.
        (Sullivan, 1893)
30. Midway the path of life that men pursue
    I found me in a darkling wood astray,
    For the direct way had been lost to view
        (Anderson, 1921)
31. Midway this way of life we're bound upon,
    I woke to find myself in a dark wood,
    Where the right road was wholly lost and gone
        (Sayers, 1949)
32. MIDWAY upon the course of this our life
    I found myself within a gloom-dark wood,
    For I had wandered from the path direct.
        (Bodey, 1938)

33. MIDWAY upon the journey of my days
I found myself within a wood so drear,
That the direct path nowhere met my gaze.
(Brooksbank, 1854)

34. MIDWAY upon the journey of our life,
I found me in a forest dark and deep,
For I the path direct had failed to keep.
(Wilstach, 1888)

35. Midway upon the journey of our life,
I found myself within a forest dark,
For the right road was lost.
(Vincent, 1904)

36. MIDWAY upon the journey of our life
I found myself within a forest dark,
For the straightforward pathway had been lost.
(Longfellow, 1867)

37. Midway upon the journey of our life
I found that I had strayed into a wood
So dark the right road was completely lost.
(MacKenzie, 1979)

38. MIDWAY upon the journey of our life
I woke to find me astray in a dark wood,
Confused by ways with the straight way at strife
(Bickersteth, 1955)

39. Midway upon the pathway of life
I found myself within a darksome wood
wherein the proper road was lost to view.
(Edwardes, 1915)

40. MIDWAY upon the road of our life I found myself within
a dark wood, for the right way had been missed.
(Norton, 1891)

41. On traveling one half of our life's way,
I found myself in darkened forests when
I lost the straight and narrow path to stray.
(Arndt, 1994)

42. Upon the journey of my life midway,
      I found myself within a darkling wood,
        Where from the straight path I had gone astray
           (Minchin, 1885)

43. UPON the journey of our life half way,
      I found myself within a gloomy wood,
        For I had missed the oath and gone astray.
           (Pike, 1881)

44. Upon the journey of our life midway
      I came unto myself in a dark wood,
        For from the straight path I had gone astray.
           (Fletcher, 1931)

45. Upon the journey of our life midway,
      I found myself within a darksome wood,
        As from the right path I had gone astray.
           (Cayley, 1851)

46. When half-way through the journey of our life
      I found that I was in a gloomy wood,
      because the path which led aright was lost.
           (Langdon, 1918)

47. When I had journeyed half of our life's way,
      I found myself within a shadowed forest,
      for I had lost the path that does not stray.
           (Mandelbaum, 1980)

Caroline Bergvall, "VIA," in *Fig* (Salt Books, 2005). Reprinted with permission of Caroline Bergvall.

In 1999, in an article called "Deformance and Interpretation," scholars Jerome McGann and Lisa Samuelson suggested that readers of poetry would do well to follow Emily Dickinson's proposal to read poems backward.[1] They argued that the disordering of our normal reading routines (through isolating parts of speech, through mapping word frequencies, through reading backward) can reveal the "special inner resources" of a poem and open up possibilities for interpretation.

A year after "Deformance and Interpretation" was published, poet Caroline Bergvall embarked upon a deformative reading of Dante's *Inferno* at the British Library. She requested the forty-seven unique English translations of the work held in the library's collection at the time and transcribed the first tercet of Canto I from each. Once collated (alphabetically), those transcriptions became the poem "Via."

"Via" began its public life as a sound poem and was then published in a number of contexts, with slight variations. I first became aware of the poem in 2003, when it was submitted to *Chain*, a literary journal I coedited with Juliana Spahr.[2] The special topic for the journal that year was "Translucinación," a word brought to us by Cecilia Vicuña via Chilean writer and translator Andrés Ajens. Ajens invented this word in order to highlight how translation is always a conversation across borders of space and time. In the *Chain* version of "Via" (which was the first version to be published), the poem appeared in two parts: a first series and a second series. The first series presents all of the tercet translations alphabetically in one solid stream of text, each translation identified with a number. When read aloud, the acoustic impact is like a rolling wave, as each translation echoes and slightly modifies the previous one. The reader becomes attuned to listening for the slight differentiations.[3]

The second series lists the full names of the translators chronologically, alongside the number of the corresponding translation as it appears in the first series. One can quickly ascertain from the second series the historical breadth (from 1805 to 2000), as well as the fact that these translations were generated on both sides of the Atlantic. The earliest translation represented was by a British vicar, Rev. Henry F. Cary, followed by John Carlyle—a Scottish doctor and brother of the writer Thomas Carlyle. Twenty-three years later American poet Henry Wadsworth Longfellow took up the task, followed in

1891 by his friend Charles Eliot Norton. Though American, Norton traveled extensively in Europe and was good friends with Thomas Carlyle, and no doubt knew John Carlyle. In 1993, Irish poet Seamus Heaney translated *Inferno*, while his friend, American poet Robert Pinsky, translated it in 1994. In 1996, at the request of Pinsky, Heaney sent a poem to the newly created *Slate* magazine; Pinsky described the three stanzas of "The Little Canticles of Asturias" as "a capsule version of Dante's *Commedia*." The list of the second series also suggests less intimate connections, as it brings British painter Tom Phillips's translation (accompanied by an artist's book version) in fairly close proximity to American poet Armand Schwerner's radical and visually spacious translation. Thus the series maps a web of previously invisible transatlantic links.

In 2005, "Via" was reprinted in Bergvall's poetry collection *Fig*, with what seems to be a fairly significant alteration. No longer divided into two series, the poem follows each translated tercet with the translator's last name and the date of the translation. While the musicality of "Via" is more disrupted in this form, the poem reveals its process more immediately; the reader/listener knows exactly what "Via" is made of without having to wait to learn the source of the translated variations. The labor of the translator is no longer delegated to a "second series" but identified as a crucial part of the whole. This change in presentation is actually a return to how Bergvall first read the poem when she recorded it in collaboration with composer Ciarán Maher in the summer of 2000, and it is the version that has been reprinted in anthologies such as *The Noulipian Analects* (Les Figues, 2007) and *Against Expression* (Northwestern, 2011).

As idiosyncratic as the 2003 *Chain* version of "VIA" might be in the publication and performance history of the poem, it gets closest to McGann and Samuelson's concept of deformance and thus anticipates the computational text processing at the center of current research in digital humanities. Text mining and computational procedures allow a "distant reader" to sort a collection of texts (a corpus) according to a particular query—for words, names, or syntactical constructions. Such sorting highlights that the literature is a system of relationships. Conventional textual analysis looks at relationships between words and images within individual works, but computational analysis proposes a means of mapping relationships between a large number of works (say, two hundred translations of Dante's *Inferno* written over two hundred years). In her note that precedes "VIA" in *Fig*, Bergvall wrote: "The minutia of writing, of copying out, of shadowing the translators' voicing of the medieval text, favoured an eery intimacy as much as a welcome distance." This is exactly the position of the reader when executing a computational sort on a corpus: both close and distant. The brilliance of "Via" is that it translates those newly discovered relationships into sound.

Procedures such as reading backward, manual deformance, and computational text mining can change our assumptions about where the meaning of a work resides. They bring us closer to the material realities of the text as such, and also make it clear that texts are never made in (or remain in) a vacuum. Literary interpretation—of works as canonical as Dante's *Commedia* or as quotidian as a newspaper— requires interactivity and circulation. In that regard, every text is part of a cultural conversation, a translucinación.

NOTES

1 Jerome McGann and Lisa Samuelson, "Deformance and Interpretation," *New Literary History* 30:1 (Winter 1999): 25–56. The Dickinson letter fragment they refer to reads: "Did you ever read one of her Poems backward, because the plunge from the front overturned you? I sometimes (often have, many times) have—a Something overtakes the Mind" (*The Letters of Emily Dickinson*, ed. Thomas H. Johnson [Cambridge, MA: Harvard University Press, 1958], 916).

2 For a detailed accounting of the poem's publication history, see Genevieve Kaplan's essay on "VIA" in *Jacket* 38, http://jacketmagazine.com/38/bergvall-by -kaplan.html. Issue 10 of *Chain* can be found at *Jacket2.org* in the "Reissues" section of the site.

3 Two recordings of Bergvall reading "Via" can be found on PennSound, both recorded in 2000, the year the poem was created; interestingly, they are significantly different.

46

Imaad Majeed

on **Charles Bernstein, "In a Restless World Like This Is"**
(2004)

Not long ago, or maybe I dreamt it
Or made it up, or have suddenly lost
Track of its train in the hocus pocus
Of the dissolving days; no, if I bend
The turn around the corner, come at it
From all three sides at once, or bounce the ball
Against all manner of bleary-eyed fortune
Tellers—well, you can see for yourselves there's
Nothing up my sleeves, or notice even
Rocks occasionally break if enough
Pressure is applied. As far as you go
In one direction, all the further you'll
Have to go on before the way back has
Become totally indivisible.

Charles Bernstein, "In a Restless World Like This Is," in *Girly Man* (Chicago: University of Chicago Press, 2006). Reprinted with permission of the author.

There are certain moments in time that alter the trajectory of the world. They cannot be anticipated and within those moments you know that something has changed. I believe that Charles Bernstein's book of poetry *World on Fire* is about these moments. The titles of the poems come from music of the 1940s—for instance, the poem "A Flame in Your Heart" gets its title from a lyric in "I Don't Want to Set the World on Fire," which came out just before the events of Pearl Harbor.

"In a Restless World Like This Is" gets its title from "When I Fall in Love," first released in April 1952, the month when the San Francisco Peace Treaty went into effect, ending Operation Blacklist, the Allied occupation of Japan. Bernstein, born in 1950, has said that the 1940s exist to him as an "always already" shadow in his mind, and of the work in his chapbook *World on Fire* he said, "The poems don't address history—they are not historiographic but lyric—they suggest a way in which one can exist in history without being consumed by it." Can it then be said that the poet exists in history—given that the book came out in 2004, following the events of September 11, 2001—without being consumed by it?

This poem suggests a way. It offers a way for poets like me to write about these moments. My own country, Sri Lanka, is riddled with its own moments: a thirty-year civil war, continuing ethnic and ethno-religious conflict, most recently manifesting in the Easter Sunday attacks of 2019 that left over 250 dead, for which ISIS claimed responsibility, that has further exacerbated tensions between the Sinhala-Buddhist majority and Muslim minorities, inciting anti-Muslim violence that claimed the life of an innocent civilian. It is fractured, and it is difficult to write. A poem like this is reassuring. Even the most harrowing moments can be addressed.

The form of the poem resembles a sonnet. It consists of 14 lines that do not follow a rhyme scheme. It has a volta, or "turn," as sonnets do. The tone, however, is almost satirical, even though we are reassured that "there's / Nothing up [his] sleeve." There is a feeling of nostalgia, even sadness, that is evoked, and perhaps the humor helps the poem go down without bringing the reader down with it. While reading it you feel as though you're losing track; you feel the words bend and bounce. There is a sense of the dissolving, the dreaming, and the breaking, of which the poem speaks. This comes across in how the poem is constructed. There is work to be done by the reader to bring out the meaning of the text. This is to be expected of a Language poet.

The enjambment at the fourth line is itself the bending of the "turn around the corner." Does this turn, then, refer to the volta that is yet to come? Or is that very line the turn? I cannot say for certain, but I am inclined to believe that the turn comes much later, as it would in a Shakespearean sonnet. To "come at it / From all three sides at once" could be the act of reading a line as a self-contained meaning, reading it along with the line that precedes, and reading it along with the one that follows, all allowing for different meanings. Just what is "it"? Is "it" "this" that "is" "restless," that is, the poem? The "hocus pocus" could then simply be the devices that the poet has employed in the writing of the poem. Or the nature of how time, memory, and history can often dissolve and become unclear.

What of the "bleary-eyed fortune / Tellers," though? To address this, I want to return to the "always already." It comes from the German *immer schon* and refers to an action or condition that has continued without any identifiable beginning. Althusser, Derrida, and Heidegger have used this term differently, but I want to interpret it here as referring to what could not be predicted. Who foresaw the world consumed by fire?

The image that we do see in the poem is that of rocks breaking under pressure. Can we take the rock to mean the nation, its people, "indivisible"? If so, what is the pressure that breaks it down? As a poet who perceives the United States from afar, I find it difficult to put my finger on it. I know that indivisible is a national word, yet the United States of today seems far from that. We see the cracks, the crumble, the division—the rock is broken.

Then comes the volta. Bernstein's final lines take Robert Frost's two roads and subvert them, ironizing them. With Frost, the further you go in one direction, the further you have to go if you turn back. With Bernstein, the further you go in one direction, the further you have to go "on before the way back has / Become totally indivisible." Initially I took this to be about the arrow of time and how you cannot turn it.

However, the more that I read this poem, in the years since I first attempted a close reading of it, it seems to me that the poet is saying that there was a moment, "not long ago," a point in time at which a different path could have been taken, a way back that was divisible.

Again, "always already" returns to me, this time, in the sense that Heidegger popularized. We project ourselves onto the possibilities of our world, in the way that we construct ourselves or, in this case, construct a poem and the possible ways for it to be. What does this mean for the reader? The reader also projects a self onto the possibilities of the poem. By the end of the poem, though, there seem to not be many possibilities, and the poem itself becomes "totally indivisible."

Bernadette Mayer

on **Laynie Browne, "Sonnet 123"**
(2007)

In Chinese astrology you are a snake
but at home you are a kitty-knight
You don't have any bunny in your body
You ate a bunny but you're not a bunny-king
To make a person you need two people
Otherwise you'll just get a big belly
And the baby will never hatch
Your favorite food is syrup
Jewel Jim "the pig," our pet caterpillar
Red, gray, yellow, and black
Is searching for a bramble leaf to eat
My rice bowl is not full
Jacob kicked me in the top of my nose
We pushed each other off of the couch

Laynie Browne, "123," in *Daily Sonnets* (Denver: Counterpath Press, 2007).
Reprinted with permission of the author.

Some sonnets have more than 14 lines. The last words in each line of
Laynie Browne's "Sonnet 123" are: snake, kitty-knight, body, bunny-
king, people, belly, hatch, syrup, caterpillar, black, eat, full, nose, and
couch. The first words are: in but you you to otherwise and your jewel
red is my Jacob and we. I don't really like punctuation or capitals, do
you? Unless we say, "Should I get a watch. Should I get a watch?"
Astrologically is a snake a bunny, or bunny a snake? Sticks often look
like snakes—you think it's a snake, but it's a stick, right? It could be
kitty-king and/or bunny-knight, or bunny-night. Who's on first? Who

goes first? Who's last? et cetera. I fall asleep and dream you wrote these poems with me, I am Jacob in the month of Jacobs in the Chinese calendar but neither I nor Jacob is a snake, at the very least, we'd be bunnies.

This is "Sonnet 123"—is that a coincidence? it's hard to list the middle words, unless you make a river, but here I'll list them as a poem:

called astrology
you and any
but and you
you'll and will
food and pig
yellow and for
is and me
and at last other

Of course the *ands* are just a prop, holding up the wall of the, say, rabbit hutch. I don't know what the word *called* is, in the *title*. But let's make the best of it. When Lisa and we were on a trip together we ate rabbit! But she didn't know what it was. People in the United States don't seem to eat rabbit. In the United States people eat a lot of animals but they don't eat the ones they see except chickens. If you ate rabbits, maybe you wouldn't call them *bunnies*. In westerns, people even eat snakes, if they have to. (In Florida, a lot of Burmese pythons have escaped as have tegu lizards, formerly kept as pets, but nobody eats them.) All the punctuation marks it's my own fault, I'm so sorry, I mean I just shouldn't have done it. It's because I fell into a bramble bush once. There aren't many bunnies here because, I think, there are a lot of farmers who scare the bunnies off so they won't eat their delicate little growing broccolis but now I want to talk about conception. Bunnies reproduce at a faster rate than humans do. Mostly humans can only give birth to one or two other humans at a time. Humans need new couches too, at times. Their couches get all squishy and hard to get up from. At first it was just that you easily fell asleep on it. And then, before the imitation Noguchi lamp, a frog flew

out of the dictionary and leapt over to me and Laynie, who happened
to be visiting at the time and we both thought: that dictionary's acting
weird, but then we remembered that the dictionary had made love to
another (etymological) dictionary and this was their offspring, we
named it bunny. So we had our fill of our favorite dish, rice and peas,
giving some to anybody who could say *bunny* and then we ambled
like brambles over to the sugar shack to pick up some syrup to put on
the sonnets Laynie wrote but no, syrup doesn't go on sonnets, it's for
pancakes and other edible things. So we licked our noses and fell off
the couch, or couches, because by this time there was the couch in
the poem and my couch is the one that's squishy. If I remember correctly both these couches were bought with grant money—Laynie's
is the Pew couch and mine the Guggenheim couch, no it was the
Foundation for Contemporary Performance Arts couch.

There's bunny, body, baby, bramble, bowl and big belly bunny-king
and kitty-knight. Thank the lord nobody got a bruise. The colors—
red, gray, yellow, and black—are in the middle like a nun reading a
newspaper, while rolling down a hill. My dictionary's the color of a
bunny—you could call it a bunny-dictionary. The dictionary's sinking
into the cushions. What a cushy job it is to write sonnets, so many
people have written so many words already, all you have to do is re-
arrange them like a caterpillar, or pig. Yet the symptoms of caterpillar-
hood or pig-hood don't just fall into your sonnet, willy-nilly. They
edge toward the words *jewel* and *Jim*. Hey, what's with all this alliteration? Can I go to bed yet? Will you fill up my bowl? Pets prove to be
bowls, pretty parsnipishly, don't you feel? To snooze is to search for
sonnets under the cushions of the award-winning couches until kitty
or the king come home.

48

Douglas Kearney

on **Tracie Morris, "Africa(n)"**
(2008)

Recordings of Morris performing this poem can be found
at her PennSound page:
https://writing.upenn.edu/pennsound/x/Morris.php

A sound poem, yes. But what kind of sound?

In the performance composing the poem—the poem itself a de- and
re-composition of the sentence

> *It all started when we were brought here as slaves from*
> *Africa—*

a tension reverberates between a particular version of improvisation,
the kind some might be inclined to name "jazz," and something a bit
more machinic. Machinic, hear here, as what seems sprung less by
the self-possession filmmaker Arthur Jafa associates with the jazz
soloist,[1] and the aleatory, which is engined by "glitch" or an inability
to run as intended. Seems. *This* machine, the mechanics Tracie Morris
works with and through, is operational and operative: it works. What's
more, *this* machine composes its nature by way of at least two means.
The first, sonic. And that is to say in "Africa(n)," Morris plays a drum
machine playing a voice. The second, conceptual/content driven. The
poem is (pre)occupied[2] with the slavery machine.

> *It all started—*

you remember, or someone's telling you. Here, someone is Morris,
but also not, as she is in voice as "character," a voice she calls "Afro-
Shakespearean."[3] I'd offer TransMidAtlantic—a timbre with Negro

Oratory lilt, but pitch-swung and dragged through a song-ish shiver, that heebie jeebie on *slaAaAaAves*. This is not Brooklynite Morris talking but Morris playing a sample: a repurposed segment of audio. That the sample's textual content references a Middle Past but severs temporality between the speaker and that past (. . . we *were brought here* . . .) is important as ancestral memory making passage through the TransMidAtlantic speaker, then Morris, whose body becomes a crate from which that record is dug. Dig the popular sample that says:

> *What we're gonna do right here is go back.*
> *Way back.*[4]
> *It all started . . .*

Musicians may use drum machines to play a sample, mapping it—or multiple clips—over the machine's pads. Changing the order and frequency by which you work the pads reconfigures the recording into new sequences. Alterations via processing the found sound are possible, but you are not playing a new performance of the recording.

> *It all started when we were brought here as slaves from*
>   *Africa.*

Throughout the poem, when Morris says "slaAaAaAves" she is set on saying "slaAaAaAves" mostly the same way she said "slaAaAaAves" the first time she said it. This meaning-to-repeat signifies a *beatmaker's improvisation*, playing fifteen sampled syllables, clipping them into new syntaxes, while not escaping the sentence.

Compositionally, "Africa(n)" cuts an inexhaustible line. From:

> *It all started when we were brought here as slaves from*
>   *Africa.*

to:

> *It all started—en Africa—*

and:

> *It all started when we were—Africa—*

but also:

> When we wuh Wh Wh Wh we when—

or:

> It all—It all—It all—It all—[5]

These techniques spin in sample-based hip-hop production and poetic composition (as the cut-up, for one). Meet and met in Morris' work. Since

> It all started when we were brought here as slaves from
> Africa.

I find "all" slant rhymes with "so much" from Williams's "The Red Wheel-barrow." What we are meant to measure, to weigh is unclear—*what* starts? *What* depends? That both poems speak, at least in part, on labor adds echo to chime. In not getting to *read* the work, with "Africa(n)," I grapple with what Fred Moten might call "the outwork and/or mad absence of the work":[6] what and how is the poem doing what it does?

The anatomical work of sounding the poem may get Front Street attention. But that's nubbing Morris's virtuosity. She is thinking through the sentence(s) as she goes.[7] You can't see the thinking if you're busy not hearing it. Morris, with fifteen syllables, makes a way out of no way. As it all started, as it all started.

But at this here's start, regarding Morris's second meaning of machine, I promised slavery as concept, and by the Royal African Company, I'll deliver!

The imperial enterprise the transatlantic slave trade facilitated is, itself, a machine. An industrial system that, as Stephanie E. Small-wood puts it, turned "African captives to Atlantic commodities" through brutal abstraction,[8] the Middle Passage

> —when we were brought here as slaves from Africa—

operated, its gears lubed with drums of Black blood.

Yet, the machinic sonic and conceptual Voltron-up into a third machine. Morris's performance suggests the Black figure as automaton. As cyborg. Morris has *made herself* part drum machine, her voice curtailed to a single sample of scant syllables (one and a half lines of a typical Elizabethan sonnet) with which to produce "Africa(n)." The trap of the constraint breaks me.

> *It all started when we were brought here as slaves from Africa.*

The sentence includes no word that says "it" ends. Morris's searing insistence and discipline mean I can hardly read the *can* in "Africa(n)" as an affirmation of ability. No. It's a container for a grocery.

NOTES

1 See Arthur Jafa, *My Black Death* (Hudson, NY: Moor's Head Press, 2016).

2 Haunted and haunting.

3 More specifically, a vocalese re-rendering of the late Trinidadian American actor Geoffrey Holder saying the line (Tracie Morris, "Conceptual Poetry & Its Others" at the University of Arizona Poetry Center, 2008).

4 From the Jimmy Castor Band's "Troglodite."

5 Which refrains (as in *repeats* and *doesn't start*). Delaying the trauma of slavery while shivering about it.

6 Part of "a natural history of inequality," from the essay "Black Kant."

7 I'll cite here, briefly, another recording of "Africa(n)," in which sudden stereo feedback disrupts her performance. After signifyin(g) that the interference is the result of a haunting in the name of Caroline Rothstein (for whom the performance series is named), Morris references soundchemist Val Jeanty, her collaborator, who it seems previously called to dedicate her performance to her Afro-diasporic ancestors. When Morris begins again, she changes the intonation of "we" in the original sentence to one of correction. This is about *our* ghosts. See *Reading for the 3rd Annual Caroline Rothstein Oral Poetry Program at the Kelly Writers House, University of Pennsylvania, October 28, 2008*, http://writing.upenn.edu/penn sound/x/Morris.php.

8 See Stephanie E. Smallwood, *Saltwater Slavery: A Middle Passage from Africa to American Diaspora* (Cambridge, MA: Harvard University Press, 2008).

49

Tracie Morris

on **Jayne Cortez, "She Got He Got"**
(2010)

A video recording of this performance can be found at
https://media.sas.upenn.edu/file/227821

In such brief space, there's a lot that will inevitably be left out of a
commentary on Jayne Cortez's masterful poem "She Got He Got."[1]
One aspect of her spectacular artistry is her refinement of our understanding of what the list poem can do. Each line in "SGHG" is crystalline on its own yet heightens tension between lines and throughout
the entire poem in context. Who's "she" and who's "he"? What does
degree mean in the poem? Relativism and abstraction work to great
effect in this work. "She" and "he" are at once references to very specific people many of us know (and aspects of ourselves) as well as
overall considerations of how gender plays out in a gender-biased
society.[2] This poem tells us that, while patriarchy values one gender
above others, all genders lose in this unfair, up-is-down patriarchal
world we all try to survive in. What each "she" and "he" is seeking
is *love and its promise*. This poem also makes me consider the idea
of gendered binaries, or that binaries overall are flattening and
unsuccessful.

In addition to the larger gender issues the poem expertly presents,
in word and in presentation in the video recording of the poem from
2010 with Jayne and drummer Denardo Coleman (who also happens
to be Jayne's son), there is the explicit rhythmic focus that is the
engine of the poem. One can think of the compelling rhythm as a
metaphor for inevitability ("she" will never be "warm," "he" will never
be "cool"). That rhythm builds from monosyllabic to bisyllabic to

multisyllabic rhythm and also the density of what her hotness "got" her within each line:

> got happy got hot got thrilled got hot got degreed got hot got
>   silly got hot
> got possessive got hot got disappointed got hot
> got hurt got hot
> got nurtured got hot got bitter got hot
> got drunk got hot
> got drugged got hot got rastered got hot got pregnant got hot
>   got rejected got hot
> got indifferent got hot got lost got hot

After the first six lines, with the pattern established, Cortez goes into a rhythm that is contrapuntal to Coleman's playing for the most part before it syncs up (also indicated by Cortez's subtle hand gestures and body movements), keeping her rhythm consistent with the poem and independent of Coleman's drumming until he catches up with her text.

I find "rastered" a fascinating word choice in this list poem. It's the only word that seems to reference a more specialized vocabulary, outside of ordinary language[3] (computer/pixilation language), that gender bias is also technological. This term is a great, efficient way of indicating this aspect of "she" being lost in alcohol, drugs, and unwantedness (both her pregnancy and herself in the context of the two previous and subsequent lines above and below the "rastered" line).

In the poem, Cortez indicates "her" trying to "move on up" through the narrow space that patriarchy creates for women—all women. Women get "happy," "degreed," even "silly," then "possessive," "disappointed," and "bitter" (maybe realizing that she can't "win") before succumbing to the aspects of life that were always available, designed to make her fail. And yet "she" tries: religion, politics, being skinnier, more fashionable, a feminist, a cultural gadfly, an exile, and so forth. The motivation for all this, how it all became personally debilitating in the life of "she"? A lack of unconditional love. The couplet:

all because a certain person didn't say
"I will love you forever baby"

becomes all the more heartbreaking. It could be a lover that didn't say this, but it could also be that no one said that to "she" when *she* was a baby. What does it mean to have to be strong and on your own from infancy? What does it mean to have been alone since then? This "she" has no other reference point to others in her spinning-out-of-control societal downspin. It's so hot, so very hot, in the hell of one's own making, the road leading to it based on society's bad intentions. The "she" does her best but gets pulled under. Patriarchy is ultimately "unloving" to men and to women. It's a "war game" we all lose.

The cold "he" in this poem of counterpoints refreshes the rhythm established in the first part by adding a new word: "before." In other words, the "fix" was in. What turned him from "happy" to "cold"? It was as he "learned" something along the way. As Cortez explicitly says, referencing James Brown's brilliant song "It's a Man's World." In Brown's lush song, the counterpoint is the indelible presence of women and girls to make this (unfair?) man's world worth living, even for men ("It wouldn't be nothing, *nothing* without a woman or a girl . . .").[4]

Cortez's choice to explicitly reference this musical phrase emphasizes the failure of patriarchy for men too. "He got broken-hearted and warlike," among other things, as Cortez explains, this time in a tercet:

all because somebody stole his lollipop
& no one could chip through the ice
to say "I'll love you forever baby don't be so cold"

The foundational warping of the child's/infant's mind through cruelty so the child fashions him/herself to the rules of this unfair game is "set in stone," impossible to "chip through." Here Cortez elicits another popular cultural reference in my mind, Orson Welles's opus *Citizen Kane*. I thought of this film many times in multiple viewings of

Jayne's poem. In her poem, and in Welles's story, there was never a resolution to that childhood pain. The world became, and continues to be, a worse, dystopian place because of the psychic breaks we all must make to accept and survive its fundamental cruelty that binaries and misogyny foster, fester.

NOTES

1 My first spontaneous inclination, in fact, was to examine this poem using Pound's schema of phanopoeia, logopoeia, and melopoeia, and Cortez's poem works exceptionally well in all of these levels applying Pound's tools. However, given Pound's highly problematic politics, and out of respect for Jayne's activism, I narrowed my focus to just one aspect of analysis that I wanted to include and chose to focus on the core gender dynamics that are explicitly referenced in her title. This poem is extraordinarily rich and there is much to say, in many ways, about it using other tools including close reading, accentual verse, class- and race-focused contrasts, and speech act theory analyses of "ordinary language." It would require a much longer consideration of the poem than space allows here.

2 It is my sense that Jayne Cortez references gender dynamics in racially specific ways too within the poem, but her choice to say "she" instead of terms that are more pointedly Black, White, Latina, Asian, etc., to me means that the overarching ideas throughout the poem prioritize gender across cultures.

3 I mean this phrase in the philosophical context.

4 One of the most extraordinary examples of Brown's emphasis on this counterpoint (in terms of gender, rhythm, and musical styles) is his performance of this song with Luciano Pavarotti in the filmed version of the concert "Pavarotti and Friends for Angola" in 2002: https://www.youtube.com/watch?v=gb-B3lsgEfA.

50

Erica Hunt

on **Evie Shockley, "a one-act play"**
(2017)

> a man in blue sees the black in man, sees the black boy as man,
> sees the black man as bear, bears the black bear ill will, makes
> the black man ill, sees the black man on the make, seizes upon
> the man's black make-up, makes up what he will(s). the black
> man sees the man in blue, be's the blues in man, demands the
> blues back (off), deems the blues black, does the blues deed,
> deeds the blues back, lacks what blacks need, needs the true
> blue, bleeds the true black. blue and black: z'that a fact? black
> and blue: re-do. re-do.

"a one-act play" (p. 68), from *semiautomatic* © 2018 by Evie Shockley.
Published by Wesleyan University Press and reprinted with permission.

Evie Shockley's "a one-act play" is a *blues play*, a tongue-torquing
poem that recounts perception and bias in the deaths of Black people
by police hands. In staccato rhythms that bring to mind Gwendolyn
Brooks's seminal *The Pool Players*—"we real cool"—Shockley
deploys nouns that skew and sketch how racism names and un-
names its protagonists:

> *a man in blue sees the black in man*

The words "a man in blue" are generic, specify no race; its omission
often signals a default—"white." Note that the "blue" in this phrase is
not the same as the "blues" that occurs later in the play.

The verb "sees" is an oxymoron in this usage, because what is seen
from the first glance is a color, not a person: "the black in man."

There's an expression common among Black folks: "to call someone out of their name," that is, to disrespect someone by not calling them by their proper name but by a distant, chilly pronoun. For instance, if I was ever so heedless as to call my mother "she" in her hearing, it would trigger a tongue-lashing check on grammar and a read out of "She" as a pronoun of dispossession.

There are no names used in "a one-act play," but the reader senses the reenactment of the death of Michael Brown at the hands of policeman Darren Wilson in Ferguson, Missouri. In this blues play, the dispossession begins in the third phrase:

> sees the black boy as man, sees the black man as bear

Here the "see"-ing erases childhood and innocence from a young person, echoing the anxious racist tic that tries to demean Black men by calling them "boy." It's a short trip through anti-Blackness to "see" no person at all but a nonhuman, a "bear."

In actuality, Wilson likened Michael Brown to a "demon" (what's in a name?). Wilson exercised his power (whiteness) to call a Black person out of his name and to un-name Michael Brown with a nonhuman classification. Wilson was later acquitted of repeatedly shooting and killing Brown as he walked toward him. To call a person out of their name, to liken them to a "bear" or a "demon," is part of the arsenal of undoing life, reflexive white supremacy that manifests as anti-Blackness.

The verbs of "a one-act play" animate. They tell the story of a quickly unfolding blues drama. We plunge through the territories of perceiving and naming in a cycle we recognize (or ignore) in everyday life. If one of poetry's functions is to slow down the quick summaries that blur and blunt experience, the *verbs* in Shockley's prose poem compel awareness to slow down the "facts" that splinter our humanity:

> "the man in blue" *sees, bears, makes, seizes, makes up,* and
> *wills*

> "the black man" *sees, be's, demands, deems, does, deeds,*
> *lacks, needs,* and *bleeds*

The verbs draw readerly attention: the verb "sees" in its repetition is *reactive* and highlights that "see"-ing empowers belief: "the man in blue" *sees* what he *will.*

Seeing is an act of fabrication, a series of gestures foretelling a made-up ("makes up") story in which the man in blue is the hero, and his willpower (gun power) is positioned to complete *his* narrative arc.

When the play turns to the black man, he "sees," too, and differently. The "man in blue" summons the blues in the black man.

Here I hear LeRoi Jones/Amiri Baraka's *Blues People.* Jones/Baraka frames the blues art as the creation of African American people making "blues verse" from "the life of the individual and his individual trials and successes" and the "expression of Negro individuality within the superstructure of American society."[1]

"Blues" then is an expression of the Black American condition *and* the Black "I am," an assertion of personhood in the face of constant oppression. The "be's" in the poem signal the shift of focus, invoking the infinitive—"to be"—*and* the unconjugated vernacular—"we be walking"—*and* implicitly, the ontological predicate—at this time, "for the time, being."

Let's unpack that idea further: "be" echoes "to be or not to be," Hamlet's question about existential choice amid difficulty or doubt.

"Be" also signals a continuous present, an ongoing-ness. "He always be harassing the brothers when they go into that store."

A third example of the "be's" in this poem swims in the semantic river as the "be's" winding through Black Arts poetry such as Sonia Sanchez's "Last Poem I'm Gonna Write 'Bout Us" as in:

times I turn a corner of my mind
& u be there looooking

And also in the anaphoric "bees"/"be's" in Tonya Foster's *A Swarm of Bees*—where the "be" connects one ligament to the next from which one composes a day, a river of moods:

be low be lack be ridge and grudge
be longing be sotted be ramble and hold
be come and go

As poetics, "be" is a cognate of Black being and ontology insisting that Black life matters, expressed as a *continuous present* in the will to thrive even in an environment hostile to Black life.

The remaining verbs: *demands, deems, does, deeds, lacks, needs,* and *bleeds* position the "black man" of the play as the driver of independent actions. He "demands" his blues back; he "deems" the blues black; he "does" "the blues deed."

What is "the blues deed?" Context is all we have here and so the reader brings the phrases together:

does the blues deed, deeds the blues back, lacks what
blacks need, needs the true blue, bleeds the true black,
blue and black. z'that a fact?

Cycling through the dictionary's definitions of the word "deed" and its usages the reader finds *feat, exploit; illustrious action; the act of performing; a signed sealed instrument.*

The poem pulls many senses of the word "deed" into a web of signification, connecting *feat* (a demanding task) and *performance* with *pledge.* The "blues back" invites comparison to blues music's heroes and heroines, outlaws, drama, and destiny.

The final lines of "one-act play":
Black and blue: re-do, re-do

Repeat the concatenation of blues and Black(ness), and call for rescripting the "fact before the fact," its deathly drama, meted out in swift and devastating tempo.

NOTE

1 LeRoi Jones, *Blues People: The Negro Experience in White America and the Music That Developed from It* (New York: William Morrow, 1963), 86–87.

List of Contributors

Rae Armantrout's most recent book, *Conjure*, was published by Wesleyan University Press in 2020. Her 2010 book *Versed* won the Pulitzer Prize for Poetry and the National Book Critics Circle Award.

Herman Beavers has taught at the University of Pennsylvania since 1989, holding joint appointments in the departments of English and Africana Studies. His recent poems appear in *MELUS*, *Langston Hughes Colloquy*, *Versadelphia*, *Cleaver Magazine*, and *American Arts Quarterly*. He has published essays on August Wilson, Charles Johnson, Ralph Ellison, and Toni Morrison. His recent book, *Geography and the Political Imaginary in the Novels of Toni Morrison*, was published in 2018 by Palgrave Macmillan. He also serves as an advisory editor at *African American Review*, *Modern Fiction Studies*, *Langston Hughes Review*, and *Black Scholar*.

Charles Bernstein is the winner of the 2019 Bollingen Prize for *Near/Miss* (University of Chicago Press, 2018) and for lifetime achievement in American poetry. He is the author of *Topsy-Turvy* (University of Chicago Press, 2021) and *Pitch of Poetry* (University of Chicago Press, 2016).

Julia Bloch is the author of three books of poetry—*Letters to Kelly Clarkson* (Sidebrow Books, 2012), a finalist for the Lambda Literary Award; *Valley Fever* (Sidebrow, 2015); and *The Sacramento of Desire* (Sidebrow, 2020)—and of numerous essays on modern and contemporary poetry, focusing on race, gender, and lyric. She is a recipient of a Pew Fellowship in the Arts and lives in Philadelphia, where she is director of the Creative Writing Program at the University of Pennsylvania and an editor at *Jacket2*.

Christian Bök is the author of *Eunoia* (Coach House Books, 2001), a best-selling work of experimental literature, which received the Griffin Prize for Poetic Excellence. Bök is working on *The Xenotext,* a project that requires him to encipher a poem into the genome of a bacterium capable of surviving in any inhospitable environment. Bök is a Fellow in the Royal Society of Canada, and he teaches at Charles Darwin University.

Laynie Browne is a poet, prose writer, teacher, and editor. She is the author of thirteen collections of poems and three novels. Her recent books include *In Garments Worn by Lindens* (Tender Buttons Press, 2018), *Periodic Companions* (Presses universitaires de Rouen et du Havre, 2018), and *The Book of Moments* (Tinderbox Editions, 2018). Her honors include a Pew Fellowship (2014), the National Poetry Series Award (2007) for her collection *The Scented Fox,* and the Contemporary Poetry Series Award (2005) for her collection *Drawing of a Swan Before Memory.* Her poetry has been translated into French, Spanish, Chinese, and Catalan. Recent collaborations include a public art project, "Dawn Chorus," a constellation of poetry in thirteen languages engraved in the Railpark in Callow Hill, Philadelphia with visual artist Brent Wahl. She teaches at the University of Pennsylvania.

Stephen Collis is the author of several books of poetry, including *On the Material* (Talonbooks, 2010) and three parts of the ongoing "Barricades Project": *Anarchive* (New Star, 2005), *The Commons* (Talonbooks, 2008, 2014), *To the Barricades* (Talonbooks, 2013), and *A History of the Theories of Rain* (Talonbooks, 2021). He is also the author of three books of nonfiction: *Almost Islands: Phyllis Webb and the Pursuit of the Unwritten* (Talonbooks, 2018), *Dispatches from the Occupation* (Talonbooks, 2012), and *Phyllis Webb and the Common Good* (Talonbooks, 2007).

Michael Davidson is Distinguished Professor Emeritus of Literature at the University of California, San Diego. He is the author of *The San Francisco Renaissance: Poetics and Community at Mid-Century* (Cambridge University Press, 1989); *Ghostlier Demarcations: Modern Poetry and the Material Word* (University of California Press, 1997); *Guys Like Us: Citing Masculinity in Cold War Poetics* (University of

Chicago Press, 2003); and *Outskirts of Form: Practicing Cultural Poetics* (Wesleyan University Press, 2011). He has written extensively on disability issues, most recently *Concerto for the Left Hand: Disability and the Defamiliar Body* (University of Michigan Press, 2008) and *Invalid Modernism: Disability and the Missing Body of the Aesthetic* (Oxford University Press, 2019). He has published eight books of poetry, including *Bleed Through: New and Selected Poems* (Coffee House Press, 2013).

Mónica de la Torre's most recent book of poems and translations is *Repetition Nineteen* (Nightboat, 2020). Other books include *The Happy End/All Welcome* (Ugly Duckling Presse, 2016)—a riff on Kafka's *Amerika*—and *Public Domain* (Roof Books, 2008). With Alex Balgiu, she coedited the anthology *Women in Concrete Poetry, 1959–79* (Primary Information, 2020). She teaches at Brooklyn College and the Bard MFA program.

Sarah Dowling is the author of three books of poetry, *DOWN* (Coach House, 2014), *Security Posture* (Snare, 2009), and *Entering Sappho* (Coach House, 2020), as well as numerous chapbooks and shorter works. A scholar as well as a poet, Dowling has also published *Translingual Poetics: Writing Personhood Under Settler Colonialism* (University of Iowa Press, 2018), a study of contemporary poetry written across and between languages. She teaches in the Centre for Comparative Literature and Victoria College at the University of Toronto.

Rachel Blau DuPlessis, poet, critic, and collagist, is the author of the multivolume long poem *Drafts* (1986–2012) from Salt Publishing and Wesleyan University Press. Post-*Drafts* poetry includes *Interstices* (Subpress, 2014), *Graphic Novella* (Xexoxial Editions, 2015), *Days and Works* (Ashahta Press, 2017), and *Around the Day in 80 Worlds* (BlazeVOX, 2018). *NUMBERS*, a book of collage-poems, came out from Materialist Press in December 2018. *Purple Passages: Pound, Eliot, Zukofsky, Olson, Creeley and the Ends of Patriarchal Poetry* (University of Iowa Press, 2012) is part of a trilogy of works about gender and poetics that includes *The Pink Guitar: Writing as Feminist*

Practice (University of Alabama Press, 2006) and *Blue Studios: Poetry and Its Cultural Work* (University of Alabama Press, 2006). She has also edited *The Selected Letters of George Oppen* (Duke University Press, 1990) and *The Oppens Remembered: Poetry, Politics, and Friendship* (University of New Mexico Press, 2015), and has coedited *The Objectivist Nexus*.

Craig Dworkin is the author, most recently, of *Dictionary Poetics: Toward a Radical Lexicography* (Fordham University Press, 2020) and *Radium of the Word: A Poetics of Materiality* (University of Chicago Press, 2020) .

Al Filreis is Kelly Professor of English at the University of Pennsylvania, where he is also Faculty Director of the Kelly Writers House, publisher of *Jacket2* magazine, and co-director of PennSound. He is the creator and lead teacher of the open online course on modern and contemporary poetry, ModPo. His most recent book is *1960: When Art and Literature Confronted the Memory of World War II and Remade the Modern.*

Robert Fitterman is the author of fourteen books of poetry including *Rob's Word Shop* (Ugly Duckling Presse, 2019), *Dave* (Counterpath, 2019), *This Window Makes Me Feel* (Ugly Duckling Presse, 2018), *Nevermind* (Wonder Books, 2016), *No Wait, Yep. Definitely Still Hate Myself* (Ugly Duckling Presse, 2014), *now we are friends* (Truck Books, 2010), *Rob the Plagiarist* (Roof Books, 2009), *war, the musical* (Subpress, 2006), and *Metropolis*, a long poem in four separate volumes. He has collaborated with several visual artists, including Serkan Ozkaya, Sabine Herrmann, Nayland Blake, Natalie Czech, Tim Davis, and Klaus Killisch. He is the founding member of Collective Task, an artists and writers collective. He teaches writing and poetry at New York University and at the Milton Avery School of Graduate Studies of Bard College.

Adam Fitzgerald lives in New York City, cofounded the Ashbery Home School, has published *George Washington* (Liveright, 2016), among other books, and has been at work on a novel about someone trapped inside a pig.

Tonya Foster is the author of *A Swarm of Bees in High Court* (Bella-donna, 2015) and the bilingual chapbook *La Grammaire des Os; A History of the Bitch* (Sputnik and Fizzle, 2020) and coeditor of *Third Mind: Creative Writing Through Visual Art* (Teachers & Writers Collaborative, 2002). Her writing and research focus on ideas of place and emplacement and on intersections between the visual and the written. She is an editor at *Fence Magazine* and at *African-American Review.* Her poetry, prose, and essays have appeared in *Callaloo, Tripwire, boundary2, MiPOESIAS, NYFA Arts Quarterly, Poetry Project Newsletter,* and elsewhere.

Lyn Hejinian teaches in the English Department at the University of California, Berkeley, where her academic work is addressed principally to modernist, postmodern, and contemporary poetry and poetics, with a particular interest in avant-garde movements and the social practices they entail. She is the author of over twenty-five volumes of poetry and critical prose, the most recent of which are *Positions of the Sun* (Belladonna*, 2019) and *Tribunal* (Omnidawn, 2019).

Erica Hunt is a poet and essayist, the author of several collections of poetry, including *Veronica: A Suite in X Parts* (selva oscura Press, 2019). A volume of new and selected poems, *Jump the Clock,* was published in 2020 by Nightboat Books. With poet and scholar Dawn Lundy Martin, Hunt is coeditor of the anthology *Letters to the Future: Black Women/Radical Writing* (Kore Press, 2018). Hunt has received awards from the Foundation for Contemporary Art, the Fund for Poetry, and the Djerassi Foundation and is a past fellow of Duke University/the University of Cape Town Program in Public Policy. Hunt is a Bonderman Visiting Professor at Brown University.

Amber Rose Johnson is a creative and critical thinker from Providence, Rhode Island, pursuing a joint PhD in English and Africana Studies at the University of Pennsylvania. As an editor, she has produced exhibition catalogues for the Institute of Contemporary Art in Philadelphia and Richmond, Virginia, and her writing has been featured in *BOMB.* Johnson is the curator of a conversation and workshop series titled

Mess + Process and is the coordinator of the Black Cultural Studies Collective in Philadelphia.

erica kaufman is the author of *INSTANT CLASSIC* (Roof Books, 2013), *censory impulse* (Factory School, 2009), and *POST CLASSIC* (Roof Books, 2019). Prose and critical work can be found in *MLA Guide to Teaching Gertrude Stein* (2018) and in *Reading Experimental Writing* (ed. Georgina Colby, Edinburgh University Press, 2019). kaufman is the director of the Bard College Institute for Writing & Thinking.

Douglas Kearney has published six books, including the award-winning poetry collection *Buck Studies* (Fence Books, 2016); libretti, *Someone Took They Tongues* (Subito, 2016); and criticism, *Mess and Mess and* (Noemi Press, 2015). His collection of poems, *Sho*, was published in April 2021 (Wave). A Whiting Writer's and Foundation for Contemporary Arts Cy Twombly awardee with residencies/fellowships from Cave Canem, the Rauschenberg Foundation, and others, Kearney teaches Creative Writing at the University of Minnesota, Twin Cities.

Davy Knittle earned a PhD from the University of Pennsylvania and works in the fields of feminist, queer, and trans theory, environmental humanities, and multiethnic U.S. writing. His dissertation, "Queer with the City: Environmental Justice, Racial Capitalism, and the Poetics of Urban Change," uses literary accounts of gender, sexuality, and kinship as lenses for reading the relationship between natural and built environments in the globalizing U.S. city. His critical work has appears in *Women's Studies Quarterly*, *GLQ: A Journal of Lesbian and Gay Studies*, *Planning Perspectives*, and *Modern Language Studies*.

Imaad Majeed is a poet based in Colombo, Sri Lanka. They are also cofounder of Poetry P'lau, one of the city's most active and consistent gathering of poets since 2011. Their poetry has been published in *Frieze*, *CITY: A Journal of South Asian Literature*, and *ARTRA*, as well as the local small-press chapbooks *Lime Plain Tea* and *Annasi & Kadalagotu*. Their spoken-word performance of "Thambivamsa" was screened at the 46th NeMLA convention during the panel "The

Migrating Word: Imagining Collectives Outside State Boundaries" as an example of diasporic writing. They also performed a spontaneous poem constructed of language found in Ananda Guruge's *Society of the Ramayana* at documenta 14 in Kassel, Germany, at the historic Fridericianum for the "Parliament of Bodies" public program.

Jake Marmer is a poet, performer, and educator. He is the author of *The Neighbor Out of Sound* (2018) and *Jazz Talmud* (2012), both published by the Sheep Meadow Press, and *Cosmic Diaspora* (Station Hill, 2020). He regularly writes about poetry for *Tablet Magazine*. Born in the provincial steppes of Ukraine, in a city that was renamed four times in the past hundred years, he considers himself a New Yorker, even though he lives in the Bay Area.

Bernadette Mayer is an award-winning poet and artist who lives in upstate New York. Her influence in the contemporary avant-garde is felt widely. Among her many books of poems are *A Bernadette Mayer Reader* (New Directions, 1992), *Poetry State Forest* (New Directions, 2008), and *Midwinter Day* (Turtle Island Foundation, 1982).

Sharon Mesmer's recent poetry collection, *Greetings from My Girlie Leisure Place* (Bloof Books), was one of Entropy's "Best of 2015." Her other collections are *Annoying Diabetic Bitch* (Combo, 2008), *The Virgin Formica* (Hanging Loose, 2008), *Vertigo Seeks Affinities* (Belladonna*, 2007), *Half Angel, Half Lunch* (Hard Press, 1998), and *Crossing Second Avenue* (ABJ Press, Tokyo, 1997). Her fiction collections are *Ma Vie à Yonago* (Hachette Littératures, in French translation, 2005), *In Ordinary Time* (Hanging Loose, 2005), and *The Empty Quarter* (Hanging Loose, 2005). She is a coeditor of *Flarf: An Anthology of Flarf* (Edge Books, 2017), and was a member of the flarf collective from 2003 to 2010. Four poems appear in *Postmodern American Poetry: A Norton Anthology* (second edition, 2013). She teaches in the undergraduate and graduate programs of New York University and the New School.

Nick Montfort's computer-generated books of poetry include *#!* (Counterpath, 2014), the collaboration *2×6* (Les Figues, 2016), *Autopia* (Troll Thread, 2016), *The Truelist* (first in the new Using Electricity series from Counterpath, 2017), and *Hard West Turn* (Bad Quarto, 2018). Among his more than fifty digital projects are the collaborations *The Deletionist*, "Sea and Spar Between," and *Renderings*. He performs and shows digital artwork internationally. He has six books out from the MIT Press, most recently *The Future.* He is professor of digital media at MIT, teaches at the School for Poetic Computation, and lives in New York and Boston.

Tracie Morris is writer/editor of nine books and is a poet, professor, performer, voice teacher, and theorist. She holds an MFA in poetry from CUNY Hunter College and a PhD in Performance Studies from New York University, and she studied British Acting technique at the Royal Academy of Dramatic Art in London. Tracie served as the CPCW Fellow in Poetry and Poetics at the University of Pennsylvania from 2008 to 2009 and the Woodberry Poetry Room Creative Fellow at Harvard University from 2018 to 2019. Tracie was the inaugural Distinguished Visiting Professor of Poetry at the Iowa Writers Workshop before joining the permanent faculty as their first African American Professor of Poetry in the fall of 2020.

Eileen Myles came to New York from Boston in 1974 to be a poet, subsequently a novelist, public talker, and art journalist. A Sagittarius, their twenty-two books include *For Now* (Yale Press, 2020) *EVOLUTION* (Grove/Atlantic, 2018), *Afterglow (a dog memoir)* (Grove/Atlantic, 2017), *I Must Be Living Twice/new and selected poems* (Ecco/HarperCollins, 2015), and *Chelsea Girls* (Repress, 2015). Eileen is the recipient of a Guggenheim Fellowship, an Andy Warhol/Creative Capital Arts Writers grant, four Lambda Book Awards, the Shelley Prize from the PSA, and a poetry award from the Foundation for Contemporary Arts. In 2016, Myles received a Creative Capital grant and the Clark Prize for excellence in art writing. In 2019 they taught at NYU and Naropa University and they live in New York City and Marfa, Texas.

Aldon Lynn Nielsen is the Kelly Professor of American Literature at Penn State University. His two most recent books are *The Inside Songs of Amiri Baraka* (Palgrave Macmillan, 2021) and *Back Pages: Selected Poems* (BlazeVOX Editions, 2021).

Mark Nowak's books include *Shut Up Shut Down* (2008; a *New York Times* "Editor's Choice"), *Coal Mountain Elementary* (2009), and *Social Poetics* (2020), all from Coffee House Press. He is a Guggenheim and Lannan fellow. Nowak has been editing a revised and expanded edition of writings from the Attica poetry workshops of Celes Tisdale (1972–74). A native of Buffalo, he is the founding director of the Worker Writers School at PEN America and a professor at Manhattanville College.

Gabriel Ojeda-Sagué is a poet and writer living in Chicago. He is the author of three books of poetry, including most recently *Losing Miami* (The Accomplices, 2019), which was nominated for the Lambda Literary Award in Gay Poetry. His fourth poetry book is *Madness* (Nightboat Books, 2022). He is also the coeditor of a book of selected sketches by the artist Gustavo Ojeda (Soberscove Press, 2020). He is a PhD student in English at the University of Chicago where he works in the study of sexuality.

Jena Osman's books of poems include *Motion Studies* (Ugly Duckling Presse, 2019), *Corporate Relations* (Burning Deck, 2014), *Public Figures* (Wesleyan University Press, 2012), *The Network* (Fence Books 2010, selected for the National Poetry Series in 2009), *An Essay in Asterisks* (Roof Books, 2004), and *The Character* (Beacon Press, winner of the 1998 Barnard New Women Poets Prize). She cofounded and edited the literary magazine *Chain* with Juliana Spahr. Osman was a 2006 Pew Fellow in the Arts and has received grants from the National Endowment for the Arts, the New York Foundation for the Arts, the Pennsylvania Council on the Arts, the Howard Foundation, and the Fund for Poetry. She is a professor of English at Temple University, where she teaches in the MFA Creative Writing Program.

Bob Perelman has published numerous books of poems, including: *Jack and Jill in Troy* (Roof Books, 2019); *Iflife* (Roof Books, 2006); *Playing Bodies*, in collaboration with painter Francie Shaw (Granary Books, 2004); and *Ten to One: Selected Poems* (Wesleyan University Press, 1999). His critical books are *The Marginalization of Poetry: Language Writing and Literary History* (University of California Press, 1994); *The Trouble with Genius: Reading Pound, Joyce, Stein, and Zukofsky* (Princeton University Press, 1996); and *Modernism the Morning After* (University of Alabama Press, 2017). His work can be heard on PennSound; his website is writing.upenn.edu/pepc/authors /perelman; a feature on his work appears in *Jacket* 39. He is Professor Emeritus of English at the University of Pennsylvania and lives in Berkeley, California.

Marjorie Perloff is Sadie D. Patek Professor of Humanities Emerita at Stanford University and Florence Scott Professor Emerita of English at the University of Southern California. A member of the American Academy of Arts and Sciences and the Philosophical Society of America, she is the author of many books and articles on twentieth- and twenty-first-century poetry and poetics, including *Frank O'Hara: Poet Among Painters* (University of Chicago Press, 1998, orig. Brazillier, 1977), *The Poetics of Indeterminacy: Rimbaud to Cage* (Northwestern University Press, 1981), *Radical Artifice: Writing Poetry in the Age of Media* (University of Chicago Press, 1992), *Unoriginal Genius: Writing by Other Means in the New Century* (University of Chicago Press, 2011), and *Infrathin: An Experiment in Micropoetics* (University of Chicago Press, 2021). Her book *Edge of Irony: Modernism in the Shadow of the Habsburg Empire* (University of Chicago Press, 2016) enlarges on the theme of her 2004 memoir, *The Vienna Paradox. Circling the Canon: The Collected Book Reviews of Marjorie Perloff, 1969–2016* was published in two volumes by the University of New Mexico Press in 2019.

Sina Queyras is the author of *Lemon Hound* (2006), *MxT* (2014), *Expressway* (2009), and *My Ariel* (2017), all from Coach House Books. *Rooms: Women, Writing, Woolf*, is being published by Coach House in winter 2021-22.

Anna Strong Safford is an Upper School English teacher at the Episcopal Academy. Previously, she was an instructor and curriculum specialist at the University of Pennsylvania's School of Liberal and Professional Studies and the Course Coordinator for ModPo. She has taught at Temple University, the Community College of Philadelphia, and Boston College, and her poems and essays can be found in *Supplement, Cleaver*, and other publications.

Jennifer Scappettone is the author of two full-length poetry collections, *From Dame Quickly* (Litmus, 2009) and *The Republic of Exit 43: Outtakes & Scores from an Archaeology and Pop-Up Opera of the Corporate Dump* (Atelos, 2016), and of the critical study *Killing the Moonlight: Modernism in Venice* (Columbia University Press, 2014), as well as editor and translator of *Locomotrix*, a collection of selected poetry and prose by the modernist Italian poet and refugee from Fascist Italy, Amelia Rosselli (University of Chicago Press, 2012). She teaches courses in poetics, alternative histories of modernity, writing and social change, translingualism, and exploratory translation across multiple departments at the University of Chicago.

Lytle Shaw's books include *The Lobe* (University of Michigan Press, 2002), *The Moiré Effect* (Bookhorse, 2012), *Frank O'Hara: The Poetics of Coterie* (University of Iowa Press, 2006), and *New Grounds for Dutch Landscape* (OEI editör, 2021). He is a professor of English at New York University and a contributing editor for *Cabinet* magazine.

Ron Silliman has written and/or edited forty books and has had his poetry and criticism translated into sixteen languages. Silliman was a 2012 Kelly Writers House Fellow, the 2010 recipient of the Levinson Prize from the Poetry Foundation, a 2003 Literary Fellow of the National Endowment for the Arts, a 2002 Fellow of the Pennsylvania Arts Council, and a 1998 Pew Fellow in the Arts. Silliman has a plaque in the walk dedicated to poetry in his hometown of Berkeley and a sculpture in the Transit Center of Bury, Lancaster, a part of the Irwell Sculpture Trail. He lives in Chester County, Pennsylvania, and teaches at the University of Pennsylvania.

Danny Snelson is an assistant professor of English at UCLA and is a writer, editor, and archivist. His online editorial work can be found on *PennSound*, *Eclipse*, *UbuWeb*, *Jacket2*, and the *EPC*. See also http://dss-edit.com.

Yosuke Tanaka is the author of three poetry collections: *A Day When the Mountains Are Visible* (Shichōsha, 1999); *Sweet Ultramarine Dreams* (Michitani, 2008); and *I'd Love to Go to Mont Saint-Michel* (Shichōsha, 2018). Since 1989 he has served as the editor of Japanese poetry magazine *Kisaki* and as a regular poetry reviewer for *Gendaishi-techō*, *Tanka Gendai*, and *Shikaku*. He graduated the ModPo course 2014 and has contributed recordings to ModPo and *Jacket2* since his first visit to Kelly Writers House at the end of that year. When he is not writing poetry, Tanaka works as a molecular cell biologist.

Edwin Torres is a New York City native and the author of ten books of poetry, including *XOETEOX: the infinite word object* (Wave Books, 2018), *Ameriscopia* (University of Arizona Press, 2014), and *In the Function of External Circumstances* (Nightboat, 2010), and he is the editor of the intergenre anthology *The Body in Language: An Anthology* (Counterpath Press). He has performed his multidisciplinary *bodylingo* worldwide. His fellowships include NYFA, the Foundation for Contemporary Art, and the DIA Arts Foundation. His anthologies include *American Poets in the 21st Century: The Poetics of Social Engagement* (Wesleyan University Press, 2018) and *Aloud: Voices from the Nuyorican Poets Café* (Henry Holt and Company, 1994).

Rodrigo Toscano's books of poetry include *The Charm and The Dread* (Fence Books, 2021), *In Range* (Counterpath, 2019), *Explosion Rocks Springfield* (Fence Books, 2017), *Deck of Deeds* (Counterpath, 2012), *Collapsible Poetics Theater* (Fence Books, 2008, a National Poetry Series selection), *To Leveling Swerve* (Krupskaya, 2004), *Platform* (Atelos, 2003), *Partisans* (O Books, 1999), and *The Disparities* (Green Integer, 2002). His poetry has appeared in over fifteen anthologies, including *Voices Without Borders* and *Best American Poetry*. Toscano lives in New Orleans.

Divya Victor is the author of *Curb* (Press at Colorado College, 2021); *Kith* (Fence Books/Book*hug, 2017), a book of verse, prose memoir, lyric essay and visual objects; *Natural Subjects* (Trembling Pillow, 2014, Winner of the Bob Kaufman Award); *UNSUB* (Insert Blanc); and *Things to Do with Your Mouth* (Les Figues, 2014). She has been a Mark Diamond Research Fellow at the U.S. Holocaust Memorial Museum, a Riverrun Fellow at the Archive for New Poetry at the University of California, San Diego, and a Writer in Residence at the Los Angeles Contemporary Exhibit (LACE). Her work has been performed and installed at the Museum of Contemporary Art (MoCA) Los Angeles, the National Gallery of Singapore, the Los Angeles Contemporary Exhibit (LACE), and the Museum of Modern Art (MoMA). Victor is an assistant professor of poetry and writing at Michigan State University.

Fred Wah is a poet, novelist, scholar, and former Canadian Parliamentary Poet Laureate. His books include *Music Is at the Heart of Thinking* (Talonbooks, 1987), *Sentenced to Light* (Talonbooks, 2008), *Is a door* (Talonbooks, 2009), and *Faking It: Poetics and Hybridity Critical Writing, 1984–1999* (NeWest Press, 2000).

Simone White is the author of *Dear Angel of Death* (Ugly Duckling Presse, 2018), *Of Being Dispersed* (Futurepoem Books, 2016), *House of Envy of All the World* (Factory School, 2010), and the chapbooks *Unrest* (Ugly Duckling Presse, 2013) and *Dolly* (Q Avenue Press, 2008). Her work has appeared in *e-flux*, *BOMB*, *New York Times Book Review*, *Harper's*, and *Frieze*, among other places. In 2017, she received the Whiting Award for poetry. She lives in Brooklyn and teaches in the English Department at the University of Pennsylvania.

Tyrone Williams teaches literature, literary theory, and cultural studies at Xavier University in Cincinnati, Ohio. Among his books of poetry are *On Spec* (Omnidawn, 2008) and *As iZ* (Omnidawn, 2018).

Christie Williamson is a poet and essayist who lives in Glasgow and runs Tell It Slant Books, Scotland's only bookshop dedicated to poetry. *Arc o Möns* (Hansel Cooperative, 2009) was a Spanish/Shetland bilingual edition of Federico García Lorca's poems and won the

Calum MacDonald Memorial Award. His first full collection, *Oo an Feddirs*, was published by Luath Press in 2015 and his second, *Doors tae Naewye*, in 2020. He comes fae Yell.

Elizabeth Willis is the author of *Alive: New and Selected Poems* (New York Review Books, 2015), which was a finalist for the Pulitzer Prize. Her other books of poetry include *Address* (Wesleyan University Press, 2011), *Meteoric Flowers* (Wesleyan University Press, 2006), *Turneresque* (Burning Deck, 2003), *The Human Abstract* (Penguin, 1995), and *Second Law* (Avenue B, 1993). She was awarded the PEN New England/L. L. Winship prize for *Address*; and her second book, *The Human Abstract*, was selected for the National Poetry Series. Her poems have appeared in recent issues of *Hambone*, *Harper's*, *Nation*, *New Yorker*, *Poetry*, and *A Public Space*. Willis is also the editor of a collection of essays titled *Radical Vernacular: Lorine Niedecker and the Poetics of Place* (University of Iowa Press, 2008). Since 2015 she has taught at the Iowa Writers' Workshop.

Rachel Zolf's writing tends to queerly enact how ethics founders on the shoals of the political. Their five full-length books of poetry include *Janey's Arcadia* (2014), *Neighbour Procedure* (2010), and *Human Resources* (2007), all from Coach House Books. Films Zolf has written and/or directed have shown internationally at venues including White Cube Bermondsey and the International Film Festival Rotterdam. Their work has won a Pew Fellowship in the Arts and a Trillium Book Award for Poetry, among other honors. *No One's Witness: A Monstrous Poetics* was published by Duke University Press in 2021. Zolf lives in Philadelphia.

Index

245

CPSIA information can be obtained
at www.ICGtesting.com
Printed in the USA
JSHW031734060222
22612JS00005B/5